D1473138

WORKING WITH CULTURE

PSYCHOTHERAPEUTIC INTERVENTIONS WITH ETHNIC MINORITY CHILDREN AND ADOLESCENTS

LUIS A. VARGAS AND JOAN D. KOSS-CHIOINO, EDITORS

Jossey-Bass Publishers · San Francisco

For international orders, please contact your local Paramount Publishing International office.

Manufactured in the United States of America

10% POST CONSUMER WASTE

The paper used in this book is acid-free and meets the State of California requirements for recycled paper (50 percent recycled waste, including 10 percent postconsumer waste), which are the strictest guidelines for recycled paper currently in use in the United States.

Library of Congress Cataloging-in-Publication Data

Working with culture : psychotherapeutic interventions with ethnic
 minority children and adolescents / Luis A. Vargas, Joan D. Koss-
 Chioino, editors.
     p.   cm.—(The Jossey-Bass social and behavioral science
series)
    Includes bibliographical references and index.
    ISBN 1-55542-469-4
    1. Children of minorities—Mental health—United States.   2. Child
psychotherapy—Social aspects—United States. 3. Adolescent
psychotherapy—Social aspects—United States. I. Vargas, Luis A.,
[date]. II. Koss-Chioino, Joan. III. Series.
    [DNLM: 1. Ethnic Groups—psychology. 2. Minority Groups—
psychology. 3. Psychotherapy—in adolescence. 4. Psychotherapy—
in infancy & childhood.   WS 350.2 W9268]
RJ507.M54W67   1992
618.92'89'008693—dc20
DNLM/DLC
for Library of Congress   92-8187
                                                                   CIP

FIRST EDITION
HB Printing   10 9 8 7 6 5 4 3   *Code 9266*

Contents

ix

Part Four: Working with American Indian
Children and Adolescents

To our children and stepchildren,
who give us the most important lessons:

Katherine and Elizabeth Vargas
Rhea, Judith, and Hugh Koss
Colleen, Aaron, and Rachael Chioino

Preface

In the last decade, increased attention to cultural factors in psychotherapy and counseling with ethnically diverse populations has resulted in a number of important contributions to the mental health literature. Most of these contributions, however, have focused on adult clients or families and, by comparison, only a few books have addressed clinical concerns in working with ethnic minority children and adolescents. Yet these young people often face unique problems in their development and in their adjustment to mainstream society. Other books have highlighted what is different about various ethnic minority children and adolescents and how to approach these differences in providing mental health services. The perspectives of these authors, however, are global in scope rather than oriented toward providing detailed material on how to conduct psychotherapy with ethnic minority children and adolescents.

What is lacking in the mental health literature on this subject are texts that address psychotherapeutic interventions for specific problems commonly experienced by young people of certain minority groups. For example, how does a therapist deal with a troubled African American adolescent girl from an upwardly mobile family in which the parents cannot understand their daughter's distress because it seems so out of proportion to the material goods and social status that she enjoys? What approach can the therapist use to treat substance-abusing American Indian adolescents? How can a therapist establish a therapeutic alliance with immigrant Asian American families in order to be more effective in treating their children? Or how can a clinician better treat the Hispanic gang member who seems so out of reach of any psychotherapeutic endeavor? Many therapists involved with ethnic minority children, adolescents, and their families are likely to face these types of questions.

In addition to an introductory and a concluding chapter, this book presents twelve chapters that discuss models of and approaches to carrying out individual psychotherapies with African American, Hispanic American, Asian American, and American Indian children and adolescents. The contributors have focused on in-depth discussions of treatment processes and methods as they are affected by, and interwoven with, the cultural dimensions of the child's or adolescent's life. As editors, we do not deny the value of group, family, or other treatment modalities, but these are brought into the discussions of culturally responsive treatment only when they are considered necessary adjuncts or extensions to an individualized approach.

The contributions by the chapter authors and our own concepts and model of culturally responsive psychotherapeutic intervention are based on a long history of interest in the topic and on interactions with many psychologists, psychiatrists, social workers, and anthropologists who have given careful thought to it. We have been organizers and presenters in a series of conferences at the University of New Mexico School of Medicine on multicultural approaches to working with children and adolescents. Moreover, each of us teaches parallel seminars in child and adult psychiatry that review cultural issues in treatment and assessment. In addition, we have organized a number of symposiums at national meetings of various associations on cultural issues in psychotherapeutic interventions and on training therapists to be culturally responsive. This book derives from all of these experiences. The contributors have also been involved with one or more of the conferences, symposiums, or seminars and represent some of the best work presented there.

Our intention as editors was to enlist as many ethnic minority therapists as possible, or persons highly identified with a particular ethnic group. This strategy was not based on the assumption that only ethnic minority persons can discuss or practice culturally responsive psychotherapy. Rather, we felt that therapists of the same ethnicity as their clients are more likely to relate to the theoretical and practical aspects of being culturally responsive in the therapeutic task.

This book restricts its focus to particular problems that affect certain ethnic minority groups more than others, problems that we, as therapists, believe are of critical importance. Our approach is a significant departure from much of the other literature in the multicultural mental health field in its limitation of breadth in favor of depth, especially regarding the more practical aspects of treatment. We acknowledge that this book is not exhaustive in its coverage. Although we have not given full justice to the diversity within the general ethnic minority groups addressed, the chapters do provide greater detail on topics that often have received only cursory coverage. We have not been able to include chapters on Puerto Ricans, Cubans, Dominicans, or other specific Central and South American communities within the overall Hispanic population. Overall, we have not given full coverage to the ethnic heterogeneity in the United States, since our book is limited to only four minority groups. In this regard, our book represents only one step toward fulfilling the need for a literature that provides instrumental and culturally responsive approaches to the treatment of all ethnic minority children and adolescents. However, we hope that this book will add impetus to more works that can assist therapists to do this.

Audience for the Book

Working with Culture is intended for mental health practitioners who work with African American, Hispanic American, Asian American, and American Indian children and adolescents. The chapters take a "how to" approach; they stress the praxis aspect of working with clients from the particular ethnic group that they discuss. The book is also intended for those who teach clinical psychology, psychiatry, counseling, social work, and applied medical anthropology, as well as for graduate students in these fields. Although we have focused on four specific ethnic minorities, the creative solutions presented by the chapter authors offer fruitful suggestions that can generalize to other groups with similar problems.

Overview of the Contents

The chapters are organized into four parts, after the introductory chapter. Every effort was made to include a variety of viewpoints and theoretical orientations; in no way did we, or the contributors, intend the individual chapters to represent a consensus of opinion. Chapter One offers a multidimensional model that describes various ways in which psychological interventions can be innovated or modified so that they become culturally responsive.

Part One focuses on African American children and adolescents. This section presents three treatment-related issues that therapists working with African Americans are likely to experience in their clinical work, issues that are often ignored in the mental health literature. Chapter Two, by Arthur C. Jones, presents a clinical exposition of the salient psychological issues that confront African American adolescents from upwardly mobile families who are in treatment for behavioral or adjustment problems. As are all chapters in the book, this is illustrated with clinical case material. Helen L. Jackson and George Westmoreland, in Chapter Three, discuss developmental, cultural, social, and political issues essential to treating African American children and adolescents in foster care. In Chapter Four, Beverly A. Greene discusses the role of racial socialization in aiding psychotherapy with African American children and adolescents.

Part Two addresses Hispanic American children and adolescents. Chapter Five, by Kenneth J. Martinez and Diana M. Valdez, introduces and describes a "therapist-facilitated" transactional and contextual model of play therapy in which the therapist promotes the inclusion of relevant sociocultural and contextual elements into the play of the child. In Chapter Six, Joseph M. Cervantes and Oscar Ramírez describe how Latino spirituality, deriving from both Catholic and Indian religious beliefs, can be incorporated into the treatment of Latino children and their families. A culturally responsive therapeutic approach emerges from their synthesis. Armando T. Morales, in Chapter Seven, examines how Latino youth gang members can be treated in order to minimize their resistance to psychotherapy.

Part Three considers Asian American children and adolescents. In Chapter Eight, Christine M. Chao shows how she creates an Asian cultural ethos in working with her clients to establish more effective alliances with families from this population. In Chapter Nine, Man Keung Ho discusses the differential application of treatment modalities within a conceptual framework that considers the Asian American child's phenomenology, cultural experiences, biculturalism, acculturation, language, traditional family structure, and help-seeking behavior. Chapter Ten, by Nga Anh Nguyen, explores the interaction between cultural and developmental processes in treating first- and second-generation Asian American children and adolescents within a psychodynamic, object-relations theoretical framework.

Part Four directs attention to treatment issues in working with American Indian children and adolescents. In Chapter Eleven, Martin D. Topper presents a clinical approach to the treatment of emotionally disturbed American Indian adolescents that focuses on the environmental context of the adolescent across four dimensions: medical, psychological, socioeconomic, and cultural-historical. Joseph E. Trimble, in Chapter Twelve, describes a cognitive-behavioral approach to drug abuse prevention and intervention that builds on the strengths of many American Indian communities, that is, on their sociocentric organization and the high value they place on familial and kinship relationships. In Chapter Thirteen, Diane J. Willis, Antonio Dobrec, and Dolores Subia BigFoot Sipes address cultural considerations in treating sexually abused American Indian children.

Chapter Fourteen, our conclusion, uses the descriptive model presented in Chapter One to compare and contrast the ways in which the chapter authors developed culturally responsive interventions. We believe that readers will agree that the topics are timely and, from the standpoint of many therapists, the attention that the authors give them is long overdue.

Acknowledgments

We express our great appreciation to Irene Trujillo and Mercedes Herrera for their excellent clerical support. Our deep gratitude is extended to our spouses, Janet Hodde-Vargas and Craig C. Chioino, for their patience and tolerance during the many late nights and weekends when we worked on this manuscript. We also wish to thank all of the trainees (psychology interns, child psychiatry fellows, psychiatry residents, and postgraduate social work fellows) whom we supervised and taught in seminars, as well as our clients, for their inspiration in helping us to become more culturally responsive in our formulations and our work. To all of our chapter authors, we give a hearty *abrazo* as an expression of our gratitude for their contributions. We have very much appreciated the support, patience, and guidance of Lesley Iura, Christie Hakim, and Frank Welsch at Jossey-Bass. Finally, we thank Paul Pederson and three anonymous reviewers, whose feedback helped us to develop the ideas in our own chapters and to produce a better integrated book. We wish to note that this book is the result of collaboration between us as editors; the order of our names in the byline is arbitrary.

July 1992   Luis A. Vargas
                                        Albuquerque, New Mexico

                                          Joan D. Koss-Chioino
                                              Tempe, Arizona

The Editors

Luis A. Vargas is director of the Clinical Child Psychology Internship Program and associate professor in the Division of Child and Adolescent Psychiatry, Department of Psychiatry, University of New Mexico School of Medicine. He is also the chief psychologist at the University of New Mexico Children's Psychiatric Hospital. He received his B.A. degree (1973) in psychology from St. Edward's University in Austin, Texas; his M.S. degree (1976) in psychology from Trinity University in San Antonio, Texas; and his Ph.D. degree (1982) in clinical psychology from the University of Nebraska, Lincoln. Vargas's main clinical and research interests are multicultural issues in assessment and treatment of ethnic minority children and adolescents; education curricula to teach trainees, inpatient unit staff, and supervisors to be culturally responsive; treatment of severely disturbed children; schizophrenia-spectrum disorders in children; and bereavement following violent death.

Joan D. Koss-Chioino is professor of anthropology at Arizona State University; visiting professor in the Department of Psychiatry, University of New Mexico (professor of psychiatry until 1992); and visiting professor in the Department of Psychiatry and

Neurology, Tulane Medical Center, New Orleans, Louisiana. She is also adjunct professor at the School of Public Health, Tulane Medical Center. She received her B.F.A. degree (1955) in fine arts, English, and philosophy from Temple University and her M.A. (1959) and Ph.D. (1965) degrees in anthropology from the University of Pennsylvania. Koss-Chioino is a member of the board of the Society for the Study of Psychiatry and Culture and has been a fellow of the American Anthropological Association for many years.

Koss-Chioino's main research activities are interdisciplinary, focusing on cross-cultural approaches to psychological and psychiatric clinical concerns with regard to traditional healing, psychotherapy, and psychiatric nosology, particularly among Hispanic peoples. Her recent book *Women as Healers, Women as Patients: Mental Health and Traditional Healing in Puerto Rico* (1992) encompasses diverse anthropological, psychiatric, and psychoanalytic perspectives. Her numerous articles and chapters reflect these interests, as well as her most recent research project, which deals with family treatment for substance-abusing Hispanic youths. Other publications include a special issue of the *Journal of Community Psychology*, June 1987, on "Minority Children and Families in the Southwest" and a chapter, "Sociocultural and Behavioral Influences on Health" (with H. Kloss), in the medical textbook *Tropical Medicine and Parasitology* (1989).

The Contributors

Joseph M. Cervantes is a diplomate of the American Board of Professional Psychology (ABPP); an adjunct assistant clinical professor in the Department of Psychiatry at the University of California, Los Angeles; and an adjunct professor in the Department of Psychology at Chapman University, Orange, California. He received his B.A. degree (1972) in sociology from Divine Word College and his Ph.D. degree (1977) in clinical psychology from the University of Nebraska, Lincoln. He also serves as director of Cervantes Institute, a mental health consulting practice for children, adolescents, and families.

Christine M. Chao, a clinical psychologist, received her B.A. degree (1972) from Manhattanville College with a major in religion and her M.A. (1979) and Ph.D. (1981) degrees from the University of Denver, where she was a Danforth Foundation graduate fellow. She is currently in part-time private practice because of child-rearing responsibilities. Most recently, she worked at the Asian Pacific Center for Human Development, where she served as clinical director and interim executive director. She studied at the C. G. Jung Institute in Zurich, Switzerland, and completed the two-year Curriculum Training Program at the C. G. Jung Center in Denver.

She is also assistant clinical professor of psychiatry at the University of Colorado School of Medicine in Denver.

Antonia Dobrec has served as the president and director of projects for Three Feathers Associates since 1981. She received her B.A. degree (1966) in social welfare from California State University, Humboldt, and her M.S.W. degree (1976) from the University of Kansas. She was assistant director and assistant professor for the University of Oklahoma School of Social Work and directed the American Indian Social Work Education Program from 1979 to 1984. During her tenure with Three Feathers Associates, she has served as the director of a subcontract with CSR, Inc. to study the implementation of the Indian Child Welfare Act and Section 428 of the Adoption Assistance and Child Welfare Act of 1980. She coauthored *Indian Child Welfare: A Status Report*, the report of the study. She has been project director for the Child Protection Team Training Project, which is funded by the Muskogee, Oklahoma, area office of the Bureau of Indian Affairs. Dobrec has over fifteen years of experience in providing training and technical assistance to American Indian tribes and organizations, and she currently serves on the council of Social Work Education's House of Delegates as an American Indian representative.

Beverly A. Greene is associate clinical professor of psychology at St. John's University, Jamaica, New York. She received her B.A. degree (1973) in psychology from New York University and her M.A. (1977) and Ph.D. (1983) degrees in clinical psychology from the Derner Institute of Advanced Psychological Studies of Adelphi University. A fellow of the American Psychological Association, Greene received the 1991 Women of Color Psychologists' Publication Award for the paper "A Perspective on Psychotherapy with African American Women." She is coeditor of *Women of Color and Mental Health* and *Contemporary Perspectives in Lesbian and Gay Psychology*. The latter is an official publication of the American Psychological Association, Division 44.

Man Keung Ho is professor of social work and director of the Transcultural Family Institute at the University of Oklahoma. He

received his B.A. degree (1965) in sociology from Tulsa University
and his M.S.W. degree (1967) and Ph.D. degree (1969) in counseling
psychology from Florida State University. Ho's main research activities have been in transcultural therapy with ethnic minority
children and families and interethnic and interracial couples and
families. He has been the director of two children's treatment centers as well as external examiner for the University of Hong Kong,
and he is on the editorial boards of six professional journals. He
received the 1979 Distinguished Service Award and the 1981 Social
Worker of the Year Award, both from the National Association of
Social Workers, Oklahoma chapter. In 1981 he was the honor lecturer of Mid-American State Universities Association.

Helen L. Jackson is clinical assistant professor of psychiatry at the University of New Mexico and is in private practice in
Albuquerque, New Mexico. She received her B.A. degree (1962) in
psychology from City College in New York, her M.A. degree (1965)
in psychology from City University in New York, and her Ph.D.
degree (1980) in clinical psychology from Teachers College, Columbia University. Jackson has worked for many years with children,
parents, and families in a children's outpatient clinic; in residential
treatment programs; in public schools; and in a children's inpatient
setting. She was formerly the director of the Clinical Child Psychology Internship Program at the University of New Mexico School of
Medicine.

Arthur C. Jones is a senior lecturer in the Department of
Psychology at the University of Denver. He is also a clinical asso-
ciate professor of psychiatry at the University of Colorado School
of Medicine and maintains a part-time psychology practice in
Denver. Jones received his B.A. degree (1967) in psychology from
Drew University in Madison, New Jersey, and his M.A. (1969) and
Ph.D. (1974) degrees in clinical psychology from the University of
Iowa. In addition to his long-standing involvement in the field of
African American mental health, he has a subspecialty in Jungian
psychology and has been involved in numerous professional and
community activities. He was the recipient of the Colorado Psycho-
logical Association's 1990 E. Ellis Graham Award for distinguished

career contributions to psychology. Jones also works as a professional singer of classical and African American traditional folk music and is currently working on a psychohistorical study of folk songs composed during slavery. He is currently involved in a touring lecture-recital program in which he sings a sampling of these songs and presents lecture material from his research.

Kenneth J. Martinez is clinical assistant professor of psychiatry in the Division of Child and Adolescent Psychiatry at the University of New Mexico School of Medicine. He received his B.A. degree (1974) with distinction in psychology from Stanford University and his Psy.D. degree (1978) from the University of Denver School of Professional Psychology. He also maintains a private practice in Albuquerque, New Mexico, specializing in child, adolescent, and family therapy. He is a consultant to the University of New Mexico Department of Pediatrics and to the New Mexico Human Services Department.

Armando T. Morales is professor and director of clinical social work at the Neuropsychiatric Institute at the University of California, Los Angeles, School of Medicine, where he has been teaching since 1971. He received his B.A. degree (1957) in sociology from Los Angeles State College and his M.S.W. (1963) and D.S.W. (1972) degrees from the University of Southern California. He is a former gang group worker and senior deputy probation officer, having worked with juvenile and adult forensic populations in the field and in institutions. Currently, he is a mental health consultant and gang group therapist with the California Youth Authority, as well as a gang homicide prevention program and research consultant with the Kellogg and Eisenhower Foundations. He has authored numerous publications; his most recent (with B. W. Sheafor, 1991) is the sixth edition of *Social Work: A Profession of Many Faces.*

Nga Anh Nguyen, a native of Vietnam, is a child and adolescent psychiatrist and an associate professor in the Department of Psychiatry and Behavioral Sciences at the Oklahoma University Health Sciences Center. She received her M.D. degree (1969) from the College of Medicine of the University of Saigon in Vietnam and completed her residency in general psychiatry (1979) and her fellowship in child and adolescent psychiatry (1981) at the University of Oklahoma Health Sciences Center. Nguyen is board certified in general and child psychiatry. Her main clinical interest is in loss and mourning, and her areas of clinical and research expertise include children of Southeast Asian refugees and immigrants, children of divorce, and adopted children suffering from depressive disorders. She is currently completing a National Institute of Mental Health research fellowship in child and adolescent affective disorders.

Oscar Ramírez is clinical assistant professor of psychiatry at the University of Texas Health Sciences Center in San Antonio. He received his B.A. degree (1970) in psychology from the University of Texas, Austin, and his M.A. (1974) and Ph.D. (1980) degrees in clinical psychology from the University of Michigan, Ann Arbor. Ramírez maintains a private practice and specializes in working with children, adolescents, and couples, with particular expertise with adult survivors of childhood sexual abuse. In addition, he is currently interested in addressing clinical issues relating to domestic violence, child sexual abuse, and spiritual issues as applied to psychotherapy.

Dolores Subia BigFoot Sipes is a postdoctoral fellow at the Child Study Center, Department of Pediatrics, University of Oklahoma Health Sciences Center. She received her B.S. degree (1979) in psychology and sociology from Southwestern Oklahoma State University and her Ph.D. degree (1989) in counseling psychology from the University of Oklahoma. Sipes has lived and worked on American Indian reservations, has consulted with American Indian organizations, and has authored several publications on American Indian concerns. She serves on American Psychological Association committees and is involved with the Society of Indian Psychologists. She is a member of the Caddo tribe of Oklahoma.

Martin D. Topper is an applied anthropologist who lives in Falls Church, Virginia. He received his B.A. degree (1968) from the

University of Illinois, Urbana, and his M.A. (1969) and Ph.D. (1972) degrees in anthropology from Northwestern University. He conducted postdoctoral studies at the University of Chicago and the University of California, San Diego. Topper did field research among the Navajo on several occasions between 1969 and 1977. He served as cultural anthropologist for the Indian Health Service (IHS) from 1978 to 1980 and as both cultural anthropologist and assistant director of the IHS mental health branch of the Navajo area from 1980 to 1987. He is currently the national Indian program coordinator for the U.S. Environmental Protection Agency.

Joseph E. Trimble is professor of psychology at Western Washington University (WWU), and he serves as a research associate at the National Center for American Indian and Alaska Native Mental Health Research at the University of Colorado Health Sciences Center. In addition, he is a technical adviser for the National Institute on Drug Abuse Office of Special Populations and research associate in WWU's Center for Cross-Cultural Research. Trimble received his B.A. degree (1961) in psychology from Waynesburg College, his M.A. degree (1965) in psychology from the University of New Hampshire, and his Ph.D. degree (1969) in psychology from the University of Oklahoma. Since 1986, he has been working on drug abuse prevention research models with American Indian youth through grants from the National Institute on Drug Abuse and the National Cancer Institute. Trimble has held offices in the International Association for Cross-Cultural Psychology and the American Psychological Association. He has written nearly 100 publications on American Indian and Alaska Native topics.

Diana M. Valdez is assistant professor of psychiatry at the University of New Mexico School of Medicine, Division of Child and Adolescent Psychiatry, and is a staff psychologist at Programs for Children and Adolescents, University of New Mexico Mental Health Center. She received her B.A. degree (1975) in psychology from the University of California, Los Angeles, and her Ph.D. degree (1983) in social psychology from the University of California, Riverside. Valdez completed her postdoctoral training in clinical child psychology at the University of New Mexico. Her interests include cross-cultural issues in the assessment and treatment of minority children, forensic psychology, and cross-cultural training and consultation.

George Westmoreland received his B.A. degree (1972) in psychology from the State University of New York (SUNY) College at Old Westbury, his M.S.W. degree (1974) from SUNY at Stony Brook, and his Psy.D. degree (1978) in clinical psychology from Rutgers University. His internship was in clinical psychology at the College of Medicine and Dentistry of New Jersey Community Mental Health Center, where he was instrumental in the development of a psychoeducational day treatment program for adolescents. Westmoreland's postgraduate training has been in neuropsychological assessment of learning disabilities, ego psychology, computer science, and stress management. He earned a diploma in clinical psychology from the American Board of Professional Psychology (ABPP) and is a fellow and diplomate in medical psychotherapy of the American Board of Medical Psychotherapists.

Diane J. Willis is professor of medical psychology in the Department of Pediatrics and director of Psychological Services at the Child Study Center of the University of Oklahoma Health Sciences Center. She received her B.S. degree (1960) in biology from Northeastern Oklahoma State University, her M.A. degree (1965) in psychology from George Peabody College at Vanderbilt University, and her Ph.D. degree (1970) in experimental psychology from the University of Oklahoma. She completed a two-year postdoctoral fellowship in clinical child (pediatric) psychology in the Department of Psychiatry and Behavioral Sciences at the University of Oklahoma Health Sciences Center. Willis is a voting member of the Kiowa tribe in Oklahoma and consults with the Indian Health Service. She is author of numerous publications and past editor of two journals. She is also a past president of Division 37 and of the Clinical Child Psychology Section of Division 12 of the American Psychological Association, and a past president of the Society of Pediatric Psychology.

WORKING WITH
CULTURE

1

Through the Cultural Looking Glass: A Model for Understanding Culturally Responsive Psychotherapies

JOAN D. KOSS-CHIOINO
LUIS A. VARGAS

> *"Where do you come from?"* said the Red Queen. *"And where are you going? Look up, speak nicely, and don't twiddle your fingers all the time."* Alice attended to all these directions and explained as well as she could that she had lost her way.
> *"I don't know what you mean by* your *way,"* said the Queen. *"All the ways about here belong to* me—*but why did you come here at all?"* she added in a kinder tone. *"Courtsey while you're thinking what to say. It saves time."*
> —Through the Looking Glass, *Lewis Carroll, 1977, p. 36.*

As Alice reacted to the world on the other side of the looking glass, so ethnic minority children often find their mainstream psychotherapies outside the realm of their previous experience. They may experience psychotherapy to be emotionally unsettling, perhaps thought provoking but confusing, and out of line with their expectations and views of the world. They may even see their therapists as "Red Queens."

In this introductory chapter, we first review selected literature on background factors and techniques, especially with children

This chapter is the result of equal contributions by both authors.

and adolescents, for the clues they provide for fulfilling the task of developing culturally responsive psychotherapeutic treatment models. We then present our own conceptual model as a lens through which to explore, assess, and develop culturally responsive therapeutic approaches. Our overall goal in this book is to facilitate the integration of ethnic minority children's cultures into the form and process of the therapies used to treat their emotional and behavioral problems.

Before proceeding further, it is necessary to discuss terminology. We prefer the phrase "culturally responsive" to describe the process through which culture can be integrated into psychotherapeutic interventions. It is somewhat synonymous with "culturally sensitive" but is meant to emphasize an active stance rather than a more passive appreciation of the psychotherapeutic task. We use the phrase "ethnic minority" to denote ethnic groups whose members are numerically fewer in the overall population of the United States and who are unequal in status and power relative to the larger, majority group. Ethnic minority also calls attention to those political and economic factors that relate to societal position. We use the term "ethnic" to indicate a sociological distinction regarding a social group or category that differs in its values, worldview, and traditions (that is, "culture") from the other social groups in a complex society. Culture, in our view, refers to an ideological dimension of the human condition that guides and motivates behavior. Ethnic groups express their differences in customs, ideas, and attitudes within a societal context that includes a number of other ethnic groups of both minority and majority status. For example, in New Mexico there are two numerically large ethnic populations, Hispanics and Anglos. Within each population there are cultural variations, such as Mexican-born persons as compared to Hispanic New Mexicans whose families have lived in New Mexico for many generations, adapting to years of Spanish colonialism, invasions from Mexico, and Southwestern Indian cultures. The Anglo population, defined locally as "non-Hispanic white," is also somewhat ethnically diverse, slightly larger than the Hispanic one, and, from many perspectives, politically dominant. In addition, smaller ethnic minority populations such as American Indians from different tribes and nations (Navajo, Pueblo, and Apache), African Americans, and Asian Americans each exhibit their own type of cultural diversity.

Acknowledging Ethnopsychologies

As Alice experienced discomfort with the world on the other side of the looking glass, so therapists and their clients are most comfortable in *their* everyday worlds. However, therapists often act as if there is only one paradigm that defines the parameters for behavior, that is, one psychology. An emerging body of literature on ethnopsychologies has important implications for psychotherapy (Heelas and Lock, 1981; Sampson, 1988; Cushman, 1990). Sampson (1988) argues for paying more attention to how indigenous psychologies conceptualize individualism, making a distinction between "self-contained" and "ensembled" individualism. Self-contained individualism is characterized by firm self-other boundaries, emphasis on personal control, and an exclusionary concept of the self. In contrast, ensembled individualism is characterized by a fluid self-other boundary, field control, and an inclusive concept of the self. Sampson's approach shows how self-contained individualism has influenced major theories in psychology. Cushman (1990) extends this perspective to a critique of the ways in which current psychologies of the self are in fact historically and culturally situated. He notes that "there is no universal transhistorical self, only local selves; no universal theory about self, only local theories" (Cushman, 1990, p. 599). With respect to the United States, he contends that there has been a "historical shift from the Victorian, sexually restricted self to the post-World War II empty self" (p. 599). The empty self is predicated upon what Cushman calls the "bounded masterful self" or what Sampson refers to as "self-contained individualism." The recent history of the United States is a deterioration of "community, tradition, and shared meaning" (Cushman, 1990, p. 600). The empty self is the result of these deficiencies, characterized by the need for fulfillment with consumer goods and other material and idealized objects rather than a firm, internal sense of self-worth. Since self psychologies are gaining in popularity in the treatment of children, our model for culturally responsive psychotherapy can be helpful in understanding those therapies in which concepts of the self are central. In our view, psychotherapies should attend to the emerging "local selves" of culturally different children in the context of their families, their ethnic communities, and the impinging, dominant society.

A number of older studies focused on the behavior of Mexican American children in school settings. They drew attention to their seeming lack of motivation for achievement and their preference for cooperation over individualistic striving and performance (Ramírez and Castañeda, 1974; Bender and Ruiz, 1974; Buriel, 1975). However, when cultural factors were explored in relation to these "problems" in underachievement, it became clear that the process of socializing children in Mexican American families resulted in children manifesting what Sampson (1988) has now labeled an "ensembled self." In other words, Mexican American children are reported to have performed in school and elsewhere in terms of family-defined rather than individualistically defined goals and needs.

Issues around the self are crucial in both assessment and treatment of ethnic minority children and adolescents and central to major treatment approaches based upon self psychology, ego psychology, and object relations theories. For example, the therapist, working from the theoretical perspective of Kohut's self psychology, may assume that all children experience isolation as a result of common developmental events (Elson, 1986). However, this therapist is working within a therapeutic paradigm that basically denies the presence of cultural factors in its emphasis on the structural aspects of self psychology. Attending to cultural dimensions raises an important issue regarding the extent to which historical and developmental assumptions, utilized by mainstream American therapists (see Cushman, 1990), apply, for example, to the Mexican American child. These children, reared in extended families with values and practices that mediate the content of the self, are most likely to emerge with selves that cannot be described as "empty" (that is, the condition for which Kohut's therapy seems primarily intended). In other words, we must consider the locally situated history of Mexican American children as directly relevant to the configuration of self. If we utilize Cushman's conceptualization of the historically situated self as central to culturally responsive psychotherapy, this then permits the inclusion of culturally contextualized formulations and interventions.

Understanding the Role of the Therapist

Although the ethnic minority child has much in common with Alice, the therapist often behaves more like the Red Queen. In therapy "all the ways" (see epigraph on page 1) belong to the therapist; it falls to the child to figure out what therapy is about and how to behave. The therapist may assume that the young client knows what therapy is about and the expected behaviors or changes. If the child does not respond adequately to treatment, the result may be attributed to resistance rather than to a deeper cause such as a poor match between the therapist's approach and the client's experience and expectations. One outcome of this unfortunate state of affairs is that many children and adolescents go untreated even if initially enrolled in therapy. For example, Latino and African American gang members do not often receive effective intervention in mental health settings because they are viewed as antisocial and too "hard core" to benefit from treatment. Armando T. Morales, in Chapter Seven, explores the special processes of successful engagement and treatment of this type of client. Christine M. Chao in Chapter Eight and Nga Anh Nguyen in Chapter Ten counter the widespread perception that Asian American children are too constrained in expressing emotions to benefit from many types of psychotherapy based on insight or emotive techniques. Other stereotypes are found in anecdotal clinical material: American Indian adolescents who use alcohol or drugs are seen as beyond the possibility of change (see Joseph Trimble in Chapter Twelve); African American teenage girls are thought of as inherently promiscuous because many become pregnant before completing school and therefore are unable to respond to therapies that motivate them to seek job training or higher education (Ann Dean, personal communication, Oct. 4, 1991).

In examining cultural responsiveness in interventions, therefore, the therapist-client alliance is especially important in terms of how the interaction of expectations of each party may affect the course and outcome of treatment of children and adolescents. Being

open to contrasts—some subtle, others extreme—in ways of thinking, perceiving, and feeling, and particularly in ways of relating, is
essential to effective psychotherapeutic work with *any* client. Such
openness and flexibility is necessary to developing a personal capacity to take on the perspectives and understand the identifications of
the child client. For those clients who are culturally different, this
capacity in the therapist may be necessary to obtain any therapeutic
result at all. To quote Pederson (1984, p. 340), "Cultural differences
introduce barriers to understanding in those very areas of interaction that are most crucial to the outcome of therapy, through dis-
crepancies between counselor and client experiences, beliefs, values,
expectations and goals." Carrying out culturally responsive psychotherapy itself is an exercise in how to conduct "good enough" psychotherapy, not only in learning how to deal with a child's or
adolescent's confusions or resistances but also in providing the therapist with a ready arena within which to deal with his or her own
confusions and resistances.

    We are not supporting our emphasis on culturally responsive
psychotherapy with ethnic minority children on the basis of their
numbers or the severity of the problems they manifest. We leave the
enumeration and description of these factors to Gibbs, Huang, and
Associates (1989), as well as to books and articles on individual
minority populations, such as Canino, Earley, and Rogler (1980);
Powell, Yamamoto, Romero, and Morales (1983); and Phinney and
Rotheram (1987). Instead, we base our position regarding cultural
responsiveness as necessary to a "good enough" psychotherapeutic
method on the absolute value of integrating cultural meaning and
culturally relevant form and process into therapy with children,
who are most often perceived as passive vehicles rather than active
recipients and partners in the therapeutic exchange. As partners
(whether of equal or unequal status), the therapy must be meaningful to them, in the sense that the child client already has a mind-
set and patterned images of self and other. The content of his or her
culture—that is, the pattern of religious beliefs, worldviews and
self-views, and so on—provides a matrix for the therapy. In a parallel way, culture as context—that is, particular features of the
child's environment, such as racial prejudice, poverty, and so on—

provides constraints that can prevent psychological fertility in the therapeutic endeavor.

Theoretical and Practical Issues in
Culturally Responsive Psychotherapy

Developmental Perspectives

Models of culturally responsive psychotherapy with children and adolescents are based on particular notions regarding development, which is clearly a crucial variable in the psychotherapeutic task. A relatively large literature examines developmental markers in children of non-Western cultures and suggests that Western developmental schedules need to be revised for other cultural contexts. (See, for example, Whiting and Whiting, 1975; Munroe and Munroe, 1975.) This issue has been raised in relation to ethnic minority children, but with some few exceptions, such as Powell, Yamamoto, Romero, and Morales (1983), it has not been systematically investigated or utilized. Specifically, we need to consider the ways in which culture (both content and context) directly affects the expression and scheduling of certain behaviors considered age and/or gender appropriate for mainstream American children but possibly not for non-Western, ethnically different children. We define cultural *content* as the specific meaning through which social phenomena are constructed, deconstructed, and reconstructed: patterns of behavior, interpersonal interactions, emotions, the scheduling of developmental landmarks, beliefs about gender and role, and attitudes about sexuality and identity. Cultural *context* refers to social environments such as family, school, and community and their patterns of interpersonal relationships, which affect behavior and cognition in many spheres, including the therapy itself and the clinical setting in which the therapy takes place. A discussion of how culture affects development is a topic far too complex for the scope of this introductory chapter; however, awareness of its relevance is crucial to carrying out culturally responsive psychotherapy with ethnic minority children and adolescents.

Although many studies of psychological development in ethnic minority children are concerned with cognition, we focus here on other types of behaviors that we believe to be of greater importance to the therapeutic task. With Hispanic children and adolescents, for example, an important issue is the development of autonomy and individuation-separation from the family of origin (Erikson, 1950; Mahler, Pine, and Bergman, 1975). Traditional Puerto Rican and Mexican American families normatively exert heavy centripetal pulls on their offspring, especially on females (Nieves Falcon, 1973; Zayas and Bryant, 1984). Canino and Canino (1982), discussing "culturally syntonic" family therapy for Puerto Ricans in relation to Minuchin's measure of enmeshment, describe the "normal enmeshment" they find in families, which is at the extreme of the measure. When Hispanic parents do not lead children into autonomous behaviors that prepare them for separation from the family at the cessation of high school, and when they groom their female (and often male) children to remain at home until they marry, therapists who insist upon a certain degree of adolescent autonomy provoke misunderstandings and confusion in their clients.

Developmentally oriented discussions of treatment that focus on how cultures pattern social development in children usually only address culture as content and often assume that the therapist's knowledge of cultural content automatically transfers into the therapeutic situation. Although cultural awareness on the part of the therapist is important to a moment-by-moment management of the therapeutic task, this in itself is not enough.

Only a few discussions in the literature show how cultural dimensions interrelate with those of technique or process in conducting psychotherapy. Zayas and Bryant (1984), after detailing aspects of cultural patterning in the life and problems of an adolescent Puerto Rican girl, integrate them into the therapeutic process in a number of ways. For example, they suggest that "since age and gender are important variables in the Puerto Rican family" (p. 248), the therapist's age and sex will assuredly have an impact. In a clinical vignette, their strategy was that the female therapist would enter into a working alliance with the client, but she would deflect parental perceptions that she was fostering independent, assertive behavior in the girl and at the same time would model the potential benefit of the client's achieving the vocational success that her parents envisioned. The male co-therapist would establish a direct relationship with the father, who expressed the least confidence in the treatment, supporting him in his ideal roles as caretaker and protector in a situation in which the client was asserting the primacy of her needs over her father's strict traditional rules for behavior. Each family member, including the mother, who was caught between father and daughter, was appropriately supported through a process of negotiating a looser attachment to the family for the client—one that could stem the headstrong rebellious rush into teenage sexuality. The therapeutic approach described was one of acknowledging cultural values, expectations, and directives on familial roles and dynamics, while, as the authors explicitly point out, not necessarily sharing those values. Zayas and Bryant recommended that the therapist become "empathic and congruent" with the cultural patterning of a client's family life, while at the same time examining his or her own values.

Environmental Impacts on the Patient and the Therapeutic Task

The complex social situations surrounding ethnic minority populations in the United States provide background factors important to the enterprise of psychotherapy with children and adolescents. Significant social environmental factors—that is, culture as context—include poverty, racism, generational differences in sexual mores and behavior, the stress of immigration and resettlement, and acculturation.

Poverty. Although economic factors in general are always a part of the therapeutic picture, the most important is that of poverty. A number of studies have shown that African Americans, Puerto Ricans, Mexican Americans, and American Indians are disproportionately poor; the majority suffer the effects of poor housing, inadequate schooling, and poor health. External poverty produces an internal poverty of hope and expectation about the future. This can have destructive effects on the therapeutic task, if, on the one hand, unrealistic goals are assumed for the child or adolescent, or on the other, if he or she is made responsible for what is lacking materially or in opportunities. Thus the therapist who regularly encourages the child to be more ambitious and goal oriented is assuming that "anything is attainable" and may lack an empathic understanding of the realistic social constraints suffered by the child, an approach that denies the value of alternative forms that assume that the child may not have control over his particular social environment.

Racism and Prejudice. Persons of color—African Americans, Puerto Ricans, Mexican Americans, and Asian Americans—are all regularly subjected to the effects of racist attitudes and various types of prejudice. Even where prejudice is not severe, such as in communities characterized by homogeneous economic status and diverse ethnicity, there are always social stereotypes about difference, which pose a number of difficult considerations for the therapeutic task. First, clients' self—and social—identification take on added complexities in that a child's or adolescent's sense of identity may be significantly related to behavior problems, regardless of ethnic group affiliation (see Phinney and Rotheram, 1987; Rotheram-Borus, 1989). For ethnic minority adolescents in comparison to white majority youth, the personal exploration of ethnic role is complex and may be resolved only during adulthood when limitations of opportunity and choice have greater impact (Rotheram-Borus, 1989). The results of the studies cited above show that ethnicity itself may not mediate the relationship of identity to behavior problems, social competence, or self-esteem but rather that some youths within each ethnic group are in a state of "moratorium" regarding their "identity status"; that is, their identity is still at issue and frequently associated with high anxiety.

A second aspect of the therapeutic task is understanding and working with the relationship between the effect of "racial socialization," its positive or negative valences, and other problems associated with the child's or adolescent's early experiences. Beverly A. Greene (1990; also in Chapter Four) explores the mother-daughter relationship in the light of the effects of both sexism and racism: how mothers teach daughters about them as stressors and model adaptive responses to these stresses for their daughters.

Still a third aspect of the therapeutic task focuses on the therapist-client relationship as it pertains to the ethnicity of each party. Awareness of and emphasis on how attitudes and stereotypes about race and color are processed within the therapeutic arena, given either the same or different ethnicity of therapist and client, is a crucial part of the therapeutic process (Hobbs, 1985; Jackson, 1983; López, López, and Fong, 1991). Comas-Díaz and Jacobsen (1987) describe the assessment of "ethnocultural identification" as "an auxiliary therapeutic tool" with clients undergoing the stress of acculturation. This is a five-stage process, the last stage of which focuses on the therapist's ethnocultural background in relation to that of the client. Some therapists/researchers suggest that the form of the therapy be arranged to include the factor of therapist ethnicity depending on whether the clinician is "highly dominant" and therefore more successful with clients with similar ethnic backgrounds or "less dominant" and therefore more effective with culturally different clients (Hall and Malony, 1983).

Acculturation. The impact of elements of the dominant majority culture on ethnic minority clients may vary in intensity depending on a number of factors, such as how recently they have resettled in the United States, the ethnicity and social organization of the community in which they settle, their preparation for resettlement and preimmigration experiences, and their personal adjustment prior to the full impact of the acculturation process. A number of papers (Lee, 1988; Chao and Nguyen in Chapter Eight and Chapter Ten) demonstrate that adolescents born elsewhere, or the first generation born and reared in the United States, seem to be literally caught between two cultures. The case of the adolescent Puerto Rican girl described above, in which a parent refused to change his values regarding the timing of her autonomy and initiation of sexuality, is replicated in other ethnic minority groups, especially among recently resettled Southeast Asians. Lee (1988) frames the problem as one of "rate of acculturation" influenced by five different cultures: "(1) the Southeast Asian culture; (2) the American culture; (3) the refugee culture; (4) the adolescent culture in America; and (5) the refugee adolescent culture" (p. 171). She suggests three areas of focus for treatment: first, the therapist should assess the major stresses, including "life cycle stress"; second, he or she should assess the strengths of both the client and family; and third, the therapist should assess the culturally specific responses to mental health problems.

Normative Behavior. The issue of a definition of normative behavior is central to the purpose of psychotherapy, because its main goal is to bring a child within normative behavioral standards. However, what is "normative" is culturally determined. From this viewpoint, psychotherapy is a culturally defined enterprise (Vargas, 1991); yet it is ironic that most psychotherapists do not see psychotherapy in this light. As a result, theories of development and psychotherapy are developed from the vantage point of one culture—invariably, the dominant culture. For example, a psychodynamically oriented therapist might implicitly assume an optimal level of individuation-separation for all children, regardless of their ethnicity, ignoring other cultural standards (as in the case of the Puerto Rican girl we described earlier). In contrast, another psychodynamically oriented therapist might argue that separation-individuation is a crucial aspect of development but is negotiated through diverse cultural patterns. How that therapist chooses to view culture then determines which particular dimension is invoked, that of content or context.

Therapists need a framework in order to understand and employ cultural patterns with regard to standards for behavior. Consider the example of the Pueblo girl who has moved to an urban center from her reservation. In her school setting her "reticence" and "meekness" are now perceived as interfering with her school performance. She is thus sent for therapy in order to encourage her assertiveness. Her therapist's comments to her teachers that this behavior would not necessarily have negative consequences on the reservation are not helpful. The therapist's dilemma is that his or her therapeutic task is to assist the child to be more successful, but "success" is both content and context relevant. If a therapist decides that the girl should be assisted to increase her initiative and assertiveness in one context, an urban school "in the white man's world," while remaining unassertive at home, the therapist has made use of both the dimensions of cultural content and context. This therapist is fully cognizant of changing the client's behavior in one context (school in the urban environment) in the direction of what is normative for that setting. However, he or she might also advocate that the child should remain unassertive at home. Realizing only cultural content, that is, the normative value of reticent behavior for a Pueblo girl, will not necessarily result in cultural responsiveness in therapy.

A Working Model for Understanding
Culturally Responsive Psychotherapies

Recent discussions of culturally responsive therapies can be examined along various dimensions. For example, Sue and Zane (1987) have suggested attending to two process-oriented variables—"credibility," which can be either ascribed or achieved, and "giving"— that are more directly related to positive outcomes than are approaches that emphasize cultural knowledge or culture-specific techniques. In contrast, D. W. Sue (1990) proposes a conceptual framework that includes three major domains: culture-bound styles of communication, sociopolitical facets of nonverbal communication, and therapy styles (for example, a client-centered approach versus a rational-emotive approach). Thus his formulation is primarily framed within cultural dimensions and considers both content and context but does not address the process dimensions as do Sue and Zane (1987).

A detailed comment on the cultural dimensions of content and context is necessary before defining them. Studies in cross-cultural psychology and cultural psychiatry often utilize one of two types of interpretation of data. The universalistic interpretation assumes that people basically behave in similar ways because they have biological and psychological characteristics in common. An opposite type is the relativistic, interpretive approach, which views culture as molding and shaping people's behavior so that each population with a common culture is wholly or partially unique. A related paradigm is the two-dimensional "emic-etic" dichotomy (that is, "insider view" versus "outsider view"; Trimble, Lonner, and Boucher, 1983; Headland, Pike, and Harris, 1990), which derives from structural linguistics, that distinguishes "phonetic" (referring to physical sounds of assumed universal distribution) from "phonemic" (referring to the particular sounds that are meaningful in each language). Thus "etic" and "emic" have come to be used as labels for the universalistic and relativistic perspectives on human behavior.

The emic-etic paradigm has at least two major problems. First, the twin processes of cultural conservatism (retention of traditions) and acculturation (cultural change or interchange) blur the emic-etic dichotomy as each ethnic group either loses aspects of its cultural difference or exaggerates aspects of its ethnic integrity (Vargas, 1991). Second, etic is often claimed to be the objective or professional/scientific perspective and emic the subjective or lay/client perspective. From a cultural viewpoint, both perspectives are actually emic, in the sense that they are based on subjective phenomena such as cognitions, values, and worldview (Trimble, Lonner, and Boucher, 1983; Koss and Peña, forthcoming). From a sociopolitical viewpoint, the etic is constructed out of the value system of the dominant (Western) society that insists that scientific method and its products have universal validity. The emic is then based on the value system of the "other," which, in the case of the United States, is represented by various ethnic minority cultures.

In order to understand the arena of psychotherapy, we offer a multidimensional lens through which to view the relationship between the culture of the client and process and method in psychotherapy. Rather than advocating a culturally relativistic *or* a universalistic approach—which has been a well-used paradigm—we propose a model to describe culturally responsive psychotherapies that is based upon two pairs of dimensions: the cultural, comprising *content* and *context,* and the structural, comprising *form* (method and modality) and *process.* Figure 1 lays out these dimensions in relationship to one another.

Cultural content refers to the specific meanings through which social phenomena are constructed, deconstructed, and reconstructed, including patterns of individual behavior, interpersonal interactions, emotions, and so on. Cultural content as a dimension includes the perception and scheduling of developmental landmarks; beliefs about gender and role; and attitudes about sexuality, identity, and world- and self-views that run through an almost infinite number of guidelines for rearing and socializing children. The direct effect can be seen in relatively simple expressions, such as in a Navajo girl's respectful downcast eyes when facing her therapist, or a Mexican American boy's expression of fear of the witch who resides in a nearby *arroyo.* Or it can be appreciated in more

Figure 1. Multidimensional Model for
Understanding Culturally Responsive Psychotherapies.

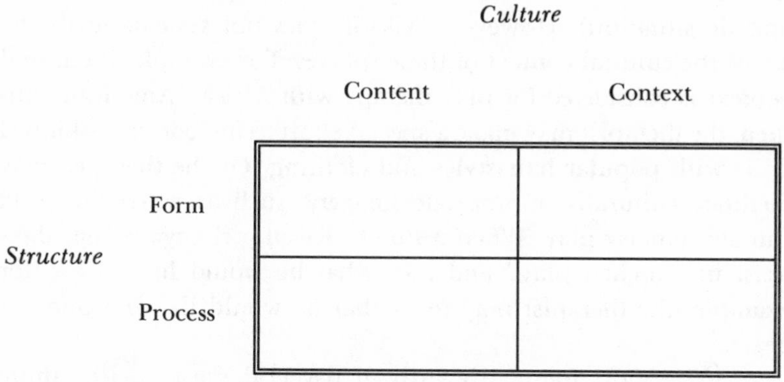

Culture

		Content	Context
Structure	Form		
	Process		

complex forms, such as a Mexican American mother's excuse for withdrawing her child from therapy because she feels that the curandero's explanation for the child's emotional distress has greater validity.

Content can be appreciated, for example, in the Freudian and Kleinian schools of child psychotherapy, or in cognitive-behavioral therapies, in which words and expressions of many types are meaningful within the range of connotations of Western European tradition, within which these therapies were developed. In contrast, if a client is from another cultural background, the approach might be to utilize that client's traditions, worldviews, and self-views as the source of meaning in his or her psychotherapy, rather than impose alien meanings embedded in psychotherapies developed within Western culture. However, neither approach is necessarily exclusive, that is, a therapist might attend to or utilize both sources of meaning.

Cultural context refers to those elements of the psychotherapeutic endeavor as defined and experienced by the client's culturally patterned expectations in interaction with those defined and experienced by the therapist. There are also extraclinical spheres pertaining to social environments (such as family, school, and community) that influence the child in ways that significantly affect his or her therapy. Contextual variables as such can be appreciated in Erikson's approach (1950), in his notions of autosphere (the child's own body and body functions), microsphere (the world of play objects and the materials themselves), and macrosphere (the larger world of the therapeutic situation). However, Erikson does not systematically describe the cultural context of these spheres. For example, if cultural context is considered for play therapy with African American children, the therapist may make a special effort to include dark-skinned dolls with popular hair styles and clothing. Or the therapist may facilitate culturally appropriate imagery, such as when the child initiates fantasy play. When a Puerto Rican girl engages her therapist in "kitchen play" and asks what he would like to eat, for example, the therapist may reply that he would like rice and red beans.

The most frequently utilized psychotherapies with ethnic minority children have been developed within Western culture, and therapists most often uncritically assume that their form and process are universally applicable. Culturally indigenous therapies in the non-Western world (traditional or ethnomedical healing systems) have received a great deal of attention from anthropologists and psychiatrists in the last several decades (Kiev, 1964; Koss, 1975; Kleinman, 1980). There are also descriptions of "new" therapies based in part on Western notions but comprising elements of the worldviews of the non-Western cultures in which they were developed, such as Morita therapy in Japan (Reynolds, 1990). These therapies comprise structural elements—process and form—that blend universal and relativistic conceptualizations.

The first structural dimension in our model, process, refers to the gradual steps or changes that produce a particular result in psychotherapy. Certain types of family therapy are easily described as process-oriented. As Ho (1987) has illustrated, the approaches by Haley, Satir, and the Mental Research Institute group focus on the interactive processes between individual family members and subsystems within the family. Individual psychotherapies can also be process-oriented, such as, for example, the relationship-oriented approaches of Moustakas (1973) and those described by Schaefer and O'Connor (1983). Proponents of self psychology for treating children are also process-oriented in that they commonly focus on the process of developing and utilizing empathic understanding by the therapist (Tolpin, 1978; Elson, 1986). Examples of how psychotherapy can be culturally responsive along the process dimension primarily involve the relationship between the child and the therapist. A first-generation Mexican American child reared in traditional ways of respect for older persons with authority, for example, will likely approach the therapist with considerable deference, although the therapist who desires to convey his sense of empathic understanding to the child may request that he or she address the therapist in a more familiar way. However, the child may experience discomfort because he or she perceives such familiarity as disrespectful. This can then defeat the therapist's goal.

The second structural dimension, *form,* refers to the manner or style of carrying out psychotherapy according to guidelines or recognized standards, encompassing both method and modality, over a limited number of sessions. Psychotherapies are form-oriented when they emphasize a specific method, such as codifying the form in which the therapist relates to the client or specifying the scheduling and length of sessions. Brief Strategic Family Therapy for adolescents with problem behaviors (Szapocznik and Kurtines, 1989) is form-oriented in its careful attention to guidelines for therapist-client relations, in its specific concern with techniques for engaging the youth and family members, and in its particular focus on the initial evaluation of family behaviors (communication, alliances, and so on). Szapocznik and Kurtines's approach was developed specifically for Cuban youths in Miami, Florida, and is aligned with the cultural dimensions of content and context. As one example, the therapist's style is strongly directive. The therapist takes charge of the family's behaviors during the session, in accordance with the traditional role of the strong father who directs the family in Cuban society.

All psychotherapeutic approaches, with their diverse orientations, can be described along the four dimensions of culture as *context* and as *content,* and structure as *form* or as *process,* according to the ways the therapist assesses the goals of therapy and the needs and problems of her client. However, psychotherapies can differ substantially in the extent to which they emphasize one or more of these dimensions with regard to the aspect of cultural responsivity. For example, in play therapy, toys can be approached through the form dimension without cultural responsiveness when "any doll will do" as a vehicle for children to express themselves. Alternatively, toys can be approached through the dimension of cultural content, for example, when the meaning and importance of "Barbies" for mainstream American girls, or origami for Japanese children, are specifically considered as a part of the therapeutic work. When culturally relevant dolls are used to elicit or clarify problems around ethnic or racial identity, the therapy is also oriented around the dimension of cultural context.

Applying the Model

Although each of the four dimensions can be separately described in relation to a particular psychotherapeutic intervention, cultural responsiveness depends most upon the dynamic interactions among any of the four. The purpose of the model is to describe approaches that make psychotherapies culturally responsive in order to facilitate the innovation and development of culturally responsive interventions. A number of examples in the literature illustrate the descriptive potential of the model. If we examine Cuento Therapy, for example (Costantino, Malgady, and Rogler, 1986), we see that it uses culture as both content and context. It clearly includes culture as content in terms of its use of traditional Puerto Rican stories and the cultural values and role definitions that typify their themes. It includes culture as context by specifically cultivating a sense of Puerto Rican identity in the midst of the strong acculturative forces to which Puerto Rican children in New York are subjected. If we look at its structural dimensions, we see that Cuento Therapy is primarily form-oriented. This is evident in its storytelling design, which intentionally mimics traditional storytelling in Puerto Rico and presents popular characters that model functional familial relationships. Thus, in Cuento Therapy, storytelling interrelates content and form, which communicate traditions, values, and normative behavior, as well as focusing on developing ethnic identity as a therapeutic tool.

Each of the twelve chapters that follow represents a different solution to the task of making psychotherapy culturally responsive for a particular ethnic group in relation to a specific problem prevalent in that group. Moreover, each chapter takes a unique approach to the dimensions of the model. Each author describes how he or she conducts therapy with ethnic minority children or adolescents in a somewhat different way. Prior to writing their chapters, the authors were given broad parameters to guide their efforts. They were requested to take a "how-to" approach to working with the ethnic group they were addressing and were given a set of three very general instructions:

1. Describe how you work with children and adolescents from a particular ethnic group with respect to a selected problem.
2. Describe the model or conceptual framework for your particular approach to intervening in the problem you will address.
3. Include ample case material to illustrate clinical processes in your work with ethnic minority children or adolescents who manifest the particular problem you have selected.

In meeting our general criteria, each author has creatively developed a unique, culturally responsive approach to his or her therapeutic work. We hope that the reader of these chapters will share our appreciation of the skill and sensitivity of these authors as therapists who mainly work with ethnic minority child and adolescent clients.

References

Bender, P. S., and Ruiz, R. A. "Race and Class in Differential Determinants of Underachievement and Underaspiration Among Mexican Americans." *Journal of Educational Research,* 1974, *68,* 51–56.

Buriel, R. "Cognitive Styles Among Three Generations of Mexican Children." *Journal of Cross-Cultural Psychology,* 1975, *6,* 417–429.

Canino, G., and Canino, I. A. "Culturally Syntonic Family Therapy for Migrant Puerto Ricans." *Hospital and Community Psychiatry,* 1982, *33,* 299–303.

Canino, I. A., Earley, B. F., and Rogler, L. H. *The Puerto Rican Child in New York City: Stress and Mental Health.* Monograph no. 4. New York: Hispanic Research Center, Fordham University, 1980.

Carroll, L. *Through the Looking Glass.* New York: St. Martin's Press, 1977.

Comas-Díaz, L., and Jacobsen, F. M. "Ethnocultural Identification in Psychotherapy." *Psychiatry,* Aug. 1987, *50,* 232-241.

Costantino, G., Malgady, R. G., and Rogler, L. H. "Cuento Therapy: A Culturally Sensitive Modality for Puerto Rican Children." *Journal of Consulting and Clinical Psychology,* 1986, *54,* 639-645.

Cushman, P. "Why the Self Is Empty: Toward a Historically Situated Psychology." *American Psychologist,* 1990, *45*(5), 599-611.

Elson, M. *Self Psychology in Clinical Social Work.* New York: Norton, 1986.

Erikson, E. *Childhood and Society.* New York: Norton, 1950.

Gibbs, J. T., and Huang, L. N. "A Conceptual Framework for Assessing and Treating Minority Youth." In J. T. Gibbs, L. N. Huang, and Associates (eds.), *Children of Color: Psychological Interventions with Minority Youth.* San Francisco: Jossey-Bass, 1989.

Greene, B. A. "What Has Gone Before: The Legacy of Racism and Sexism in the Lives of Black Mothers and Daughters." *Women and Therapy,* 1990, *9,* 207-230.

Hall, G.C.N., and Malony, H. N. "Cultural Control in Psychotherapy with Minority Clients." *Psychotherapy: Theory, Research and Practice,* Summer 1983, *20*(2), 131-142.

Headland, T. N., Pike, K. L., and Harris, M. (eds.). *Emics and Etics: The Insider/Outsider Debate.* Newbury Park, Calif.: Sage, 1990.

Heelas, A., and Lock, A. (eds.). *Indigenous Psychologies: The Anthropology of the Self.* London: Academic Press, 1981.

Ho, M. K. *Family Therapy with Ethnic Minorities.* Newbury Park, Calif.: Sage, 1987.

Hobbs, S. R. "Issues in Psychotherapy with Black Male Adolescents in the Inner City: A Black Clinician's Perspective." *Journal of Non-White Concerns,* Apr. 1985.

Jackson, A. M. "Treatment Issues for Black Patients." *Psychotherapy: Theory, Research and Practice,* Summer 1983, *20*(2), 143-151.

Kiev, A. (ed.). *Magic, Faith and Healing: Studies in Primitive Psychiatry Today.* New York: Free Press, 1964.

Kleinman, A. *Patients and Healers in the Context of Culture: An Exploration of the Borderland Between Anthropology, Medicine, and Psychiatry.* Berkeley: University of California Press, 1980.

Koss, J. D. "Therapeutic Aspects of Puerto Rican Cult Experiences." *Psychiatry,* 1975, *38,* 160–171.

Koss, J. D., and Peña, J. "A Dance of Paradigms: Clinical Research Design, Substance Abuse Treatment and Culture." In J. Trimble, C. Bolek, and S. Niemyk (eds.), *Conducting Cross-Cultural Drug Abuse Research.* New York: Howarth, forthcoming.

Lee, E. "Cultural Factors in Working with Southeast Asian Refugee Adolescents." *Journal of Adolescence,* 1988, *11,* 167–179.

López, S. R., López, A. A., and Fong, K. T. "Mexican Americans' Initial Preference for Counselors: The Role of Ethnic Factors." *Journal of Counseling Psychology,* 1991, *38,* 487–496.

Mahler, M. S., Pine, F., and Bergman, A. *The Psychological Birth of the Human Infant.* New York: Basic Books, 1975.

Moustakas, C. *Children in Play Therapy.* (rev. ed.) New York: Jason Aronson, 1973.

Munroe, R. L., and Munroe, R. H. *Cross-Cultural Human Development.* Monterey, Calif.: Brooks/Cole, 1975.

Nieves Falcon, L. *Diagnóstico de Puerto Rico.* Rio Piedras, Puerto Rico: Ediciones Edil, 1973.

Pederson, P. "The Intercultural Context of Counseling and Therapy." In A. J. Marsella and G. M. White (eds.), *Cultural Conceptions of Mental Health and Therapy.* Dordrecht, Holland: Reidel, 1984.

Phinney, J. S., and Rotheram, M. J. (eds.). *Children's Ethnic Socialization: Pluralism and Development.* Newbury Park, Calif.: Sage, 1987.

Powell, G. J., Yamamoto, J., Romero, A., and Morales, A. (eds.). *The Psychosocial Development of Minority Group Children.* New York: Brunner/Mazel, 1983.

Ramírez, M., III, and Castañeda, A. *Cultural Democracy, Bicognitive Development, and Education.* New York: Academic Press, 1974.

Reynolds, D. D. *Flowing Bridges, Quiet Waters.* New York: State
University of New York Press, 1990.

Rotheram-Borus, M. J. "Ethnic Differences in Adolescents' Identity
Status and Associated Behavior Problems." *Journal of Adolescence,* 1989, *12,* 361–374.

Sampson, E. E. "The Debate on Individualism: Indigenous Psychologies of the Individual and Their Role in Personal and Societal Functioning." *American Psychologist,* 1988, *43,* 15–22.

Schaefer, C. E., and O'Connor, K. E. "Major Approaches to Play
Therapy: Advances and Innovations *(Part One).*" In C. E.
Schaefer and K. E. O'Connor (eds.), *Handbook of Play Therapy.*
New York: Wiley, 1983.

Sue, D. W. "Culture-Specific Strategies in Counseling: A Conceptual Framework." *Professional Psychology: Research and Practice,* 1990, *21*(6), 424–433.

Sue, S., and Zane, N. "The Role of Culture and Cultural Techniques in Psychotherapy: A Critique and Reformulation." *American Psychologist,* 1987, *42*(1), 37–45.

Szapocznik, J., and Kurtines, W. *Breakthroughs in Family Therapy
with Drug Abusing and Problem Youth.* New York: Springer,
1989.

Tolpin, M. "Self-Objects and Oedipal Objects: A Crucial Distinction." *The Psychoanalytic Study of the Child,* 1978, *33,* 167–184.

Trimble, J. E., Lonner, W. S., and Boucher, J. D. "Stalking the
Wily EMIC: Alternative to Cross-Cultural Measurement." In
S. H. Irvine and J. W. Berry (eds.), *Human Assessment and Cul-
tural Factors.* New York: Plenum, 1983.

Vargas, L. A. "Evaluating Outcome in a Multicultural Inpatient
Setting." In R. L. Hendren and I. N. Berlin (eds.), *Psychiatric
Inpatient Care of Children and Adolescents: A Multicultural Ap-
proach.* New York: Wiley, 1991.

Whiting, B., and Whiting, J.W.M. *Children of Six Cultures.* Cambridge, Mass.: Harvard University Press, 1975.

Zayas, L. H., and Bryant, C. "Culturally Sensitive Treatment of
Adolescent Puerto Rican Girls and Their Families." *Child and
Adolescent Social Work,* 1984, *1*(4), 235–253.

Working with African American Children and Adolescents

PART ONE

2

Self-Esteem and Identity in Psychotherapy with Adolescents from Upwardly Mobile Middle-Class African American Families

ARTHUR C. JONES

As mental health services become more acceptable among African Americans, increasingly large numbers of African American families are seeking help from professional psychotherapists (Baker, 1988). Middle-income families are a growing clinical subpopulation whose recent occupational and economic prosperity is accompanied by a unique set of psychological issues (Coner-Edwards and Spurlock, 1988). Children and adolescent members of these families often experience problems that demand keen understanding and creative intervention. This chapter provides a discussion of some of the salient psychological issues for adolescents and the treatment strategies that seem most appropriate and effective.

Although the social changes of the 1960s and 1970s produced very little significant change for the masses of African Americans, some upwardly mobile families were able to take advantage of newly opened educational and career opportunities, which allowed them to move into an expanding class of professionally and economically successful African American families (Jewell, 1988). In some communities, a simultaneous breakdown in patterns of housing discrimination created a relatively new phenomenon: the ability of prosperous African American families to choose where they

25

wanted to live. And like their white American counterparts, many of these families migrated into suburban communities, seeking their vision of the American Dream, with modern, upscale housing and perceived educational opportunities in "better" schools for their children. These changes occurred rapidly; many young professionals who had themselves been reared in segregated communities, attending de facto segregated schools, now found themselves living in predominantly white neighborhoods and rearing children who were now attending predominantly white schools. Many of these young parents prided themselves on having overcome multiple obstacles on the path toward prestige and financial stability, and they rejoiced in sparing their children the personal hardships that they themselves had experienced in childhood.

Although African Americans in this newly expanding middle class have many of the same values and aspirations as most other American families, they are finding that their economic status does not buffer them completely from the persistent problems of systemic societal racism. The children in these families have to struggle with complex issues of identity and self-esteem, which are in some ways even more complicated than the perennial psychological tasks that all African Americans have had to face historically (A. C. Jones, 1985). In adolescence, these issues reach their peak (see R. L. Jones, 1989).

A Model of Treatment: A Prototype Case

When she was referred for treatment, Charisse was a thirteen-year-old African American girl whose parents were successful young corporate lawyers. The family lived in a predominantly white suburb of a large midwestern city. In the year before they consulted a psychotherapist, Charisse's parents had grown increasingly worried about escalating problems at school and at home. In elementary school Charisse had been a "perfect" student, with straight A grades and consistently positive feedback from teachers. She had lots of friends and seemed almost unaware of the fact that she was one of only six African American children in a school with a population of 350. However, when Charisse entered middle school her behavior changed dramatically. In the first semester her grades dropped to a C average, and by the end of the second semester she had failed two core subjects. At home she became increasingly sullen and withdrawn. When her parents attempted to get her to talk about what was bothering her, she was defiantly silent.

Frustrated, worried, and angry, Charisse's parents took her to see an African American psychotherapist who was a friend of one of Charisse's mother's law colleagues.

In the first session, the therapist met with Charisse and her parents. The parents talked uninhibitedly about their perception of the events of the past year, but Charisse remained silent and stonefaced. After twenty minutes, the therapist suggested that she and Charisse talk privately for the remainder of the session. After the parents left the room, Charisse became a different person. Animatedly, she talked about several painful events she had experienced during the past year. In the first week of middle school, for example, she had gone to use the bathroom and had noticed the words "Niggers should go back to Africa" scratched into the walls of one of the stalls. However, she tried not to think much about it and decided for herself that the graffiti was probably written by some crazy girl with nothing else to do. She was absolutely certain that it was not representative of how her fellow students felt, so she did not even mention it to her parents and in fact had almost forgotten about it after a week or so.

She found herself caught up in the excitement of the new school. Several of her friends had begun to date, and she herself was really attracted to a boy in her French class. One day after school she was excited when the boy came up and started talking to her. It seemed like he was interested in her. The next day they met after school and took a detour into the park across the street before going home. The boy asked her if he could kiss her; she was embarrassed and thought she should say "no," but she liked him a lot, so she let him. She discovered herself liking it but felt ashamed. The next day she was coming down the stairs toward her gym class when she thought she heard her new boyfriend's voice, and as she turned the corner she saw him, laughing and talking with two of his friends, so involved that they didn't notice her. Her boyfriend was telling his friends that he had kissed a black girl and detailing his plans to have sex with her: he had heard that sex with a black girl was the ultimate "high" and he was going to find out if it was really true. Charisse was devastated. She ran up the stairs, crying, and the boy, finally noticing her, ran up after her, recognizing immediately what had happened and trying to undo the damage. She refused to talk to him.

Over the next few weeks, she withdrew into a shell. She wanted desperately to be able to tell her mother about the incident, but she was embarrassed about her own behavior and she did not feel close enough to her mother, who was frequently absent from home as a result of her busy professional schedule. Telling her father was also out of the question. Moreover, the racial feelings that had suddenly come up for her were confusing and upsetting. All of her girlfriends were white; she did not feel she could discuss this with them and she again remembered the inscription on the bathroom wall. She felt alone and helpless, beginning to mistrust almost everyone, including teachers.

The Salient Issues

Charisse's story, with variations on the particulars, is in many ways representative of a clinical picture that is common among adolescents from upwardly mobile middle-class African American families seen in therapy. Parents of these adolescents grew up solid in their racial identities and skilled in dealing with racism; however, in their newfound economic prosperity, their children are negotiating environmental contingencies with which the parents are unfamiliar and inexperienced. Additionally, the outward trappings of success for these families mask the fact that salaries for black professionals rise at a significantly lower rate than for their white counterparts, so that both husband and wife have to work long hours to earn the incomes necessary to support their expensive life-styles. This leaves them short on quality time with their children. With the emergence of adolescence, many of these children are struggling with racial identity without adequate preparation. Their first experiences with overt racism therefore have a traumatic impact. Their parents are frustrated and confused, since they have sincerely worked very hard to make a life for their children, thinking this will protect them from the hardships the parents were happy to leave behind.

Many savvy parents understand the complexities of family and personal dynamics in their upwardly mobile life sphere. These parents often go out of their way to retain ties in the black community so that their children can be involved in supportive social and family networks, such as black churches and fraternities, sororities, and social organizations. They also frequently support educational choices for their children that help them understand the importance of developing a strong African American identity. Some parents begin talking to their children in early adolescence about the possibility of attending a traditionally black college, with the benefit of exposure to strong African American role models and professional support networks. If the children later choose to attend mainstream schools, parents support their involvement in black student organizations on campus. Many children in these families grow up with a realistic understanding of racism but also with confidence in themselves and their ability to take advantage of opportunities that become open to them in the majority culture. In effect, they learn that adaptive functioning as an African American involves a delicate balancing act between involvement in the majority culture and grounding in African American identity (A. C. Jones, 1989). However, bringing children to this point of healthy adaptation is a tall order for most parents, and it is certainly not surprising that some children show up in mental health treatment settings. The most frequent referrals for treatment come in adolescence.

Intervention Strategies

The therapist working with Charisse (actually this case is a carefully disguised composite of several cases from the clinical files of the author and therapists he has supervised) had to develop a creative intervention strategy, involving work with both Charisse and her parents, before Charisse could begin to climb out of her clinically significant depression. At the most basic level of issues to address was Charisse's emerging adolescence and the normal, awkward attempts at separation from parents that accompany this developmental phase. An approach that often helps initially is that of separate meetings with the adolescent and parents, which respects the adolescent's need for separation while helping the parents understand this need. Within this framework, attempts can be made to tackle some of the more worrisome symptoms.

It has been the author's experience that the usual rifts between young adolescents (ages thirteen to fifteen) and their parents are sometimes more intense in middle-class African American families, especially those in which middle-class economic status is new for the parents. This is because the generation gap is more exaggerated. The educational and social experiences of the children are substantially different from their parents' childhood experiences, a fact that is hard for both adolescents and parents to accept. Adolescents in these families often feel unsupported and abandoned by their parents. Charisse was attempting to find a place for herself as an African American teenager in an overwhelmingly white peer setting, with little chance to interact with peers who shared her worries, joys, and concerns. Her parents' childhoods were spent in city schools with

substantial black enrollments and numerous opportunities to interact with peers with similar stresses and aspirations.

In individual work with Charisse, the therapist devoted several sessions to helping her sort out the confusing emotional experiences of the last year. It became clear that Charisse had not
thought much about racial issues before she entered middle school.
Her parents had bought books for her about black history, had
talked to her about racism, and had emphasized the importance of
pride in being African American, but her daily life was in a largely
white environment and she did not understand why her parents had
been so preoccupied with race. In her immediate experience, people
were just people, and racial differences seemed irrelevant; from her
perspective, she had lots of (mostly white) friends who did not seem
to think of her as black, just as *Charisse*. Similarly, teachers did not
seem to treat her differently from anyone else. Thinking of herself
as black made her uncomfortable. She did not want to stand out;
she wanted to fit in. The experience in middle school came as a
shock—it simply did not match anything she had been through
before. And she found herself angry with her parents. Why had they
not prepared her for this? (Actually, they had tried to, but their
cautions and advice had seemed out of kilter with her actual
experiences.)

The therapist ended up spending considerable time in the
early sessions educating Charisse about the psychological context of
the emotional trauma she had experienced. Because Charisse's underlying pain was so accessible, they could talk easily about the
realities of racism. The therapist could help Charisse understand
her parents' struggles in trying to help her cope with a peer world
that was so different from the one they knew as children. Very early
in therapy it became clear that Charisse had employed a great deal
of denial in her early perceptions of her environment; there had
been several ugly comments from white peers, even in elementary
school. In second grade, for example, there had been an argument
with a girl who had called Charisse a "black liar." Charisse was
hurt by the comment but chose to ignore the not-so-subtle racial
overtones. The therapist empathized but also gently confronted her
use of the defense of denial. She helped Charisse see that awareness

of negative events in her environment did not conflict with her wish to have friends and ability to make friends with appropriate people.

Paralleling these discussions about race were some important talks about sexuality. Although she was clearly not interested in being sexually active at this point, Charisse welcomed the chance to talk about this in a confidential setting, outside her parents' hearing. She was embarrassed about her new awareness of her body and curiosity about boys and sex, which was intensified by the fact that she was an attractive girl whose physical development was ahead of most of the girls in her age group. The therapist's nonjudgmental attitude helped her to feel free to talk about this and also provided the occasion for some helpful corrections of misinformation about birth control, sexually transmitted diseases, and AIDS.

In terms of the incident with the boy at school, Charisse focused initially on her feelings of betrayal and the difficulty of being able to trust expressions of interest on the part of boys, especially white boys. She also expressed a great deal of anger about feeling her dating choices might be restricted because she was black. After a few sessions the emphasis shifted, and she focused on sadness over not having many black boys with whom to socialize. The therapist saw this as a beginning emergence of pride in being an African American.

Separate sessions with Charisse's parents were equally intense emotionally. Initially, the parents simply could not understand what had gone wrong. They both had felt they were especially conscious about attending to their child's emotional needs, particularly her need to feel good about herself as a black female. The therapist assumed a teaching role in helping them comprehend the difficulties Charisse had experienced in putting their parental advice into practice in her daily, essentially white world. In these discussions, both parents recognized that although they understood their daughter's personal experience intellectually, they had not really grasped her problems at a deeper emotional level. For example, they had not understood fully the critical importance of their own childhoods within nurturing African American communities. This experience, despite its economic hardships, developed their self-confidence as African American adults. In turn, this inner con-

fidence bolstered them in their daily lives, even though most of the
faces they encountered at this point, both in their neighborhood and
on the job, were white.

Talking about how their childhoods differed from Charisse's
sparked another important insight for the parents: in their eager-
ness to develop their professional careers, they had moved halfway
across the country to seek promising employment, putting
hundreds of miles between themselves and their extended families.
The move had paid off for them in professional and economic
terms; the negative side, however, was that their child had been
without the benefit of regular contact with relatives and friends in
the African American community. Naively, Charisse's parents had
believed that their love and support as parents would be enough.
They had miscalculated the extent of isolation a black child can feel
in a predominantly white environment and the extent to which
multiple family and community supports are necessary in surviving
this isolation. In their case, their daughter's isolation had been
made worse by their need to put in long hours on their jobs to
maintain their professional status and to keep up with mounting
personal expenses. And because their daughter, as a baby, toddler,
and elementary school child, had not seemed harmed by their personal and professional decisions, Charisse's parents had not, until
this point, had to deal with the negative side of their occupational
and financial success.

In separate sessions with Charisse and her parents, the therapist observed several parallel processes. First, Charisse's depressive
symptoms diminished and she began to show impressive insight
about the origins of her recent crisis. At the same time, she began
to express sympathy about her parents' situation, and her anger
toward her parents subsided significantly. Charisse's parents, in a
similar process, began to feel less frustrated and angry and were able
to empathize with their daughter's predicament.

As these changes emerged from their separate work in therapy, the therapist suggested that they begin conjoint family therapy.
All three agreed, and several productive sessions ensued. Although
Charisse maintained an outwardly defiant adolescent stance at
times, she also participated actively in plans to address the mix of
racial and personal issues that all three family members could iden-

tify as a family problem. The family decided that they did not want to move; at many levels they enjoyed their home and they affirmed for each other that they had made some genuine friends in their community. However, they also felt the need to spend more time together as a family and to make more frequent visits to the extended family "back home." Charisse's parents got her involved in Jack and Jill, a social club for children of middle-class African American families in their metropolitan area. In addition, the whole family joined a black ski club that made occasional group excursions to ski resorts in the Rocky Mountains.

When they decided to terminate therapy, Charisse still expressed frustration in her attempts to negotiate the complicated peer social scene at her school. However, she had recovered academically, and she and her parents all felt hope that they could continue to discuss problems as they emerged. All three family members seemed to have a balanced perspective on the joys and hardships connected with their life-style.

The way in which this case was managed is a prototype of a format that the author has found to be effective in work with upwardly mobile African American families in which an adolescent child is the identified client. This format consists of initial separate sessions with the adolescent and parents, followed by conjoint family sessions, including other children in the family, if there are any. In addition, the use of a teaching style in educating all family members about what is often a set of unconscious dynamics has not only been effective in stimulating change but has often been supportive. They frequently express relief when they understand that their personal predicament "makes sense," that they are not unique, and that their symptoms are attributable as much to societal problems as to personal failings. Intervention in these cases involves addressing a mixture of racial problems and common adolescent issues (identity, sexuality, and separation from parents).

Some cases involve more family pathology, sometimes including serious marital difficulties and occasionally parents who are in total denial about the racial isolation their children experience. In such cases, the interventions are necessarily more intensive and extensive and may require marital counseling in addition to attention to any number of issues, including substance abuse, delinquent behavior, and teen pregnancy (see Gibbs, 1989). In almost every case, however, racial issues also emerge and have to be addressed in combination with other personal and family problems. Skilled therapists have to recognize the infinite variety of ways these different issues emerge in African American families, regardless of social class (Boyd-Franklin, 1989).

Some Common Presenting Problems

The case of Charisse illustrates the interaction of societal and family dynamics in the mental health of adolescents from upwardly mobile middle-class African American families. However, it may be helpful to note three specific patterns of presenting problems that often bring adolescent clients and their families in for therapy: the Spiked-Hair Punk Phenomenon, Black and Bad, and Superblack.

The Spiked-Hair Punk Phenomenon

This is an apt term for adolescents who are referred for therapy because their parents think they are mimicking maladaptive white adolescent behaviors (such as the wearing of punk-style haircuts or interest in heavy metal rock music). The parents become alarmed, both by their children's potential for involvement with the juvenile justice system and by what they view as their children's obvious emotional and racial identity problems. It makes sense, of course, that African American children attending predominantly white schools and living in predominantly white residential communities would adopt many of the behaviors of the white peers they befriend. Nevertheless, parents then begin questioning their parenting, worrying that they may have participated inadvertently in their child's failure to develop a positive black identity.

A therapist working with a family such as this has an opportunity to help the family sort out emotional, behavioral, and identity problems and to discuss racial issues that may have never been discussed openly in the family. As described in the case of Charisse, separate sessions with the adolescent and parents may have to occur before initiating productive conjoint family therapy. One of the most difficult and painful issues that may emerge in the therapy is problems with black identity that can occur in children who have been raised in an environment in which assimilation is required for survival. In such a case the parents may have realistic fears about their child's lack of preparation for future experiences of rejection or exploitation based on race. Often, the child is unable to hear the parents' input, partly because of normal adolescent opposition and partly because of the lack of any life experiences to date confirming the parents' worldview. In some cases, the "seeds" planted in the therapy bear fruit only later, when the emerging young adult has experiences that confirm parents' earlier warnings. The following case illustrates this phenomenon.

Jerome, age sixteen, exhibited problems that illustrate the spiked-hair punk phenomenon. He was brought in for therapy by his mother, a single parent who was distressed after she came home early from work one day and found Jerome smoking marijuana in the living room with four white male friends, with heavy metal music blaring in the background. This incident was the climax of a series of events that had been increasingly disturbing to her. She was an architect in business for herself, and she and her son had moved into a wealthy, predominantly white suburban neighborhood three years earlier, after she had divorced Jerome's father. Jerome had seen his father infrequently since the divorce and had openly blamed his mother, both for the divorce and for the minimal contact with his father.

Over the last two years Jerome had been arrested on three occasions, for shoplifting, a violation of curfew, and an incident in which he was caught late at night with friends swimming, without permission, in a neighbor's private pool. Although she had been angry about these incidents, Jerome's mother understood that they all had to do with Jerome's anger about the divorce, and she had been reluctant to impose any strong punishments, since she felt guilty about the divorce and was hoping that Jerome, in time, would accept it and stop his acting out. However, she was greatly disturbed that Jerome's friends were exclusively white, that he had gotten a Mohawk hair-cut, and that he had developed a passionate interest in heavy metal music. Her frustrations were exacerbated by the fact that Jerome's father refused to intervene, blamed her for creating Jerome's problems, and demanded that she herself find the solutions.

Therapy in this case involved helping Jerome become more conscious of the full range of his feelings about his parents' divorce, including anger toward his father that he was afraid to express for fear of driving him away completely. In addition, the therapist helped both Jerome and his mother to understand the way in which Jerome, unconsciously, had chosen a set of behaviors intended to stir up his mother's worst fears about her son and his problems with developing a positive self-image as a black male in his father's absence. However, this required several months of intense work, including individual work with Jerome and his mother as well as some conjoint sessions. Eventually, Jerome was able to reach out to his father, who, thankfully, could reciprocate. Along with this came the development of some friendships with black male peers and the disappearance of the Mohawk haircut. However, Jerome had difficulty gaining acceptance from some of his peers and even at the time of termination continued to struggle with questions about his racial identity.

Black and Bad

Some adolescents in middle-class African American families, in discovering the need to develop a black identity, adopt negative cultural stereotypes of what it means to be black. Pervasive media images of blacks as gang members, drug dealers, pimps, and prostitutes unfortunately exert powerful influences on adolescents struggling with confused identities and searching for an authentic sense of self. Some adolescents unwittingly fall into a self-definition of blackness that Elaine Pinderhughes (1982) has referred to as the "victim system." This is a cycle of behavior in which involvement in activities experienced initially as powerful and "beating the system" (for example, gang membership, drug dealing) ultimately ends up with the participant being victimized by incarceration or death, or by creating a negative cycle of behavior that is passed on to the next generation. Middle-class adolescents who enter this victim system sometimes create an irreversible pattern that brings them the same negative consequences experienced by poor black youth who have not had the range of life choices of their middle-class peers.

Therapy with such adolescents is difficult, in part because the adolescents themselves frequently do not see themselves as needing help. They are on a temporary "high" (sometimes literally) and enthralled with the new life they have discovered. Even if the therapist is successful in engaging the adolescent in treatment, runaways are common, especially when family tensions increase as a result of open discussions that occur in therapy. Sometimes hospitalization is required when an adolescent is engaged in potentially self-destructive behavior. In one case, for example, an adolescent girl openly flaunted her relationship with a flamboyant African American boy she had met at a community theater production. In asking questions in the community, the therapist discovered that the girl's boyfriend was a pimp who preyed on naive young girls, eventually demanding that they become part of his stable of prostitutes. The girl totally denied the realities of the situation, and successful therapy was possible only via forced hospitalization in a locked adolescent treatment facility.

The key to working with adolescents who have adopted the "black and bad" pattern is to address directly in individual sessions the identity confusion that has spawned the behavior. Often these adolescents are amazed that the therapist understands the confusion and pain they have experienced and their desperate hunger to feel authentically "black." The therapist's empathic communication of this understanding is sometimes enough to establish a working alliance. Frequently the parents have no understanding of this underlying dynamic; they become preoccupied with their child's "strange" behavior and feel personally rejected and intensely worried about the child. The therapist's explanation of the behavior sometimes helps to allay their fears, to get them involved in treatment, and to bring them past their anger sufficiently to be supportive of their child's struggle. They frequently require help in understanding their own role in the child's problem and in developing more adaptive parenting styles. Eventually, some conjoint family work is almost always necessary.

Superblack

Regardless of their verbal expressions of African American pride, professionally successful African American parents are often viewed by their adolescent children as having "sold out." The adolescent with this view decides (consciously or unconsciously) to be more committed to positive African American identity than she or he perceives the parents to be. Sometimes the open hostility and contempt the adolescent expresses for the parents result in the parents demanding that the child be in therapy. The therapist's task is to do a realistic appraisal of the extent to which the adolescent's behavior is beyond the limits of normal adolescent separation. Sometimes both the adolescent and the parents simply need help in recognizing that the tension between them is temporary and will subside as the adolescent develops more comfort with self and less need to be openly hostile in relationship to the parents (who may or may not fit the projections placed on them). Occasionally, the superblack behavior is also accompanied by school failure, exploitive relationships (one adolescent client said: "The cause of African people is more important than some Eurocentric education bullshit or putting up with some stupid-ass mindless Negro sister"), or serious psychiatric symptoms. In such cases both the adolescent and family need help in separating identity issues from serious maladaptive behavior in need of treatment. In one extreme case, an adolescent in the throes of a first psychotic break masked his underlying thought disorder with black revolutionary rhetoric, and it took an evaluation by a psychologist to uncover the incipient psychotic process. Most cases, of course, are not this extreme, but therapists must be cautious in avoiding the assumption that militant behavior is necessarily an expression of a normal adolescent identity crisis. By the same token, there are times when it *is* simply an identity crisis. Thoughtful evaluation is important. The case of Mark is especially instructive.

At the time he entered treatment, Mark was fifteen. He was referred by an African American school counselor who viewed him as a bright, talented boy with a great deal of potential if he could get help with his emotional problems. Mark was president of a districtwide black student organization in a suburban school district. He was highly regarded by his peers but was having serious academic problems and was seen by many of his teachers as hostile and provocative. Mark had developed a good relationship with a school counselor, and she became concerned one day when he confessed to her that he sometimes had suicidal thoughts. She was able to convince him to cooperate with her plan for referral to an African American psychologist.

In the clinical evaluation it became clear that Mark was experiencing a major depression. An important part of Mark's history was the fact that his father had died in an alcohol-related automobile crash when Mark was three years old. Mark had only sketchy memories of his father, but conversations over the years with several extended family members had produced an impression of Mark's father as a creative man whose achievements were eclipsed by a serious drinking problem. After his death, Mark's mother had used money from a life insurance policy to return to school for a master's degree in public health administration and was now the administrator of a major regional medical facility.

Mark's mother was determined to balance her career and parenting responsibilities and felt proud of her ability to remain involved in family life despite intense professional demands. Mark, as he entered adolescence, seemed ungrateful, and his mother was puzzled about this. Mark openly accused her of "selling out" in choosing a prestigious life-style that included living in a predominantly white suburban community. His mother's strong professional commitments to a number of health projects with direct implications for black patients appeared to Mark as irrelevant to his expressed anger with his mother.

Treatment in this case required unraveling complicated underlying dynamics involving Mark's unconscious blaming of his mother for his father's death, an idealized picture of his father as a black hero, and an identity crisis fueled in large part by attempts to live out his father's unfulfilled life, all exacerbated by the family's life-style in a largely white suburban environment. A focus on grief work for Mark and his mother helped them both to release some of the tension that had mounted in their relationship. Mark was able to separate his genuine commitment to social causes from behavior motivated primarily by unresolved personal issues. Still, it was only after several years of intermittent therapy (punctuated by predictable problems with substance abuse) that Mark was able to commit himself to working on a college degree in political science, with a grade point average to match his professed passion for political issues.

Families That Remain in
the African American Community

Much of the above discussion has referenced problems that occur as a result of the migration of some newly prosperous African American families to white suburban communities. Many parents, however, cognizant of the complex identity problems their children face, decide consciously to live in communities where their children will not feel isolated from the family and community networks that the parents themselves cherished as children. In some cities, there are whole neighborhoods comprising middle-class African American families, with adult role models who are actively involved in the communal responsibility of raising a new generation of children. These social networks can have unquestionably positive effects on the psychological development of children; however, it is also important to challenge the simplistic assumption that intergenerational problems of middle-class African American families can be eliminated simply by the commitment of families to reside in the black community.

Many of the issues discussed in this chapter are ones that all middle-class African American families face. Regardless of the physical residence of families, for example, societal changes have produced expectations for some children that will continue to create conflicts for them and their families. In Denver, where the author works, many middle-class African American adolescents (including those that reside within the city limits and have contact with substantial numbers of African American adults and peers) come into therapy reporting serious emotional reactions to experiences of prejudice that have come as shocks to them. For example, one adolescent male client required several sessions to deal with the shock of several of his friends having been confronted by a gang of chain-wielding "skinheads" (white adolescent members of a racial hate group). Denver's low-key social environment had created expectations for middle-class children in the 1970s and 1980s of minimal racial conflict and an illusion that issues of color were no longer barriers to success and achievement. This client had come to value his ability to socialize with peers of all colors and was now beginning to question this long-cherished frame of reference.

Other clients are involved in similar questions. Parents who are committed to the importance of a strong ethnic identity (regardless of issues of oppression or prejudice—simply as a core part of healthy self-esteem) continue to raise concerns about how their children are faring in a complicated, changing society, where being an adolescent seems to them to be more difficult than ever before.

Of course, problems for adolescents and families are ameliorated to some extent in communities where the density of similar families is high and where children have available to them as models a greater number of professionally and economically successful African American adults who are dealing effectively with racial crises. In Denver, for example, the number of such families is lower than in cities with high-density African American communities, such as Washington, D.C., New York, or Los Angeles. However, the kinds of difficulties experienced by children in such communities, though quantitatively less severe, are similar.

Perhaps the salient point of this chapter is that upward mobility does not eradicate the need for African American children to be anchored in their personal and ethnic identities and to develop awareness of realistic interpersonal and institutional threats to their personal, educational, and vocational security. Therapists who work with middle-class African American adolescents and families must work within this frame of reference to ensure that they address the full range of issues their clients bring into the therapy setting.

References

Baker, F. M. "Afro-Americans." In L. Comas-Díaz and E.E.H. Griffith (eds.), *Clinical Guidelines in Cross-Cultural Mental Health*. New York: Wiley, 1988.

Boyd-Franklin, N. *Black Families in Therapy: A Multisystems Approach*. New York: Guilford, 1989.

Coner-Edwards, A. F., and Spurlock, J. (eds.). *Black Families in Crisis: The Middle Class*. New York: Brunner/Mazel, 1988.

Gibbs, J. T. "Black American Adolescents." In J. T. Gibbs, L. N. Huang, and Associates (eds.), *Children of Color: Psychological Interventions with Minority Youth*. San Francisco: Jossey-Bass, 1989.

Jewell, K. S. *Survival of the Black Family: The Institutional Impact of U.S. Social Policy*. New York: Praeger, 1988.

Jones, A. C. "Psychological Functioning in Black Americans: A Conceptual Guide for Use in Psychotherapy." *Psychotherapy*, 1985, *22*(2S), 363–369.

Jones, A. C. "Psychological Functioning in African American Adults: Some Elaborations on a Model, with Clinical Applications." In R. L. Jones (ed.), *Black Adult Development and Aging*. Berkeley, Calif.: Cobb & Henry, 1989.

Jones, R. L. (ed.). *Black Adolescent Development*. Berkeley, Calif.: Cobb & Henry, 1989.

Pinderhughes, E. "Afro-American Families and the Victim Sys-

42   Working with Culture

tem." In M. McGoldrick, J. K. Pearce, and J. Giordano (eds.),
Ethnicity and Family Therapy. New York: Guilford, 1982.
Wright, H. H. "Therapeutic Interventions with Troubled Children." In A. F. Coner-Edwards and J. Spurlock (eds.), *Black Families in Crisis: The Middle Class.* New York: Brunner/Mazel,
1988.

3

Therapeutic Issues for
Black Children in Foster Care

HELEN L. JACKSON
GEORGE WESTMORELAND

Black children in foster care face issues common to any child in placement, as well as issues compounded by culture, racism, and poverty. The African ancestors of black children were originally brought to this continent as slaves. Like their ancestors, many of these children have coped with environments that are not conducive to healthy physical or psychological development, in addition to living in two different cultures, one black and one Euro-American. In this chapter we will be using the term *black* to refer to people of African descent who were originally brought to America as slaves, but it will not include recent immigrants from the Caribbean or Africa whose racial experiences may be different. We chose to use the term *black* for ease in identification and for contrast with white mainstream Americans, but we consider the terms *black* and *African American* as interchangeable.

For children whose difficulties are reactive to circumstances in their families of origin and whose problems are not yet internalized, foster care offers a benevolent place where they can reconstitute their lives. For other children, foster care alone will not resolve developmental problems, heal traumatizing experiences, help chronic family disorganization, or alleviate the stress of frequent changes of residence. Foster children are not a single entity, nor do they come from a single group. We have included children with transient reactions to difficult circumstances as well as children with severe emotional problems. Some adjust to placement; those with more severe problems are often referred for mental health treatment by social workers, foster parents, or educators.

Overall, a developmental approach to understanding psychopathology in children and adolescents is extremely useful when making diagnostic assessments and developing interventions. Such an approach needs to include a review of the biological, cognitive, social, emotional, and educational aspects of the child's development. Although these aspects are all quite important in evaluating children, they fail to adequately address the impact on the development and resolution of their symptoms. There are, in fact, unique experiences that black children and families face that the developmental approach does not fully take into account. In other words, we believe there is an interaction between developmental tasks, problems and competencies, and racial experiences.

Nationally, about 30 to 33 percent of all children in foster care are black. In large cities, 63 percent are black (Shyne and Schroeder, 1978; Jenkins and Diamond, 1985). Not only are black children in foster care in disproportionate numbers, but they remain in it about one year longer than white children (Jenkins and Diamond, 1985). The population of black children in foster care has been increasing in recent years, due in great part to increased reporting of child sexual and physical abuse and parents' substance abuse that leads to family disruption (Bosnick, 1985). The special needs of this population have not been adequately addressed in the psychology literature. Because studies of therapeutic approaches for black children in foster care do not exist, this chapter will explore the authors' experiences in treating these children.

Black Families and Black Children

Dodson (1988) observed that the assumption that the black family differs in a culturally qualitative way from the white family underlies various theoretical and empirical approaches to the black family. Although the influences of Africa and of slavery have presumably had

an impact on the black family, Jaynes and Williams (1989) hypothe-
size that current differences in black and white family structure are
due to poor economic conditions in the black community and to
residential segregation. Black families and, consequently, black
children are under significant stress associated with low socioeconomic status and with living in single parent homes with a mother
who is often a teenager (Kraly and Hirschman, 1987).

Although current writers tend to focus on the strengths of the
black family (the cultural relativistic view) rather than on its deficits, it is the dysfunctional black family that usually has its children placed in foster care. The therapist working with a black child,
whether or not the child is currently living in a black foster home,
needs to understand the family of origin because it is the primary
agent of socialization. The length of time the child has had with
biological parents is therefore important because, the older the child
is at placement, the more he or she has learned about the values and
customs of the family of origin.

Strong kinship bonds, which are usually strengths of black
families (Nobles, 1974), are absent for the black child who enters the
foster care system. A social agency and staff take over the functions
of grandparents, uncles, aunts, cousins, and close friends. Family
life for black people is still greatly affected by racism and oppression, and natural parents serve an important but often ignored function of preparing their children to cope with these hostilities
(Nobles, 1988). This preparation, which recognizes children's need
to be accepted in both black and white communities, is absent when
black children are placed in white foster families. Black families
provide protection and support from racism that is unavailable
from other sources (Staples, 1976). In other words, they provide
racial socialization for black children.

Identity development of black children who experience racial
discrimination is often problematic because the way they deal with
minority status will have a significant impact on their general psychological health and functioning. Socialization patterns in the
black family, which foster group and personal identity, will thus
have a major impact on the emotional functioning of the child. The
following is an example.

Twelve-year-old Alice had a brown complexion and short, curly black hair. To all appearances she looked like a black adolescent; however, she was actually half black and half white. She was admitted to a children's psychiatric hospital because she fought with her schoolmates, was argumentative with her foster mother and teachers, and was often caught lying and stealing at home and in school. Unlike other black children whose parents or community provided them with strategies to cope with schoolyard racism, Alice had never learned those strategies. She had never met her black father or any of his family, and she had no contact with black culture. She had been raised by her white mother until she was placed with her maternal white grandparents; she had always lived in a white neighborhood. Alice thought of herself as white, and it enraged her whenever anyone distinguished her as black.

Black parents, families, and communities provide sources of positive identity and role models (Barnes, 1980), role models that are often missing from dysfunctional families, placing the children from these families at greater risk for developing dysfunctional coping strategies. In addition, black families in general have varying degrees of racial identity, thus making them heterogeneous in this respect. Despite these differences, however, black children often internalize the devaluation of their race, skin color, mannerisms, or way of life that is so prevalent in society.

Some studies indicate that dark-skinned children are likely to experience more negative feelings about themselves than light-skinned children (Spurlock, 1986). If black children experience themselves as attractive and as accepted in their first environment, they will have more positive self-esteem and be better able to cope with threats to their self-esteem later on in life, especially if they are then placed with white foster parents. Conversely, if black children feel rejected and abandoned by black biological parents, low self-esteem may result. However, without adequate black role models, black children may begin to feel that their blackness is responsible in great part for their rejection and begin to feel that being black is bad. Yet positive self-esteem in black adolescents has been found to be associated with having a pro-black attitude (Wright, 1985).

Socioeconomic problems can also affect the self-concept of black children (Powell, 1985), so that many from lower socioeconomic backgrounds exhibit feelings of intense alienation from mainstream society when they enter adolescence. Poor educational experience has prompted them to drop out of school, and seeing their parents' failure to combat many problematic situations, generated by both poverty and racism, is disheartening. The black teenager is quickly labeled delinquent, and he or she may be referred to the mental health system. (In poor black families, establishing an outer world is a special problem of ego development.)

Problems of Children in Foster Care

Most foster children do not understand why they are being placed and often blame themselves or attribute their placement to some irrelevant event. Such confusion can lead to irrational or fantasized thinking by children struggling to figure out what is required for them to return home. At initial placement, many children show transient distress marked by sleep disturbance, excessive eating, behavioral regression, and withdrawal. Preplacement evaluation, which can help make these symptoms short lived, might include determining the child's level of emotional development and ability to cope with family disruption. The therapist or social worker could then anticipate emotional and behavioral problems that the children might exhibit as they deal with changes and losses in their lives. The assessment of the children should also include an assessment of their overall level of maturity. Furthermore, the therapist or social worker needs to have knowledge of the children's past development in order to distinguish between early life experiences or developmental problems, on the one hand, and responses to a current situational difficulty on the other.

Irregular contact with natural parents, confusion about names and residences, lack of stable figures with whom to identify, transient and unstable peer relations—all contribute to children's sense of uncertainty about themselves. In many foster children, early object constancy—a stable, internalized mental representation of the mother—is tenuous. Discontinuity of experience with mothering figures, early understimulation, and abuse by caretakers distort the capacity of children to trust or form close relationships. In general, the most pervasive psychological effect is the sense of rejection and abandonment. Foster children often blame themselves for displacement from the home, a self-blame that results in feelings of low self-esteem, disillusionment, and confusion (Kaplan, 1982). Several investigators suggest that deprivation of parental affection is a major source of psychopathology in children (Kernberg, 1976; Gardner, 1976). Children fantasize parental affection even if they do not have it. Additionally, such internal dynamics are complicated by conflicting messages from social workers, community, and biological parents about the reason for the separation.

The psychological tasks confronting the child in placement thus include (1) coping with anxiety about separation from family and habitual surroundings; (2) developing or maintaining object constancy; (3) adapting to new parental authority figures and managing closeness with them; (4) defending against feelings of rejection, abandonment, and lowered self-esteem; (5) coping with the awareness of personal helplessness and inability to influence one's situation; and (6) developing a stable identity.

What happens emotionally to children after the loss of a parent has been studied by many theorists and researchers (Bowlby, 1969, 1973, 1980, 1982; Freud, 1960; Spitz, 1945, 1960; Wallerstein and Kelly, 1975). Bowlby, for example, described protest, despair, and detachment. Regardless of theoretical orientation, most researchers agree that a break in a relationship with a meaningful primary caretaker represents a significant loss to the child and has serious emotional consequences. For children in foster care, therefore, the quality of early experiences with primary caretakers, developmental level of the child at the time of separation, duration of separation and foster care experiences, number of separations, and experiences while in foster care (whether or not the child remains in familiar surroundings) will have long-term consequences for the psychological functioning of the child.

Black Children and Foster Care

The black child in foster care has usually come from a biological family, and possibly from a community, in which deprivation, powerlessness, and lack of control are common. The foster care experience compounds these feelings. Seligman's (1975) "Learned Helplessness Model" is a useful guide for understanding how the child experiences life. This model proposes that helplessness consists of four classes of deficits—motivational, cognitive, self-esteem, and affective. Helplessness results when the child believes that highly desired outcomes are improbable (returning home) or when highly aversive outcomes are believed probable (staying in foster care) and the child expects that there is nothing he or she can do that will change the likelihood of the believed outcome.

The development of self-efficacy will be difficult for the child if the underlying insecurity caused by racism and poverty is not understood by the therapist (Khan, 1982; Spurlock, 1986). Black children in foster care often experience themselves as socially ostracized and isolated, even more so than children of other races, because of their tenuous position in their communities and in society. Many black children of low socioeconomic status who enter the foster care system have been at-risk for developmental delays and poor personality adjustment since conception because of poor prenatal care. Abuse, neglect, and separations from significant caretakers add to their negative self-esteem.

Helms (1990) also notes that current research suggests that among blacks the middle range of social class is more likely to demonstrate positive racial identity and the lower range is more likely to identify out of their race. This trend is especially true for younger children of preschool and elementary age.

Black children in foster care will develop defenses to cope not only with feelings of rejection and abandonment but also with racism and feelings of low self-esteem. One defense mechanism is to deny the importance of the dominant culture; that is, the child might reject white authority figures. Another defense is denial of one's own blackness in an effort to identify with the dominant culture. Black children often learn to distrust, to be hypervigilant and defensive as an adaptive mechanism, which, although part of healthy coping in the child's original community, might contribute to initial difficulties in bonding to foster parents and in developing a treatment alliance with the therapist. Therefore, it is important for the therapist to note the degree to which these feelings of distrust and defensiveness are present and how disruptive they are. Next, the therapist must determine when they are appropriate and when they are dysfunctional.

Black children in foster care cannot be treated in a vacuum; many people have an impact on their lives and will have an impact on their therapy. Various social service agencies, for example, may be involved. The agency staff usually operates from the dominant cultural viewpoint. Foster parents are expected to follow agency standards when caring for the black child, which can result in care that is a mix of both black and dominant cultural influences if the foster parents are black or in care influenced by only the dominant culture if the parents are nonblack.

Black Children in White Foster Homes

Black children are frequently placed in white foster homes because black foster families are not available proportionate to their need. Although this practice continues to be a source of criticism and controversy, social workers often have no other placement options. When black foster children live with white families in white neighborhoods, their knowledge of the black community tends to come from the white media and white friends (Gill and Jackson, 1983). This information reflects the stereotypes of the dominant society, which view blacks as inferior. Without the benefits of family and community, these children are not exposed to the positive aspects of black culture. Sometimes, however, these children live in two cultures simultaneously, if they visit black parents or relatives. This may contribute to an identity confusion.

Mullender and Miller (1985) found that black children often do not tell white foster parents of their experiences with racism, finding the subject too uncomfortable to discuss. Furthermore, black foster children living with white families do not learn the functional survival techniques to cope with blatant and subtle racism that black children learn from their families and communities of origin. As in the case of Alice, when placed in a predominantly white social environment, some develop a defensive denial that they are black. They identify with their white foster parents and peers. This discrepancy between how they see themselves (as white) and how others perceive them, based upon their physical appearance (as black) is obviously confusing and painful to the child.

Although little research exists on black children living in

white foster homes, there is a body of research on cross-racial adoption. Most of the studies are in the social work rather than the psychology literature, making these data not readily accessible to therapists treating black children. Helms (1990) found that black children adopted by white parents exhibit ascribed and reference group racial identities similar to their white adoptive parents. If the adoptive parents consider the child not black or not mixed race, then the child adopts these attitudes about himself. If, however, the white adoptive parents raise the child within a social context that includes black friends and communicates positive attitudes about black people, the child develops a bicultural identity that incorporates positive feelings about black people and self. Younger children are obviously more influenced by parental attitudes than older ones. The following case illustrates problems that can occur.

Jeff was a twelve-year-old black boy in foster care who was initially referred for outpatient therapy because of behavior problems in school, which included exposing his penis to peers, masturbating in class and encouraging other boys to masturbate, using sexual language in class, and exposing himself to a female peer, masturbating and asking her to participate. At the home of his grandparents he was impulsive and easily frustrated when he did not get his way.

When the grandmother became too ill to care for Jeff, he was placed with a single, white male foster parent. One to four children lived in the home at any given time during Jeff's placement, but he was always the only black child. In weekly outpatient individual psychotherapy, Jeff demonstrated feelings of worthlessness and unloveableness because his biological mother was unable to care for him adequately; she had disappeared and had not contacted him for months. Jeff's biological father had remarried, and he never showed interest in his son. Jeff fantasized about expensive gifts his father would buy him and things they would do together. His powerlessness to change his family and his plight contributed to periods when he acted as if nothing mattered to him and was increasingly defiant, rude, and aggressive toward the foster father and other members of the foster family. He also lied to his peers about his accomplishments. Identity conflicts surfaced as well. Jeff described feeling alienated from other members of the household because he was of a different race. He was also uncomfortable and confused about food, behavioral expectations, behavioral management techniques, and religion in his white foster home. Jeff's maternal grandfather was minister of a black Baptist church; however, since placement, Jeff had not attended his familiar church.

Treatment with Jeff addressed these issues of neglect and abandonment by his biological mother, anxiety about his maternal grandparents' health and continued ability to care for him, and racial difference between himself and the white foster family. Treatment with Jeff helped him adjust to racial differences without reducing his self-esteem, which was already low and fragile. This was not easy, as Jeff was often withdrawn and uncommunicative, repressing the anger he felt about parental rejection and his fear of also losing his grandparents through death.

Therapy, however, provided an arena for Jeff to describe his fears and anxieties, as it would for any child. The difference was that the therapist introduced issues of racial differences and their impact on Jeff's feelings and interactions with others. The therapist also maintained regular communication with the foster father, maternal grandfather, and social worker, which helped them to be less frustrated by Jeff's behavior. All agreed that Jeff could visit his maternal grandfather on weekends so that he could attend the black church. The treatment approach not only helped reduce the deviant sexual behavior and poor peer relations but also helped improve his self-esteem and feelings of alienation.

Although some of the difficulties Jeff experienced in the foster home may have been similar to those of any child who was racially different from the foster parents, Jeff's experience was unique in some ways. For example, contact with the black church was particularly important to him because of its importance to his family of origin, and isolation from the black church and black community was disruptive to Jeff.

When black children must be placed in nonblack foster homes, they still need positive black role models. The therapist must be knowledgeable about resources in the black community and help the white foster parent or social worker understand the value of black role models to the child. Greg, a twelve-year-old black boy, developed a positive black identity, in part because his white, single foster mother had black friends with whom she and Greg socialized. The mother also made special arrangements for Greg to attend black community functions and church activities, and to participate in a black theater group.

A situation that did not work as well initially was that of Tony.

Tony was a tall, attractive twelve-year-old black girl who was admitted to a children's psychiatric hospital because of physical and verbal aggressive behaviors, defiance toward both peers and adults, and sexual acting out. She had been neglected by her biological mother and sexually abused by her maternal grandfather. Following hospitalization, Tony went to a residential treatment center; after a year she was placed with a single, white foster mother who also had a white foster daughter. Tony began outpatient therapy because of conflicts with her foster mother that threatened to disrupt placement.

Tony acted out her rage toward her biological mother on her foster mother, and racial and ethnic issues complicated these underlying, primary issues. Tony believed the white foster mother favored the white foster daughter, despite obvious dedication and warmth from the foster mother. She could do nothing to earn Tony's trust and cooperation in the family. In therapy Tony talked about how the foster mother did not understand black people and could not possibly understand her. She angrily demanded more freedom and fewer rules; her black friends were allowed to go to under-twenty-one dances and rock concerts, which were forbidden to her. From week to week in treatment, Tony vacillated between identifying to some degree both with the white foster mother and with her biological black mother. She defended against low self-esteem by acting "cool" with her schoolmates, even if this meant sacrificing her studies to win their approval. Tony also identified with both the victim and the aggressor in many situations. She frequently rescued peers she saw as victims. Identification with victims could have been associated with her sexual abuse or with perceiving black people as victims.

Eventually the therapist invited the white foster mother to bimonthly joint sessions with Tony to discuss their differences. The foster mother talked about her own family of origin and her attitudes and values regarding child rearing and Tony began to understand how they had influenced the mother's views about dances and concerts. The therapist helped Tony and the foster mother to write a behavioral contract, which contained a list of positive behaviors Tony agreed to work on increasing, rewards for accomplishing them, behaviors to be reduced, and consequences for noncompliance with rules. The improvements Tony made encouraged the white foster mother to allow Tony increased contact with black friends at concerts and dances and to fear less that Tony would abuse these privileges. Tony also began to see that it was her behavior rather than her race that often alienated her from other people.

Identity issues also surfaced for Tony later in her adolescence. At age fifteen, she ran away from her foster home to live with her biological mother, whose parental rights had been terminated by the courts years earlier. Following a tumultuous period with the mother, Tony realized she could not live with her and accepted placement in her original white foster home. In therapy Tony talked about whether she should date black or white peers or whether she should have black or white friends. She worried about proper hair care and skin lotions, how to accentuate one feature or diminish another.

This confusion about racial identity is not uncommon for black children in white foster care. In treating these youngsters, particularly as adolescents, the therapist must help the child develop a positive self-image, including positive perception of the black heritage.

In the cases described here, issues of acceptance, rejection, isolation, self-esteem, and identity are intensified by black children's experiences with racism in their schools and communities, which only compound the issues any child faces when placed in foster care. In some regions of the country, children may receive more intensive racial socialization (such as in the South or Northeast). Often black children raised in areas where there are few black families have more difficulty developing solid identities as blacks, unless their biological parents or foster parents work extremely hard to provide them with adequate racial socialization experiences.

Therapist Characteristics

Sue and Zane (1987) have pointed out that credibility and giving by the therapist to the client are two particularly important considerations in working with culturally diverse groups. If the client sees the therapist as an effective and trustworthy helper, the therapist has credibility. If the client believes that he or she has received something from the therapeutic encounter, the therapist is seen as giving. These are not new concepts; they are related to much-discussed notions of expectancy, trust, faith, and effectiveness in therapy. Credibility may not be an issue for the child initially, but it will be for the agency or parents who are referring the child. For the client and significant others to regard the therapist as credible and giving, the treatment must (1) conceptualize problems in a manner congruent with the black child's belief system (that is, the biological parents' belief system); (2) solve problems in a manner compatible with the child's primary cultural identification (black American); and (3) develop treatment goals consistent with those of the black child, the biological parent and/or foster parents, and the referring social agency. This can be difficult because at times congruity is lacking among these principals.

Initial stages of treatment can be especially complex. The

therapist must determine how many significant others are involved in the child's life, what their belief systems are, and how they will affect the course of therapy. Different cultural values and expectations will be at work, and all involved should clarify their expectations for the child's treatment as well as understand their individual roles. Differences in expectations should signal the therapist to reexamine treatment strategies in light of the child's black background.

A complete clinical evaluation of a black child should also include assessment of psychological strengths as well as expressions of psychopathology. Nonblack therapists may have difficulty understanding successful coping styles that do not fit white middle-class norms. The purposeful strutting of adolescent boys or the wearing of certain articles of clothing or hair-grooming styles are expressions of pride and solidarity with other blacks that should be appropriately valued. The white therapist, foster parent, and/or social worker, on the contrary, may feel threatened by these coping styles. In the assessment of individuals and families living through a traumatic experience, the therapist should not assume a low level of functioning for the child. In black families, children who survive stressful situations may emerge with considerable ego strength.

Treatment Goals

Gries (1986) modified the conceptual framework of Hobbs (1961) in working with children in foster care. We have further modified the model to address the specific needs of black children in foster care.

Classification

If the reasons for the initial placement are not clear, the therapist should contact the social worker, biological parent, or even attorneys, if available, to obtain a clear reason for the placement. As explained elsewhere, the therapist can then help the child separate facts from fantasy and reduce his or her confusion, self-blame, and anxiety about who or what is responsible for the displacement. Previous experiences with racism and the fact that the social worker is frequently white can incline black children and their biological parents to perceive race as part of the reason for the child being removed from the home. The therapist will need to identify these perceptions, if they exist, and help the child understand how racial issues did or did not influence placement. Exploring the racial components honestly can reduce the child's anger toward the white social worker and the white foster parents, and it can help with overall adjustment to the foster care placement.

Relating and Communicating

Most children in foster care have biological parents who are unable to care for them and/or protect them adequately. These experiences negatively affect the child's ability to trust others, to count on parental figures to meet their physical and emotional needs, or to expect other adults to meet their needs. These children have difficulty bonding with the foster parent. Developing a trusting relationship with a therapist will also be more difficult for black children in foster care when there is a racial difference between the therapist and child. The child has often received early training to be suspicious of social workers or police officers because their presence in the black community is frequently disruptive. Because treatment cannot even begin until a therapeutic alliance is established, the therapist must offer black children a positive role model to counter negative experiences the child has already had with adults.

The relationship between the black child and the therapist can be corrective, as in the case of a seven-year-old black boy who had been placed in several foster homes because of neglect by his biological mother, who was a substance abuser. The boy had a history of suicidal ideation and gestures. He began therapy with a quiet, friendly demeanor; however, after six weeks, he exhibited the behaviors for which the social worker had referred him for treatment. Only after he trusted the therapist did he express anger in his play and in his verbal communication toward adults and toward the therapist. Early experiences with a neglectful mother and with changing caretakers in numerous foster homes had fueled his anger.

Communication between the white therapist and black child might be complicated by the child's use of nonstandard English or nonverbal forms of expression. The child might distance the therapist by using slang expressions. Although the therapist might be tempted to learn and to use such language with the child, the child might view this unfavorably—adolescents might, in fact, ridicule such attempts and perceive them as fake.

Establishing Control

Once children have been placed in foster care, they begin to feel as if they do not have control over their lives in general and especially over their concerns regarding when, or if, they will return to their biological parents. From clinical experience, the authors have found that, despite frightening and painful experiences in the family of origin, black children want to return to their biological parents as much as other children in foster care want to return to their parents. Fear that abuse might be resumed if the child returns to the family of origin exists along with love for their biological parents. In addition to wishing for and fearing reunion with the biological parent (Gries, 1986), the child will simultaneously want to avenge himself or herself for abuse suffered and feel guilt for harboring feelings of revenge. The following case is an example.

A twelve-year-old black girl, Ceebee, had been in the custody of the Department of Human Services for nearly three years because she had been physically abused by her biological mother and sexually abused by a male friend of the mother. She was admitted to a children's psychiatric hospital because of defiant behavior and an oppositional manner toward her foster parent, teachers, and peers. During seven months of hospitalization, she was involved in intensive individual, group, and family therapies; art and recreational therapies; and special education. She made minimal changes.

The therapist, however, noticed that the client's human services case worker tended prematurely to share with the child placement plans that frequently failed to materialize, and the child and the therapist could seldom reach her case worker to clarify her status. The inaccessibility of the social worker compounded the child's feelings of powerlessness. She believed that the case worker would make decisions for her no matter how she felt about them and no matter how she acted. The therapist was finally able to arrange a meeting with the biological mother and other professionals involved in the case, including the mother's therapist, the guardian *ad litem* appointed by the courts, the Department of Human Services' attorney, and the human services social work supervisor. (Including the biological mother in the meeting also helped *her* exercise some control over what happened.) Treatment with this child needed to focus on her ambivalent feelings about returning to her mother, but the hospital staff observed more positive behaviors once the child was involved at the planning level with the timing of her discharge and placement.

Desensitization

Since many children are placed in foster care because of abuse or neglect by biological parents, desensitization is an important treatment goal if the child will return to the biological home. The therapist can help clarify perceptions and feelings toward biological parents. In this process, if the therapist has met the biological parents, he or she can validate the child's concerns about whether the parents are able to care for themselves and the child, as well as whether the parent is able to protect the child. Molin (1988) sees therapy with foster children as a place where they do not have the burden of loyalty to the parent by avoiding criticism. When return to the biological parent is planned, a number of preliminary visits to the home and family therapy sessions should be scheduled.

The therapist can help the biological parents, foster parents, and human services case worker to understand the child's fears about seeing his parents. The therapist can also remind the adults that an increase in acting out may follow parental visits, but reunion with a biological parent should not be dismissed as a goal simply because the child is more anxious prior to or following such visits. At this stage, children may express happiness as well as disappointment. If the biological parents have not changed substantially, the children may also be disappointed in the therapist for not magically fixing the problems that initially prompted family disruption. Black children may be reluctant to discuss these unresolved family problems, fearing, for example, that an expression of anxiety about a parent's possible substance abuse will lead to another legal or social agency involvement. Although this fear may be true for all foster children, in our experience it has often been exaggerated in black children because of their high level of suspiciousness of institutions and their feelings of powerlessness.

Black biological parents who have not sought out treatment

and are forced into it in order to get their children back are not easy to engage in therapy. They frequently feel angry but powerless, and they transfer negative feelings onto the therapist. The therapist needs to validate the anger and feelings of helplessness and appreciate clients' efforts to prove themselves good parents.

Conclusions

The therapist working with black children in foster care must integrate knowledge of (1) normal developmental issues of childhood and adolescence; (2) black culture and the impact on it of social, political, economic, and other environmental conditions; (3) issues in cross-racial foster placement; and (4) issues in cross-cultural/racial therapy. Even if the therapist is black, all problems of the therapeutic process are not eliminated, as there may be differences between the therapist and black child/black family attributed to degree of racial identity or socioeconomic level. In addition, to be effective with the black child in foster care, the therapist must be willing and able to expand his or her knowledge and conceptualization of the therapist role.

In summary, tailoring goals to the particular conflicts and needs of black foster children will enhance the possibility of successful treatment. Children in foster care are usually referred for psychological treatment by social workers when their problematic behavior threatens to disrupt placement. Therapists treating black children in foster care face unique problems due to the complicated issues generated by placement per se, issues that are compounded by culture, racism, and poverty. Many foster children are actually abandoned, rejected, neglected, and abused, but when black children have these experiences, racism has already had an impact on their identity formation and self-esteem. While the therapist and the child work to reduce disruptive behaviors, placement disruption needs to be seen as an interaction between the child, the foster parents, the social worker, and the biological parents (if the child will be returning home). Racial and ethnic differences and cross-cultural issues among all those involved can complicate interactions and have a significant impact on the psychological well-being of the child, the success of the placement, and the course of treatment.

References

Barnes, E. J. "The Black Community as the Source of Positive Self-Concept for Black Children: A Theoretical Perspective." In R. L. Jones (ed.), *Black Psychology*. (2nd ed.) New York: HarperCollins, 1980.

Bosnick, M. "Placement Trends Update." *Memorandum from Director*. Office of Management Analysis, City of New York, Human Resources Administration, Special Services for Children, Aug. 21, 1985.

Bowlby, J. *Attachment*. New York: Basic Books, 1969.

Bowlby, J. *Attachment and Loss*. Vol. 2: *Separation: Anxiety and Anger*. New York: Basic Books, 1973.

Bowlby, J. *Attachment and Loss*. Vol. 3: *Loss: Sadness and Depression*. New York: Basic Books, 1980.

Bowlby, J. "Attachment and Loss: Retrospect and Prospect." *American Journal of Orthopsychiatry*, 1982, *52*, 664-678.

Dodson, J. "Conceptualizations of Black Families." In H. P. McAdoo (ed.), *Black Families*. (2nd ed.) Newbury Park, Calif.: Sage, 1988.

Freud, A. "Discussion of Dr. John Bowlby's Paper." *Psychoanalytic Study of the Child*, 1960, *15*, 53-62.

Gardner, R. A. *Psychotherapy with Children of Divorce*. New York: Jason Aronson, 1976.

Gill, O., and Jackson, B. *Adoption and Race: Black, Asian, and Mixed-Race Children in White Families*. London: Batsford, 1983.

Gries, L. T. "The Use of Multiple Goals in the Treatment of Foster Children with Emotional Disorders." *Professional Psychology: Research and Practice*, 1986, *17*, 381-390.

Helms, J. E. (ed.). *Black and White Racial Identity: Theory, Research and Practice*. New York: Greenwood Press, 1990.

Hobbs, N. "Sources of Gain in Psychotherapy." Paper presented as presidential address, Division of Clinical Psychology, at the meeting of the American Psychological Association, New York, 1961.

Jaynes, G. D., and Williams, R. M., Jr. (eds.). *A Common Destiny:*

Blacks and American Society. Washington, D.C.: National Academy Press, 1989.

Jenkins, S., and Diamond, B. "Ethnicity and Foster Care: Census Data as Prediction of Placement Variables." *American Journal of Orthopsychiatry,* 1985, *55,* 267-276.

Kaplan, A. "Growing Up in Foster Care: One Boy's Struggles." *Journal of Child Psychotherapy,* 1982, *8,* 57-66.

Kernberg, O. *Object Relations: Theory and Clinical Psychoanalysis.* New York: Jason Aronson, 1976.

Khan, L. "The Role of the Culture of Dominance in Structuring the Experience of Ethnic Minorities." In C. Husband (ed.), *Race in Britain.* London: Hutchinson, 1982.

Kraly, E. P., and Hirschman, C. "Racial and Ethnic Inequality Among Children in the United States: 1940-1950." Paper presented at the annual meeting of the American Sociological Association, Chicago, Aug. 17-21, 1987.

Molin, R. "Treatment of Children in Foster Care: Issues of Collaboration." *Child Abuse and Neglect,* 1988, *12,* 241-250.

Mullender, A., and Miller, D. "The Ebony Group: Black Children in White Foster Homes." *Adoption and Fostering,* 1985, *9,* 33-40, 49.

Nobles, W. W. "Africanity: Its Role in Black Families." *Black Scholar,* 1974, *5*(9), 10-17.

Nobles, W. W. "African-American Family Life: An Instrument of Culture." In H. P. McAdoo (ed.), *Black Families.* (2nd ed.) Newbury Park, Calif.: Sage, 1988.

Powell, G. J. "Self-Concept Among Afro-American Students in Racially Isolated Minority Schools: Some Regional Differences." *Journal of the American Academy of Child Psychiatry,* 1985, *24,* 142-149.

Seligman, M.E.P. *Helplessness: On Depression, Development, and Death.* San Francisco: W. H. Freeman, 1975.

Shyne, A. W., and Schroeder, A. G. *National Study of Social Services to Children and Their Families.* Rockville, Md.: Westat, 1978.

Spitz, R. A. "Hospitalism: An Inquiry into the Genesis of Psychiatric Conditions in Early Childhood." *Psychoanalytic Study of the Child,* 1945, *1,* 53-74.

Spitz, R. A. "Discussion of Dr. John Bowlby's Paper." *Psychoanalytic Study of the Child*, 1960, *15*, 85-94.

Spurlock, J. "Development of Self-Concept in Afro-American Children." *Hospital and Community Psychiatry*, 1986, *37*(1), 66-70.

Staples, R. "The Black American Family." In C. H. Mindell and R. W. Haberstein (eds.), *Ethnic Families in America*. New York: Elsevier, 1976.

Sue, S., and Zane, N. "The Role of Culture and Cultural Techniques in Psychotherapy: A Critique and Reformulation." *American Psychologist*, 1987, *42*(1), 37-45.

Wallerstein, J., and Kelly, J. "The Effects of Parental Divorce: The Experience of the Preschool Child." *Journal of the American Academy of Child Psychiatry*, 1975, *14*, 600-616.

Wright, B. H. "The Effects of Racial Self-Esteem on the Personal Self-Esteem of Black Youth." *International Journal of Intercultural Relations*, 1985, *9*, 19-30.

4

~~~~~~

Racial Socialization as a Tool in Psychotherapy with African American Children

~~~~~~

BEVERLY A. GREENE

Despite a legacy of stigmatizing psychological folklore and a hostile environment fostered by the dominant culture, an examination of the personal and collective histories of African Americans reveals an undeniable pattern of adaptive survival (Billingsley, 1968). The adaptive strengths of African American families can be understood as derivatives of a process that may be conceptualized as racial socialization (Greene, 1990; Peters, 1985). This process encompasses a legacy of skills, which may be consciously or unconsciously communicated to African American children by their parents or extended family members and used to deflect and negotiate a hostile environment, and the means by which those skills are communicated. An elaboration and understanding of the constituents of racial socialization can yield information pertinent to developing tools that therapists may use for optimal outcomes in psychotherapies with African American children and their parents. These strategies can also prove useful in therapy with African American children whose families have been unable to pass along such skills.

The term *African American* will be used to refer to Americans whose ancestors came predominantly from the tribes of West Africa and were the primary objects of the United States' slave trade.

There is now great diversity within African Americans as a group, but similarities of experiences and practices exist that have their origins in African culture. African Americans are geographically and socioeconomically diverse. What they share, however, in addition to cultural origins, is that they live in the context of a dominant culture that is different and that actively and passively discriminates against African Americans on the basis of race. Forms and modes of racial discrimination may vary with geographical location, and therapists who treat African Americans should be familiar with these regional differences. The effects of discrimination may also vary depending on the family's economic and personal resources. Nonetheless, a common tie that binds African Americans is that most of them must make psychological sense out of the dominant culture's openly disparaging view of them, deflect negative messages about themselves, and negotiate racial barriers under all kinds of conditions. African American children face particular challenges in the course of their development that are not encountered by their white counterparts. Consequently, African American families have special problems in the task of socializing and rearing their children.

Peters (1985) describes the special things that African American parents do to prepare their children for being black in this society as the essence of racial socialization. In this process, African American parents must find ways of warning their children about racial dangers and disappointments without overwhelming them or being overly protective. Either extreme will facilitate the development of defensive styles that leave a child inadequately prepared to negotiate the world with a realistic perspective. According to Allen and Majidi-Ahi (1989, p. 157), "teaching African American children how to cope with racial discrimination represents a socialization issue which exemplifies all that is distinct about the Black experience in America."

African American families and their children continually confront a legacy of environmental insults, not the least of which is a body of stigmatizing social science literature that focuses on differences between African American and white American families and individuals and interprets those differences as if they were evidence of deficits in African Americans. Furthermore, this body of literature is used to suggest that the plight of many struggling African American families is due to their pathological structure and inadequacy or the inevitable debilitating effects of racism (Moynihan, 1965; Kardiner and Ovesey, 1951; Jensen, 1969). Although there are, without question, many negative developmental effects of racism, African Americans are not inevitable psychological cripples. A narrow focus on the negative effects of racism on the coping strategies of African Americans to the exclusion of a more general inquiry into the cultural values and lives of group members and their adaptive, creative coping strategies does not leave us with an accurate portrayal of them.

Challenges to the Optimal Development of African American Children

African Americans make up the only ethnic group in the United States whose members were unwilling participants in their immigration. Entry into the United States and its cultural imperatives was not a voluntary effort made to better their circumstances; rather, it was marked by significant losses. The role of derivatives of African culture and the involuntary immigrant status of African Americans must be understood if we are to comprehend the need for racial socialization. Derivatives of African culture constitute those aspects that have their origins in the values and practices of African peoples and their culture. Unlike voluntary immigrants, African Americans were legally assigned to subservient roles that were linked to physical characteristics that they could not alter. Once their subservient status became institutionalized, African Americans had fewer points of entry into America's mainstream. They were, in turn, blamed for their inability to enter this culture.

African American children are at greater risk for challenges to their optimal development than their white counterparts (Boyd-Franklin, 1989; Brenner, 1979; Comer, 1985; Garmezy and Streitman, 1974; Holiday, 1985; Norton, 1983; Spencer, 1987; Spencer, Dobbs, and Swanson, 1988; Spurlock, 1986; Willie, Kramer, and Brown, 1973; Wilson, 1978). African American children face the task of learning to be bicultural in an antagonistic environment. To succeed at this task, they must learn to imitate the dominant culture whether they accept its values or not. This is complicated by the dominant culture's insidious devaluation of persons of color. African American children thus face the realistic consequences of a legacy of racial discrimination, just as their parents do.

The higher rates of poverty for African American children, which often are a result of racial oppression, also place them at greater risk for problems. Their lives are marked by disproportionately higher levels of economic impoverishment than their white counterparts (Allen and Majidi-Ahi, 1989; Comer, 1985; Edelman, 1987; Gibbs, 1989; Powell, 1983; Norton, 1983). Economic recessions and hard times adversely affect the quality of life for most Americans; however, they have historically hurt African American families even more. The interaction between racial discrimination and economic hardship intensifies the effect of impoverishment alone.

Among the areas affected by economic disadvantage coupled with racism is health care. The basic right to timely and competent health care is not one that a majority of African American children possess (Edelman, 1985; Myers and King, 1983). The effects of the disproportionate access to health care range from mild to devastating (often life threatening). In addition, lack of health care can affect performance in other aspects of a child's life (Comer, 1985). Overall, there is a shorter life expectancy for African Americans (69.6 years) as compared to their white counterparts (75.2 years) (Allen and Majidi-Ahi, 1989). Clinically, we must be aware of how this discrepancy in life expectancy is understood by African American youth: the risk here is that they may see little point in planning for the future. This may be particularly salient for African American children in impoverished, crime-ridden areas where deaths in their families, whether due to inadequate health care, AIDS, or homicide, make the possibility of a future appear remote.

Another aspect of life affected is education. Overall levels of educational attainment between African Americans and whites continue to be significantly disparate. Private education remains largely in the reach of wealthy parents, leaving a majority of African American children dependent on public school systems that are not formally racially segregated but remain de facto segregated. Furthermore, children from lower socioeconomic groups are most likely to be referred for special class placements for problematic behaviors that their parents do not necessarily view as problems. According to Allen and Majidi-Ahi (1989), there is a conflict between what schools view as problem behavior and what parents often think is the problem. In addition to this, many African American parents do not trust their school systems or their children's teachers as agents who act in their child's best interest.

As African American parents and their children are required to function under greater levels of stress, they are at greater risk for mental illness (Comer and Hill, 1985; Myers and King, 1983). African American children may be found in state and county psychiatric and health care facilities at a rate 75 percent higher than their white counterparts (Edelman, 1985). It has also been suggested that 10 to 25 percent are at significant risk for developing clinical depression during their childhood (Edelman, 1985). Traditionally, African American families have borne the additional brunt of mental health's blame for problems that often had more to do with adverse social conditions and inequities than with the individual pathology of the families themselves (Gibbs, 1989).

The image of childhood as a protected developmental period is clearly not the case for a majority of African American children, particularly those who are economically impoverished. These children grow up under conditions that sharply contrast with those of many white children, the life-styles they view in the media, and the formally espoused values of the dominant culture. Survival becomes an ongoing struggle for most African American parents and their children. The fact that African American parents are vulnerable to the whims of racism in the dominant culture means that their children are vulnerable as well, often in ways from which their parents cannot protect them. In this atmosphere, the opportunity to succeed against the odds may require exceptional performance (Greene, 1990; Holiday, 1985). African American children may more easily resign themselves to frustration, hostility, and self-destructive behavior. As they operate in an atmosphere where they feel placed in a double bind and where different standards are applied to the conduct of African American and white persons, it is surprising that a preponderance of African American children are not dysfunctional or deficit ridden. African Americans must use a variety of adaptive strategies to cope with racism and the sequels of racial discrimination.

Coping Strategies and Adaptational Processes— Basic Ingredients of Racial Socialization

Despite the existence of pervasive racial discrimination and realistic barriers to their optimal development, African American children have succeeded against the odds for many generations. Their socio-emotional environment represents a major factor contributing to their adaptive development. In this context, African American families constitute an important buffer between the child and the outside environment (Bowman and Howard, 1985; Boyd-Franklin, 1989; Comer, 1985; Greene, 1990; Hopson and Hopson, 1990; Norton, 1983; Spurlock, 1986). An important aspect of this role of the family as a buffer, not unlike that of the therapist, is to help the child understand the outside world's messages and how to tell when those messages are true or not.

All parents face difficult challenges raising children in adverse circumstances, but African American parents face added stressors and special tasks. They must teach their children how to handle the special nuances of a bicultural existence without losing a core sense of themselves. This is particularly difficult because functioning in and between two often contradictory cultures can produce competing and conflicting developmental tasks and tensions (Baker, 1988; Chestang, 1973; Pinderhughes, 1989). African American parents must accomplish this task in the ubiquitous environment of real or potential racial discrimination, where there is always the potential for being devalued and/or physically and psychologically harmed, a condition beyond one's control. This context further changes and intensifies the meaning and impact of life's normal and catastrophic events, thus increasing the day-to-day level of stress. This pressure of racism and the effort by African American parents to minimize its damaging effects on their children is, in fact, a major stress not shared by their white counterparts. This stress is reflected in the amount of energy that must be consumed and in the distraction presented by the ongoing requirement of anticipating and coping with the dominant culture's barriers.

African Americans have used a variety of strategies to cope with racism throughout their history, yet they must be flexible in their strategies. The sensitivity of many African American persons to the potential for exploitation by white persons has been referred to as cultural paranoia (Grier and Cobbs, 1968). Faulkner (1983, p. 195) uses the term *armoring* to describe behavioral and cognitive skills used by African Americans as well as other persons of color to decrease their psychological vulnerability in encounters with racism. For the most part, such strategies have been pathologized by the mental health community of the dominant society, which often refers to such maneuvers as hypersensitivity or paranoia. This is the result of the mental health community's reluctance to view the behaviors of the African American individual in the context of a specific set of social conditions. Once viewed in that context, the adaptive value of such behaviors becomes obvious.

An important set of strategies for coping with racism consists of introducing and sharing derivatives of African cultural values and practices. According to Spencer (1987), an African American child's preparation by parents and other socializing agents to understand and take pride in their culture can be a major source of resilience and coping, a racial consciousness that provides a necessary foundation for the coping strategies needed. Sanchez (1989) notes that the first time African American children discover that they are "black" is usually through a negative experience; hence, many authors (Bowman and Howard, 1985; Boyd-Franklin, 1989; Harrison-Ross and Wyden, 1973; Hopson and Hopson, 1990; Peters, 1981; Sanchez, 1989; Spencer, 1987) strongly suggest that parents discuss the issue of race directly with their children before problems occur.

African American children find themselves surrounded by negative images of African American persons, in distorted or disparaging images of African American persons in the media. An additional problem is their conspicuous omission in these areas. Our language emphasizes the symbolic "goodness" of whiteness and its corollary, the bad unattractiveness of the color black, a symbolism particularly manifest in children's fairy tales, books, and cartoons. Hopson and Hopson (1990) suggest that while these images appear innocent enough, they are absorbed by children at an early age and can be destructive. They suggest removing racial or color-laden words from such stories and changing the stories themselves to make them more relevant to an African American child. In order to openly acknowledge racial diversity, parents may also use crayons to color in the faces of storybook figures to represent a variety of facial complexions and explain to children why they do so.

In environments where African Americans make up the numerical majority, their children can be protected in some ways from direct expressions of racism coming from whites. They may experience its effects in the form of poor or inadequate services to their communities, but these forms tend to be more indirect, so parents or other important adult figures need to make a connection between the problems in these communities and racism. African American children who are in situations, usually schools, where they are the minority may experience racism more directly from teachers or classmates. If they have not been a part of discussions about race or the unique aspects and contributions of their culture, they can be ill prepared to manage what are often painful and rejecting experiences with their peers.

In the context of pervasive negative images of African American persons, it is important that parenting figures take special care to expose their children to more accurate and positive images of African American people and their history. Reading to children and obtaining learning materials in which African American children not only are represented but are accurately and sensitively depicted are important undertakings. Sharing information about family members, family history, and African American history may be useful in developing an important sense of group identity and the child's sense that African Americans are worthy of pride. Hopson and Hopson (1990) also suggest providing children with ethnic dolls, prominently displaying pictures of African American people in the home, and doing anticipatory role-playing, preferably before, as well as after, problems occur.

Racial socialization encompasses the interpretation of the outside world's messages to an African American child about who she or he is with respect to African American and white American persons and what his or her respective place in the world can be. It requires that parenting figures communicate racial dangers and realities of the world to their children. They can thus help their children to identify racial discrimination and distinguish it from other life problems. Once helped to accurately identify racism, African American children must be provided with strategies for responding to it. Positive racial socialization may be accomplished by giving children strategies for specific problems as well as providing them with appropriate role models that show them how to handle discriminatory experiences. This process is illustrated in the case material reviewed later in this chapter. Bowman and Howard (1985) suggest that family socialization of proactive stances in response to racial barriers promotes resilience in African American children when they encounter or observe environments that are unresponsive to their abilities and efforts. This proactive stance can help maximize the chances that a child will take advantage of opportunities that can enhance his or her quality of life.

Racial Socialization as a Therapeutic Tool

In psychotherapy with an African American child, it is important to assess the level and quality of the child's self-image and the extent to which it may have bearing on the presenting problem. A relevant aspect of this self-image is racial identification and feelings about the limits that race can or should impose on his or her life chances (Bowman and Howard, 1985; Hopson and Hopson, 1990; Myers and King, 1983; Spencer, 1984). Parents are traditionally, but not exclusively, the persons responsible for positive racial socialization in guiding children through their developmental periods into adulthood. In this author's clinical experience, the therapeutic outcome is therefore maximized if the therapist works with the child's parenting figures, empowering and assisting them in fostering positive racial socialization. The key here is that in African American families, the role of extended kinship patterns and flexibility in caretaking roles makes it possible for important figures in the child's life to perform such functions in the absence of natural parents. In this context, therapists, regardless of their race, may incorporate many aspects of the racial socialization process into either verbal or play therapy if the parenting figures are unavailable or unable or unwilling to do so.

Parenting Issues and Their Impact on Children

We can identify a range of conditions or situations in which this process is enhanced for the child. Generally, good coping skills have been observed in children whose parents were models of resilience and were available to their children with encouragement, comfort, and reassurance (Anthony and Cohler, 1987). Therefore, the therapist can help parents understand that their children may imitate and internalize what they see in their parents' behavior before they necessarily understand what is said to them (Greene, 1990). An overall atmosphere of love and support for the child that conveys the feeling that he or she is a valued member of the family is perhaps the most important contribution the parents can make to the child. Here, despite the child's sense of uncertainty in the outside world, there is an important foundation of love and respect that the child, in turn, can carry into negotiations at uncertain times. The parenting figures must also maintain an open exchange of ideas and communication. Children will not always accept their parents' ideas or views in intense and emotionally charged areas such as race; however, parents must allow their children enough latitude in expressing themselves so that they will not fear rejection if they disagree.

Many African American persons who were confronted early in life with direct and open racial discrimination may have felt better prepared to manage it later than those who were either protected from it or who confronted it only in its most subtle forms. The expectation of discriminatory treatment may, in fact, represent a principal factor in the development of skills and strategies required to recognize and manage racial discrimination when it occurs (Greene, 1990).

Of perhaps greatest importance is the parents' self-examination on how they cope with racial discrimination themselves. Peters (1985) interviewed African American parents in an attempt to determine factors relevant to the development of young African American children, the parents' child-rearing behaviors, their attitudes toward their children, and their life goals for their children. Most of the parents interviewed reported their belief that having black children made a difference in the way they raised their children. They reported feeling that special things were required to prepare their children for being African American people in a racist society and that it placed additional stress on them as parents. Many of these same parents reported feeling that they had not been adequately prepared by their own parents to cope with the kind of discrimination they faced.

Just as some factors facilitate the racial socialization process, other factors undermine it. The children referred for psychotherapy and their families may have suffered from a variety of such factors and may be overrepresented in the clients we treat in the public sector. Parenting figures who have internalized the dominant culture's racism and its accompanying message of limited life options for African American persons will pass these messages on to their children. It is important for the therapist who determines that race awareness or identification plays a role in the presenting problem to explore these parameters in the life experiences of the parents.

In impoverished environments, parents who must devote a major portion of their energies simply to surviving economically have little energy available for anything else. A factor that often accompanies the financial woes of the family is the level of tension or discord in the relationship between parenting figures, who may not necessarily be natural parents. High levels of emotional tension may be reflected in other family arrangements where a grand-mother, aunt, uncle, or others who assume primary responsibility for the child have serious conflicts with the child or the child's parent. Isolation or estrangement from extended family members or friends may add more stress to an already stressful situation, as in the case example below. The presence of many young children in the home, particularly infants or sick or disabled children, exemplifies another stressful arrangement in which the racial socialization process may suffer. Psychologically ill-equipped or inexperienced parents, such as mothers or fathers in their early teens, may be so personally overwhelmed that they neglect any process that is not understood as one vital to immediate survival. Finally, the physical or serious mental illness of the parent may compromise the success of this process.

The situations in which a child might need the benefits of the racial socialization process most are, in fact, the very same situations in which the process is most apt to be neglected. The development of internal resources is crucial for impoverished children and is often among the few means they have available to mitigate the lack of anything beyond life's bare necessities.

The Case of Beth

The following case example reflects the use of the previously discussed principles in the course of psychotherapy.

Beth was a ten-year-old African American female at the time of her referral. Beth's mother (Mrs. D.), a twenty-seven-year-old nurse's aide, was concerned about her daughter's recent drop in a previously outstanding school performance. Nine months prior to treatment, Mrs. D. had Beth transferred from her previous school to her present school, a predominantly white, Catholic institution. Beth's previous school was a neighborhood school with a predominantly African American student body. Mrs. D. expressed with great pride that, despite much financial sacrifice, she had finally been able to remove her daughter from that "black school" and its "negative element" to a "better institution where she will have advantages."

It was somewhat clear from the outset that Beth had not desired a change of schools, had been doing well academically, and had many friends and playmates. According to her mother, she initially looked forward to her new school; however, after several months she made excuses for not going to school. After Beth's grades began to decline, Mrs. D. became alarmed. Beth reported that she wanted to return to her previous school, that she missed her friends, and that she did not feel like she "belonged" in this new school. She also reported feeling that her teacher did not treat her the same as her other classmates and that she did not feel "as smart" as she did in her old school. Mrs. D. felt Beth was being somewhat hypersensitive and should give the new school and her teacher a chance to work. After numerous sessions with both Beth and her mother, it appeared that most of Beth's difficulty centered around the new school placement and a feeling that she could not measure up to her mother's expectations, particularly when competing against white schoolmates. After some time, Beth could acknowledge the feeling that she was "not as good" as her classmates, in part because she was a "black girl." She also acknowledged to the therapist that her teacher often ignored her when her hand was raised and "yelled" at her for, as she put it, "little stuff . . . like when a lot of kids are talking in class and she just yells at me."

On meeting separately with Mrs. D., it became apparent that she was quite angry with Beth. Mrs. D. could not understand why Beth was not taking, as she described it, "full advantage of opportunities I struggle to give her, opportunities that I always wished for. . . ." Her failure to understand Beth's situation made it difficult for her to see that perhaps the teacher was treating her daughter unfairly and that Beth needed her mother's help in adjusting to this new and difficult situation.

As the work with this mother and daughter continued, Mrs. D. talked about her own early years, which she spent in a small midwestern town where whites and African Americans lived separately and race was not discussed. Her questions to her own parents about why African American children were not allowed to use some of the town's nicer schools and facilities were unanswered. In her own mind, Mrs. D. felt that her race predisposed her to second-class status and often caused her to question her own capabilities. Always feeling second best, she concluded that her children would have the benefits that she lacked and, consequently, they would become more equal to white children. Although her ambitions for her children were laudable, they also concealed her deeper feelings of racial inferiority. These feelings, she eventually reported, were heightened when her parents refused to discuss her feelings and observations about her race and the mistreatment she received because of it. This refusal simply reinforced her burgeoning notion, as a child, that "the white people must be right," that is, that she was not "as good" as they were.

The therapist worked toward offering Beth support for her experience in her new environment and for her loss of her friends, and she also worked directly and extensively with Mrs. D. This work focused on helping her to make connections between her early life experience with racism and racial differences and her fears about her own adequacy and the messages she communicated to Beth about her adequacy as an African American child. For example, Mrs. D. frequently voiced her feelings of dissatisfaction about Beth's old school directly to Beth or to others, in Beth's presence. Without realizing it, she also communicated her own fears about her adequacy as an African American mother, and, consequently, her fears about Beth's adequacy. If this could be corrected only by sending Beth to a white school, it implied that her own race was somehow defective. Mrs. D. thus came to understand her own racial insecurities and the ways they interfered with giving Beth a positive image of herself.

Therapy was terminated after Beth's grades gradually improved and returned to their previous level. Beth was able to express greater confidence in herself in concert with her mother's developing sense of confidence in herself and her ability to parent her child. An essential change was noted in Mrs. D.'s willingness to openly discuss race and racial incidents at school and elsewhere directly with Beth, rather than cringing and hoping racial conflicts and discrimination would go away, as she had been indirectly taught to do.

In this case, it was necessary to assist the patient's mother in understanding her own background; the role of racial pride, shame, or confusion in her life; and how these factors predisposed her to address her child's racial identity. A parent's understanding in these matters can directly affect the skills, resources, or difficulty that the child experiences. The mother had experienced many of the same feelings herself that her daughter had, and her own family had not provided her with the means of decoding and understanding her racial experiences except to refuse to acknowledge them. In turn, she reacted similarly to her own child and blamed her for many problems that were racial in nature. A parent such as Mrs. D. needs to learn how to listen to the child's concerns after exploring his or her own beliefs.

Generally, the process of racial socialization contains four major phases, which the therapist can first help the parent to understand and then to put into practice. First, there is the role of helping children to accurately label racism, identifying it when it occurs and understanding their experiences, which may be fraught with feelings of difference, rejection, and confusion. This aspect of the process may be seen as the phase of understanding and labeling, with the enhancement of cognitive skills as its major focus. The second phase involves the role of the parent as a role model. By their actions, parents send powerful communications to their children without uttering a word. Parents can benefit considerably by being helped to understand that their children will watch them and be aware of how they respond in particular situations. Hence, they may consciously fashion certain responses to situations to give their children models for action. In the case example, Beth's mother went to her school and talked directly to her teacher about Beth's complaints and her struggles. By acting appropriately as Beth's advocate, she simultaneously gave Beth a lesson in becoming her own advocate and a means for problem solving.

Providing emotional support for the predictable feelings of anger and impotence that often emerge when children experience direct and subtle confrontations with racism is of critical importance in the third phase. Despite the fact that encounters with discrimination may be analyzed and intellectually understood, both child and parent will nonetheless have feelings about such encounters. During this phase, the therapist should assist the parents, in a supportive fashion, in accepting such feelings in themselves and in doing the same for their children. The therapist must remember that the requirement to cope with discrimination, in no matter what form, constitutes a stressor, and like other stressors may be most effectively addressed in a supportive context. In the last phase, the parents need to be assisted in understanding that they have a legacy of negative stereotypes that their child will surely encounter in the outside world. The therapist must help the parents to stop reinforcing negative racial stereotypes and show them how to take an active role in mitigating these with positive racial images, which can be found in family folklore as well as any other symbols of ethnic pride. Children can be better helped if such symbols are introduced early in their development and are spontaneous occurrences in the home. Discussions about race and ethnic identity should be introduced to the child as a natural part of development rather than only as a response to a racial incident. When a parent is unavailable or unwilling to engage in this process, the therapist can incorporate it, or parts of it, into treatment directly with the child, depending on what the child's parent is able to do.

Summary

Although many constituents of racial socialization may be useful in work with other racial and ethnic groups, the author's experience is that racial socialization as a tool in psychotherapy is particularly suited for African American children. Therapists who use this approach must also be aware of differences in the socialization of black Americans of African descent as opposed to those of Caribbean or Hispanic origin. While all share the characteristics of oppressed groups, their respective socialization takes place under circumstances as different as they are similar. It is clear, for example, that black children of Caribbean origin are exposed to racial discrimination in the course of their upbringing in the Caribbean. One important difference between the experiences of this group and African Americans is that black persons of Caribbean origin are socialized in a context where they are the numerical majority. African Americans are socialized in the context of a larger dominant culture where white Americans are the numerical majority. Because institutions in the United States are dominated by white Americans, African Americans historically have had less control over access to information about their history before slavery.

There are certainly periods in the course of treating children with serious psychopathology in which the process of racial socialization should not be paramount in the mind of the therapist. Nor is it automatically an important therapy issue for all African American children in treatment. It can, however, enhance the treatment process when issues of low self-esteem are present, if they are related to racial identity.

This is an effective intervention tool that can be used directly with the child, but its effectiveness is optimized when the therapist assists the child's parent or parents in incorporating positive race consciousness into the routine of the child's socialization. The essential idea is to make the parent the expert, an approach consistent with systems family therapy approaches (Boyd-Franklin, 1989). This effort is particularly important if the therapist is white. Failure to be sensitive to this issue can result in inadvertently reinforcing the child's or parent's often unconscious belief or fear that the white person is automatically more knowledgeable. Although the author uses this approach in the context of psychodynamic psychotherapy, its usefulness is not limited to this modality. This process can be useful in different forms of psychotherapy with different practitioners in helping African American parents and the many African American children whom the dominant culture either ignores or treats with disdain.

References

Allen, L., and Majidi-Ahi, S. "Black American Children." In J. T. Gibbs, L. N. Huang, and Associates (eds.), *Children of Color: Psychological Interventions with Minority Youth*. San Francisco: Jossey-Bass, 1989.

Anthony, E. J., and Cohler, B. (eds.). *The Invulnerable Child*. New York: Guilford, 1987.

Baker, F. M. "Afro-Americans." In L. Comas-Díaz and E. Griffith (eds.), *Clinical Guidelines in Cross-Cultural Mental Health*. New York: Wiley, 1988.

Billingsley, A. *Black Families in White America*. Englewood Cliffs, N.J.: Prentice-Hall, 1968.

Bowman, P., and Howard, C. "Race Related Socialization, Motivation, and Academic Achievement: A Study of Black Youths in

Three Generation Families." *Journal of the American Academy of Child Psychiatry*, 1985, *24*(2), 134-141.

Boyd-Franklin, N. *Black Families in Therapy: A Multisystems Approach.* New York: Guilford, 1989.

Brenner, M. H. "Influence of the Social Environment on Psychopathology: The Historical Perspective." In J. E. Barrett (ed.), *Stress and Mental Disorder.* New York: Raven Press, 1979.

Chestang, L. *Character Development in a Hostile Environment.* Occasional Paper no. 3. Chicago: Social Service Administration, University of Chicago, 1973.

Comer, J. "Black Children and Child Psychiatry." *Journal of the American Academy of Child Psychiatry*, 1985, *24*(2), 129-133.

Comer, J., and Hill, H. "Social Policy and the Mental Health of Black Children." *Journal of the American Academy of Child Psychiatry*, 1985, *24*(2), 175-181.

Edelman, M. W. "The Sea Is So Wide and My Boat Is So Small: Problems Facing Black Children Today." In H. McAdoo and J. McAdoo (eds.), *Black Children: Social, Educational and Parental Environments.* Newbury Park, Calif.: Sage, 1985.

Edelman, M. W. *Families in Peril: An Agenda for Social Change.* Cambridge, Mass.: Harvard University Press, 1987.

Faulkner, J. "Women in Interracial Relationships." *Women and Therapy*, 1983, *2*(2/3), 191-203.

Garmezy, N., and Streitman, S. "Children at Risk: The Search for the Antecedents of Schizophrenia: 1. Conceptual Models and Research Methods." *Schizophrenia Bulletin*, 1974, *8*, 14-90.

Gibbs, J. T. "Black American Adolescents." In J. T. Gibbs, L. N. Huang, and Associates (eds.), *Children of Color: Psychological Interventions with Minority Youth.* San Francisco: Jossey-Bass, 1989.

Greene, B. "Sturdy Bridges: The Role of African American Mothers in the Socialization of African American Children." *Women and Therapy*, 1990, *19*(1/2), 205-225.

Grier, W., and Cobbs, P. *Black Rage.* New York: Basic Books, 1968.

Harrison-Ross, P., and Wyden, B. *The Black Child: A Parent's Guide.* New York: Wyden, 1973.

Holiday, B. "Developmental Imperatives of Social Ecologies: Lessons Learned from Black Children." In H. McAdoo and J. Mc-

Adoo (eds.), *Black Children: Social, Educational and Parental Environments*. Newbury Park, Calif.: Sage, 1985.

Hopson, D. P., and Hopson, D. S. *Different and Wonderful: Raising Black Children in a Race Conscious Society*. Englewood Cliffs, N.J.: Prentice-Hall, 1990.

Jensen, A. "How Much Can We Boost I.Q. and Scholastic Achievement?" *Harvard Educational Review*, 1969, *39*, 1–123.

Kardiner, A., and Ovesey, L. *The Mark of Oppression*. Cleveland, Ohio: World Press, 1951.

Moynihan, D. P. *The Negro Family: A Case for National Action*. Washington, D.C.: U.S. Government Printing Office, 1965.

Myers, H., and King, L. M. "Mental Health Issues in the Development of the Black Child." In G. J. Powell, J. Yamamoto, A. Romero, and A. Morales (eds.), *The Psychosocial Development of Minority Group Children*. New York: Brunner/Mazel, 1983.

Norton, D. "Black Family Life Patterns: The Development of Self and Cognitive Development of Black Children." In G. J. Powell, J. Yamamoto, A. Romero, and A. Morales (eds.), *The Psychosocial Development of Minority Group Children*. New York: Brunner/Mazel, 1983.

Peters, M. F. "Parenting in Black Families with Young Children: A Historical Perspective." In H. McAdoo (ed.), *Black Families*. Newbury Park, Calif.: Sage, 1981.

Peters, M. F. "Racial Socialization of Young Black Children." In H. McAdoo and J. McAdoo (eds.), *Black Children: Social, Educational and Parental Environments*. Newbury Park, Calif.: Sage, 1985.

Pinderhughes, E. *Understanding Race, Ethnicity and Power: The Key to Efficacy in Clinical Practice*. New York: Free Press, 1989.

Powell, G. J. "Coping with Adversity: The Psychosocial Development of Afro-American Children." In G. J. Powell, J. Yamamoto, A. Romero, and A. Morales (eds.), *The Psychosocial Development of Minority Group Children*. New York: Brunner/Mazel, 1983.

Sanchez, S. "Sonia Sanchez." In B. Lanker (ed.), *I Dream a World: Portraits of Black Women Who Changed America*. New York: Stewart, Tabori & Chang, 1989.

Spencer, M. B. "Black Children's Race Awareness, Racial Attitudes and Self Concept: A Reinterpretation." *Journal of Child Psychology and Psychiatry,* 1984, *25*(3), 433-441.

Spencer, M. B. "Black Children's Ethnic Identity Formation: Risk and Resilience of Castelike Minorities." In J. Phinney and M. J. Rotheram (eds.), *Children's Ethnic Socialization: Pluralism and Development.* Newbury Park, Calif.: Sage, 1987.

Spencer, M. B., Dobbs, B., and Swanson, D. P. "African American Adolescents: Adaptational Processes and Socioeconomic Diversity in Behavioral Outcomes." *Journal of Adolescence,* 1988, *11,* 117-137.

Spurlock, J. "Development of Self-Concept in Afro-American Children." *Hospital and Community Psychiatry,* 1986, *37*(1), 66-70.

Willie, C. V., Kramer, B. M., and Brown, B. S. (eds.). *Racism and Mental Health.* Pittsburgh, Pa.: University of Pittsburgh Press, 1973.

Wilson, A. *The Developmental Psychology of the Black Child.* New York: Africana Research, 1978.

PART TWO

Working with Hispanic American Children and Adolescents

5

Cultural Considerations in Play Therapy with Hispanic Children

KENNETH J. MARTINEZ
DIANA M. VALDEZ

Play therapy with minority children has been a long-ignored topic in the developmental and clinical literature. This chapter addresses the role of culture in a sociocultural, transactional, and contextual model of play therapy with Hispanic children. Essential to this therapist-facilitated model is the role of cultural and contextual variables that are a natural part of the Hispanic child's world, including language, beliefs, values, and traditions. The contextual variables include economic, political, racial, social, and frequently spiritual aspects of one's life experiences (Martinez, 1990).

Unlike Axline's (1947, 1969) nondirective play therapy technique, the therapist in this model takes a more active role and the child's minority group status is a central consideration. Specific stimuli are selected to encourage the playing out of certain sociocultural experiences, to reinforce a sense of identity. For example, if the therapist would like to explore cultural issues that may be relevant to understanding a child's background and worldview, he or she must create a sociocultural play environment in which such themes can emerge. In addition to the arrangement of toys that

This chapter is the result of equal contributions by both authors.

reflect ethnic content, the therapist can display visual materials that may stimulate conversation and themes about family rituals, language, or taboos. To understand and to be able to integrate the cultural themes that are elicited, the therapist should be sensitive to and well grounded in knowledge about the sociocultural world that the child comes from. Therefore, the therapist's contextual understanding of the child and family's worldview will help to determine the cultural content he or she introduces into the session. Three cases will be presented to illustrate this active model of therapist-facilitated play therapy.

This chapter will address those issues that are germane to a model of play therapy with minority children. First, the model is therapist facilitated, in that the therapist actively introduces relevant cultural and contextual elements into the play therapy. Second, the play therapy setting is an environment that is structured to access cultural and sociocultural themes. Third, the therapist needs to be knowledgeable about the real-life sociocultural context that the child lives in to be able to bring that into the play therapy setting. Fourth, the therapist assumes an advocacy role with the patient to help him or her, through play, to find healthy strategies, defense mechanisms, and methods by which to confront the shadow side of these dimensions.

Theories of Play Therapy

Play can be defined as a form of communication and expression through symbols whose language allows the therapist into the experiential and fantasy life of the child. Bettelheim (1987, p. 35) wrote that if we wish to understand our children, we need to understand their play, because he considered play a "royal road" that we must learn to walk to understand the child's inner world and to help him or her with it. Bettelheim (1987, p. 36) also stated that "play is the child's most useful tool for preparing himself for the future and its tasks."

Sutton-Smith (1986) defined play as a primitive form of communication, expression, and symbolization. From his perspective, play is a natural function that schematizes life, that is highly symbolic, and that precedes both language and art in its ability to reach out to others. He stated that play needs to be viewed within its contexts—physical, social, emotional, cultural, and ludicrous—all of which are essential to understanding play therapy.

There are various theoretical frameworks of play therapy. The psychoanalytic approach focuses on the analysis of the transference relationship through therapist interpretation of the child's play. The purpose is to provide the child with insight into his or her unconscious conflicts (Klein, 1937). Levy (1939) developed release therapy, an active therapist-directed approach in which certain toys are selected for the child to use while the therapist asks the child what he or she is thinking and how he or she is feeling about a specific problem. In this approach, play repetition is the key element to help the child master the problematic issue. Behavioral approaches to play therapy focus on the changing of behaviors, such as the conditioning of a more positive self-image by reinforcement of certain behaviors. Social learning theories involve the teaching of new approaches through the modeling of different play solutions. A hypnotic approach involves the use of imagination and pretending for self-enhancement and behavioral change (Katz, 1979). Family play therapy (Eaker, 1986) is an integration of play therapy with systemic family therapy that moves the transference relationship from the child and the therapist to the child and the family members. It also focuses on uncovering family secret(s) through play because the identified patient's problem (the child's problem) is seen as a metaphor for the family problem.

Practical applications of the more structured approaches are described in studies that attempt to teach children positive adaptive skills. Amato, Emans, and Ziegler (1973), studying the use of creative dramatics in storytelling with children, found that these techniques promoted a more positive self-image and the development of empathy within the therapeutic context. Gardner (1971) found that mutual storytelling resulted in positive therapeutic outcomes as well. In a study dealing with urban disadvantaged kindergarten children, Freyberg (1973) found that the children responded positively to systematic training in imaginative play, which led to more positive expressions of emotions as well as assisting the child in finding ways of reducing his or her sense of inadequacy. Bettelheim (1977) believed that the use of folktales with children was an effective means of fostering personality and ego development and dealing with their emotional problems. In the approaches studied by Amato, Emans, and Ziegler (1973), Gardner (1971), and Freyberg (1973), the therapist takes on a more facilitative role to promote change. Therefore, active and, at times, goal-oriented, therapist-facilitated approaches have been found to be effective in promoting a wide variety of positive outcomes in children.

The Cultural Context in Play Therapy

Researchers have stated the need to develop culturally distinct therapeutic interventions to address the needs of minority group children (Canino, Earley, and Rogler, 1980). Rogler and others (1983, p. 86) emphasized that there is a "compelling need to develop culturally sensitive modalities to remediate the psychological problems of minority youngsters in need of psychotherapy." Rogler, Malgady, Costantino, and Blumenthal (1987) proposed that more attention should be given to the development of culturally sensitive therapies with Hispanic children. They maintain that second-generation Hispanic children are often trapped between two cultures and are at high risk for mental disorders.

In reviewing the literature, only two articles were found that specifically addressed play therapy and Hispanic minority children in this country. Costantino, Malgady, and Rogler (1986, p. 639) developed "Cuento Therapy" as a modeling therapy designed to be sensitive to Hispanic culture. Their results indicated that Cuento Therapy significantly reduced children's trait anxiety relative to traditional therapy and to no intervention, and that this trend was stable over one year. They found that the cuento modalities also increased Wechsler Intelligence Scale for Children-Revised (WISC-R) Comprehension subtest scores and decreased observer-rated aggression. The authors stated that these findings indicate "the clinical utility of culturally sensitive modalities for improving Hispanic children's ability to understand, to verbalize and to evaluate socially acquired knowledge and to channel it in an adaptive manner" (1986, p. 644).

Trostle (1988) examined the effects of child-centered group

play sessions on the social-emotional growth of three- to six-year-old bilingual Puerto Rican children. In particular, the purpose of the study was to elicit greater social acceptance in young minority children and to increase their self-control and fantasy expression levels. In the areas of self-control and fantasy play, boys and girls who received systematic child-centered group play sessions outperformed children who received no play treatment. The author concluded that when used for preventive, remedial, or enrichment purposes, the effects of child-centered group play can serve to facilitate Puerto Rican children's social, representational, and adaptive skills in group settings.

The Transactional Contextual Model of Play Therapy

The transactional contextual model of play therapy emphasizes the process of empowering the child. Hispanic children and their families, like many ethnic minorities, are frequently disempowered and sometimes become institutionalized in systems in which they become involved. Individual, familial, and cultural identities are often invalidated. They enter mental health clinics with multiple problems that are not purely emotional in nature, such as poverty, unequal access to education, overrepresentation in the legal system, and the effects of oppression and racism. Elizur and Minuchin (1989) criticize the dehumanizing nature of mental health institutions that insist on maintaining an "objective stance" toward the patients they serve. They assert that patients are often separated from the contexts that maintain and confirm them. They challenge therapists to examine the "wider focus" and to look at problems within their contexts because the individual can never be isolated from his or her culture or context. Therefore, the goal of this play therapy model is to encourage children to explore their complex issues by acknowledging and bringing forth the multiple contexts of their experiences.

Because this is a transactional contextual model, an essential variable is language. In any work with bilingual children, or with children who live in a home where Spanish is the dominant language, it is useful to introduce Spanish into some sessions. The use of Spanish can (1) give the child permission to discuss his or her feelings about Spanish being the dominant or second language in

the home or, in some cases, feelings about his or her role as inter-
preter for the family; (2) help expose the child's bicultural identity;
(3) assess how much the child is willing to integrate cultural identity into the session; and (4) enable the therapist to assess negative
reactions by the child when the therapist introduces a second
language.

An important and initial step in the area of play therapy with
Hispanic minority children is for the clinician to assess the play
environment. Many play settings are kept current with contemporary superheroic figures, such as Spiderman or the Teenage Mutant
Ninja Turtles, that help facilitate the expression of a child's villain/
hero fantasies. Often missing in play environments, however, are
toy materials that encourage the discussion of sociocultural issues
that may have an impact on a child's psychological functioning.
The following section describes play materials that are recommended to create this environment.

Materials Used in Play Therapy

Display of the Cultural Context

Room decor can reflect cultural diversity with pictures, drawings,
postcards, and cultural artifacts on the walls and shelves. This stim-
ulates discussion and provides a welcome atmosphere for children
to explore a multicultural play environment. Pictures of cultural
heroic figures, such as César Chávez and Fernando Valenzuela, can
be displayed to promote ethnic identification and pride.

Dolls

In the past several years, toys, especially dolls, targeted for minority
group children have emerged—for example, Hispanic Barbie dolls
as well as Playmobil and Fisher-Price figures with dark complexions. For a time, at the height of their popularity, look-alike
Michael Jackson and Mr. T dolls served as superheroic figures for
some children. In New Mexico, dolls dressed in traditional American Indian dress are readily available. Dolls from different ethnic/
racial backgrounds or from other countries provide children the

opportunity to introduce characters from their own cultural world into their play. With dolls, a therapist can assess children's attitudes about cultures different from their own and can stimulate discussions about ethnic identification, self-perceptions, and idealized or rejected self-images.

Books

Numerous bilingual and Spanish publications can be used in the playroom. Books that present folktales, "dichos" (proverbs), or rhymes teach children about various human dilemmas within a bilingual/bicultural context. Coloring books that depict Hispanic, African, Asian, and American Indian legends and folklore expose children to their own cultures as well as to others'. Topics such as prejudice, intercultural differences, and cultural history are now appearing in children's literature and are useful in the playroom.

Music and Tapes

Tapes are available in conjunction with many bilingual books. Ethnic music can be turned on at low volume in the playroom while the therapist and child engage in play activities. Records and tapes of children's songs and rhymes in Spanish and Spanish/English can serve to encourage the acceptance and possibly the use of Spanish, at least within the play session.

Games

Bilingual games are more difficult to find. Games from other countries, such as "lotería" from Mexico (similar to bingo but pictures are used instead of numbers), can elicit discussion about a child's knowledge of games familiar to his or her parents or grandparents. During one play session with three Hispanic children whose mother was from Mexico, the game of "lotería" was introduced. The mother was very familiar with the game and talked about how it was played in Mexico. The children were initially opposed to playing the game in Spanish and preferred to play it in English; but the therapist and the mother called out the names in Spanish, and after a few games, the children also began to use Spanish more. They were praised by the mother and the therapist for their use of Spanish, because they had claimed that they did not know how to speak it.

Maps and Globes

The presence of a map or a globe in the play environment is often a visual cue for the child to discuss his or her family's place of origin or his or her own emigration experience, if that is relevant in the child's history. The following anecdote provides a good illustration of this. A clinician was seeing a child from El Salvador who was referred for adjustment problems following her placement with an adoptive white family in a southwestern city. During the session, the child noticed a globe that was in the therapist's office, and she told the therapist, "You have this globe here because you know I'm from El Salvador, right?" The presence of this one object in the playroom provided the child with the opportunity to discuss her emigration experience and helped facilitate ongoing discussion about her adjustment to the host country. It also helped the child bond with the therapist because she assumed that the therapist was showing empathy for her life experiences by having an object in the room that displayed her country. This gave the child the sense that the therapist acknowledged her cultural background, and the child was given "permission" to talk about sociocultural issues. The therapist also was able to establish more credibility with her.

Miscellaneous

Kitchen toys often elicit talk about foods that the child enjoys and about making ethnic foods such as tortillas or chile. In general, kitchen play provides an excellent context for the therapist to ask about parent-child relationships, as well as family routines, rituals, and roles. This could lead to discussions about extended family relationships and the role of the nuclear family within the larger kinship system. When play therapy incorporates cultural and sociocultural variables, the bilingual/bicultural development of the family is preserved, which is particularly critical when children are placed in foster care settings that may sabotage cultural and familial ties.

Therapist Assessment of Sociocultural Variables

The critical ingredient in a thorough assessment of any child is the assessment of his or her family, which knows the child best and therefore is one of the best resources to inform the therapist about the context in which the child lives. As in all child and family cases, a thorough family history is very important. This is especially true in working with Hispanic families because the therapist ought to be aware of the worldview with which the family enters therapy.

Castro and Cervantes (1985) developed a stress and coping interview to use with Mexican American families. Direct inquiries are made about the family's adaptation to the host culture and occupational, economic, marital, and family stressors. Many factors reflect the diversity of Hispanic families that would naturally affect their symptom presentation. Ramírez and Castañeda (1974) have delineated seven of them, which are directly related to the degree of acculturation of the family: (1) distance from the Mexican border, (2) length of residence in this country, (3) urban versus rural environment, (4) degree of political and economic strength, (5) degree of prejudice in the community, (6) extent of affiliation with the host culture, and (7) identification with ethnic Hispanic history. Others include languages spoken at home, education, and intrafamilial and ethnic group affiliation. Familial identification can be assessed as being traditional (least assimilated), atraditional (most assimilated), or having incorporated cultural norms from both the native and host cultures. Even within families, there are differences in levels of acculturation.

As the therapist becomes more familiar with the sociocultural world that the child and family come from, he or she is also asking about and becoming knowledgeable about the presenting problems and their possible context and origins. Through this process of inquiry, the therapist in a large sense is reframing the problem for himself or herself and the family, much like in the family play therapy model. For example, inquiries about gang involvement, even with children as young as eight to ten, are important in determining the degree of importance of extended social systems. For some children and adolescents, their gang is an essential part of their extended family, and they use the gang as an anchor in their otherwise chaotic world. This need for affiliation, validation, and sense of family can be incorporated into the therapy, but only if the therapist is aware of it through inquiry.

After the therapist has met with the family, including the child, he or she is now ready to begin a play assessment with the child in the socioculturally structured play setting. The therapist can proceed in the traditional manner of allowing the child to become oriented and comfortable within the play setting. This allows the child to choose those toys or activities that are appealing to him or her, as well as those that are more likely to elicit themes that the therapist can explore further. After the child has looked over the options and has chosen a toy or activity, the therapist can allow the child to develop the content, which allows the therapist to question him or her in a culturally sensitive manner. Lappin (1983) refers to this as cultural questioning. This may not occur in the first or even the third session until the therapist has developed rapport with the child and has allowed him or her to develop personally relevant psychological themes pertinent to his or her issues. For example, if the child is playing in the kitchen of a doll house, the therapist may ask what kind of food is being prepared, who is involved in making it, and whether any ethnic food is prepared at home. If the child is drawing, he or she may be asked who his or her heroes or heroines are, both real and fictional, to determine whether the child has any cultural identification with ethnic heroes or heroines. If the child is bilingual and chooses puppets, the therapist may verbalize a few sentences in Spanish to assess the child's comfort and identification with Spanish. A therapist-facilitated approach might involve setting up a doll play situation involving a brown and a white doll. The therapist might initiate a scenario in which the brown doll is ostracized by his or her peers because of skin color, especially if this was determined to be a relevant issue in the initial family assessment.

The purpose of this cultural inquiry is to assess the child's identification and affiliation with his or her ethnic group. The therapist can then proceed in the therapy portion to incorporate cultural themes depending upon the child's affiliation and comfort with the ethnic content. As will be evident in the cases that follow, the cultural content and interventions can also be used to maintain or strengthen a child's ethnic identity, depending upon the current circumstances in the case and the goal of the therapy.

The following case examples are from the authors' own cases of children from the Southwest, so application of this model to other Hispanic groups would require adapting play materials and the play environment to those specific groups. Given the heterogeneity of the Hispanic population in the United States, adaptation of materials would require the expertise of clinicians or ethnic consultants knowledgeable about the cultural histories, customs, and values of those groups.

Case Examples

The first case example shows the therapist's attempt to include cultural elements in the play therapy to address the child's cultural identity conflicts. The therapist introduced the Spanish language, music, and other visual materials such as maps to stimulate discussion of the child's issues. The therapist's cultural approach, however, was met with considerable resistance by the child. In this example, the therapist also assumed an advocacy role outside of the therapy setting to more effectively address the child's cultural identity issues.

Martín, a five-and-a-half-year-old Spanish-speaking child, was brought to therapy after his mother disclosed to the state human services department that he had been sexually abused by her adolescent brother. Several months after therapy began, he was removed from the home because of physical abuse by his mother. Martín was placed in an Anglo foster home with a single mother who provided foster care for several other non-Hispanic children. A major issue in the therapy was to help Martín cope with the loss of his family and culture. Since Martín was primarily Spanish speaking, Spanish was spoken during the play sessions. After Martín entered school and after more extended placement in his foster home, he began to speak more and more English, and he eventually refused to speak Spanish during the sessions. When playing board games, if the therapist counted in Spanish, Martín counted in English. During sessions, the therapist would have a Spanish radio station on at a low volume and would sometimes show Martín a map of Mexico in an attempt to stimulate conversation about his family background.

Through his nonverbal behavior, however, Martín expressed very little interest in participating in the therapist's "cultural agenda."

Martín's resistance to cultural material introduced in the sessions for the purposes of supporting his cultural identity was obvious. Martín seemed to associate his cultural identity with a mother who had rejected and virtually abandoned him. It was clear that Martín was having difficulty integrating both positive and negative aspects of his cultural and familial backgrounds into his self-image.

This resistance to exploring cultural identity issues was also related to the fact that his identity was not being reinforced in his Anglo foster home. It was possible that in his home and school environments outside of the playroom, Martín was better able to cope with his losses by relying on a new "Anglo identity."

This case example illustrates the therapist's attempt to guide the therapy to address cultural identity issues. Martín's resistance seemed to be related to the following factors: (1) The child had difficulty integrating both positive and negative aspects of his cultural and familial identity; (2) the child's cultural identity was not being reinforced in the foster home where he lived; and (3) there was the need for a more comprehensive response to the cultural dilemma and the child's adjustment because this was more than what could be provided in weekly play therapy sessions. The therapist urged that Martín be placed in a Hispanic bilingual foster home. Martín's placement in a more culturally compatible home was critical in bolstering his self-esteem and in providing him with a positive and nurturing environment in which to explore cultural and familial issues. Many of Martín's issues were resolved when he was able to talk about his mother and his feelings of sadness and loss.

The following case exemplifies how the therapist actively introduced cultural materials and other cultural and contextual content by using storytelling techniques, language, songs, and art. These therapist-facilitated interventions allowed the therapist to deal with the rapid process of acculturation that these children were experiencing, which was affecting their familial and cultural integrity.

The family included a twenty-eight-year-old Mexican-born mother named Gabriela who had three children: Marisol, age five; Christina, age eight; and Javier, age nine. This family became involved with the state human services department after Marisol's father, Juan, the stepfather of Christina and Javier, was charged with and found guilty of sexual abuse of Christina. Christina and her two siblings were removed from the mother's home. Javier was placed in one Anglo foster home and Christina and Marisol were placed in a separate Anglo foster home.

The therapist was a bilingual-bicultural Hispanic female. Most of the play therapy was done with all three children together. The therapist was alert in identifying emerging cultural and sociocultural themes that the children brought into the sessions with them. The children would spontaneously reenact "fiestas" in which they would elaborately describe parties that their father/stepfather would have in which he would drink a lot of "cerveza" (beer) and become intoxicated. This allowed the therapist to explore the children's feelings and reactions toward the father/stepfather and his alcoholism, especially at times when he was more likely to become aggressive or violent. Since the primary referral reason was Christina's sexual abuse, the therapist was able to further explore and deal with the trauma she experienced.

The children introduced the play theme of making "burritos" with clay. Each one would take turns making them and teaching the therapist how to do it. The therapist learned how important the issue of making burritos was in their family, because that theme was connected very much to their very positive relationship and identification with their mother. It became apparent that the mother's burrito making at home was a family activity that all participated in even if it was only a time to sit with each other and talk.

This theme was particularly relevant in the therapy with Javier. When treatment began, burritos were his favorite food. As the sessions continued, and with more extended placement with the Anglo family, he decided that he liked pancakes better. This became a pivotal point in the therapy because it signaled the obvious beginning of cultural disidentification and acculturation into the host culture as he continued to reside in the Anglo foster home.

A similar phenomenon occurred with all the children regarding the issue of language. When they began therapy, they primarily spoke Spanish with the therapist, but as they continued to be separated from their mother, they began to refuse to speak Spanish with each other and with the therapist. In a therapist-facilitated intervention, when playing games, reciting recipes, counting, or doing other similar play tasks, the therapist asked the children to speak to her in Spanish because otherwise she said to them: "Yo no entiendo" (I don't understand). Although she did not directly confront the children about their choice of English, she did intervene effectively as the children saw that she was doing this as a game and easily joined in and continued to speak Spanish at those times. This helped the children maintain their first language and keep a significant maternal and cultural connection with their monolingual Spanish-speaking mother.

Childhood songs and play were also introduced in Spanish. For example, they frequently used "tortillitas para Mamá" (pattycake) as a theme song. Cultural art was also used as a therapeutic medium. Javier drew stereotypically masculine Hispanic male figures that led to discussions about cultural heroes and other males with whom he identified.

The therapist used storytelling techniques as she related tales about her "abuelita" (grandmother). The therapist initiated stories about family lore and thereby introduced cultural content, since the stories spoke of traditional ways in the Hispanic family. This elicited storytelling by the children regarding their extended family both in description of traditional cultural ways and in dynamic content that was used by the therapist to help them deal with the issues of abuse, loss, and abandonment.

Through the active facilitation by the therapist, she was able to introduce, activate, and promote cultural aspects into the treatment of the three children. While the children were being acculturated very quickly into their Anglo foster homes over the course of six months, the therapist was using the play therapy sessions to help them more easily make the transition between cultures while still assisting them in maintaining a primary identification with their own culture and their monolingual and monocultural Spanish-speaking mother. If the therapist had not taken this course, they would have been further alienated from their culture and their mother due to the rapid process of acculturation in their Anglo foster home placement.

In the final case, the inclusion of relevant cultural and contextual elements was facilitated by the mother in conjunction with the therapist. Because the mother was a black woman who emigrated to the United States from Venezuela, her life and history were significant in helping the children develop a sense of their own identity and bolster the identity of the family. Through storytelling and oral history techniques, the children were strongly grounded in their Hispanic heritage. Their cultural identity was strengthened and family integrity was maintained.

Mrs. C was a thirty-four-year-old black woman from Venezuela who brought her oldest daughter to therapy because of oppositional behaviors at home and intense conflict with her siblings. María was ten years old and her younger sisters were six and three years of age. Mrs. C had resided in the United States for twelve years. After she moved to the United States, she married an Anglo man whom she later divorced. Mrs. C was a monolingual Spanish speaker and the children were bilingual. During some sessions María often drew herself with blonde hair and blue eyes, instead of her medium brown skin, dark eyes, and dark curly hair. She frequently chose to play with the blonde-haired dolls. In contrast, her sister would draw self-portraits that were close to her actual brown-skinned appearance.

Mrs. C also reported that María often expressed her anger over the family's poor financial situation. María wanted to be rich, she wanted to live in a big house, and she wanted to be able to dress in nice and fancy clothes. She sometimes became angry at the mother for not working to provide them with more material comforts. It seemed that María's desire to transform herself underlay some rejection of her identity, which was associated with the family's poverty.

The most important intervention in bolstering María's self-image occurred in the play therapy sessions that included Mrs. C. The mother would tell the girls about her life in Venezuela, about her rituals as a child, and about extended family members. They were able to discuss how their family was special and different from other families. The play sessions helped the family separate sociocultural stress from cultural and familial identity.

Although María continued to be angry about the family's low socioeconomic status, she became more interested in the family's ties to Venezuela, which increased her feelings of "specialness" and self-worth. Mrs. C became more aware of the importance of grounding her daughters in their Hispanic culture, and she decided that it was important to take her daughters to Venezuela to visit her family. She obtained a part-time job and began to save money.

This example provides a rich description of a child's confusion over the family's poverty and cultural identity. The child tried to reject her cultural and family background for the ideal image of a child from a more privileged background. The therapist attempted to strengthen family cohesion by (1) helping the mother provide her children with a sense of their history and value as a Hispanic family, (2) helping the mother ground her children more firmly in their culture, and (3) helping the family realize that their status and value as a family was not linked to their financial situation.

The case examples presented in this section illustrate the salient issues that the children faced in their attempts to deal with both cultural transition and family dysfunction. In each case, the children faced the potential loss of cultural identity as the acculturation process was imposed. The children's rejection of their own cultural background became an issue because of their difficulty integrating positive and negative aspects of their sociocultural backgrounds. The therapist-facilitated approach acknowledged these potential cultural losses and provided a therapeutic context to maintain cultural identity and integrity.

Summary

Dilemmas presented in a therapist-facilitated approach need to be considered. In their discussion of directed and nondirected therapeutic play interventions, DelPo and Frick (1988) state that in more direct approaches, the child's spontaneous input into this type of play is limited by a preplanned structure of the theme and place of the prescribed activity. They state that directed play interventions are usually limited to one or two sessions with a specific goal. They view the therapist as the initiator of the play, who decides what aspect of the experience is the focus for the child's play.

Other dilemmas that must be considered include (1) the child's potentially negative reaction to what he or she considers to be the therapist's "cultural agenda"; (2) the child's negative reaction to certain cultural themes that may be related to the presence of other more pressing intrapsychic issues, such as needs for safety and security (it is important for the therapist to prioritize the contextual as well as intrapsychic needs); and (3) the possibility that the therapist's reinforcement of a child's cultural identity in the play setting may create more conflicts for the child if this is not reinforced in other settings outside of therapy.

A therapist-facilitated approach also has several advantages. First, the child is allowed to bring his or her own reality into the playroom, when he or she is able to discuss sociocultural stressors and contextual variables in a prepared and supervised environment. Second, the play environment contains items that convey the therapist's openness to the child's cultural background, which may engender positive feelings toward the therapist and enhance his or her credibility, as children may perceive the therapist as being more similar to them. Third, a child is given permission to expose, express, and experience his or her bicultural and/or sociocultural identity in this approach. Fourth, the play therapy provides a validation for issues that may have an impact on the child, including poverty, discrimination, and racism. Being aware of the child's painful experiences, the therapist can empower the child and help the child develop positive adaptive skills.

Most Hispanic children are currently faced with significant stressors that result from poverty, discrimination, and minority group status. As therapists, we must address their mental health needs within their sociocultural contexts. For some Hispanic families, however, their children's involvement in individual therapy is sometimes a threat to the family's sense of integrity and values. Sociocultural stress and acculturation have usually had a detrimental effect on family cohesion. When parents and children are involved in family play therapy together, the family's strengths and coping skills can be assessed and incorporated into the treatment, and family integrity and cohesion are therefore maintained. Hispanic cultural and familial values are thus essential to the treatment process.

References

Amato, A., Emans, R., and Ziegler, E. "The Effectiveness of Creative Dramatics and Storytelling in a Library Setting." *Journal of Educational Research*, 1973, *67*, 161–162.

Axline, V. *Play Therapy*. Boston: Houghton Mifflin, 1947.

Axline, V. *Play Therapy*. New York: Ballantine, 1969.

Bettelheim, B. *The Uses of Enchantment: The Importance and Meaning of Fairy Tales*. New York: Vintage Books, 1977.

Bettelheim, B. "The Importance of Play." *Atlantic Monthly*, Mar. 1987, pp. 35–46.

Canino, I. A., Earley, B. F., and Rogler, L. H. *The Puerto Rican Child in New York City: Stress and Mental Health*. Monograph no. 4. New York: Hispanic Research Center, Fordham University, 1980.

Castro, F. G., and Cervantes, R. C. "Stress, Coping and Mexican American Mental Health: A Systematic Review." *Hispanic Journal of the Behavioral Sciences*, 1985, *7*, 1–73.

Costantino, G., Malgady, R. G., and Rogler, L. H. "Cuento Therapy: A Culturally Sensitive Modality for Puerto Rican Children." *Journal of Consulting and Clinical Psychology*, 1986, *54*(5), 639–645.

DelPo, E. G., and Frick, S. B. "Directed and Nondirected Play as Therapeutic Modalities." *Children's Health Care*, 1988, *16*(4), 261–267.

Eaker, B. "Unlocking the Family Secret in Family Play Therapy." *Child and Adolescent Social Work*, 1986, *3*(4), 235–252.

Elizur, J., and Minuchin, S. *Institutionalizing Madness*. New York: Basic Books, 1989.

Freyberg, J. T. "Increasing the Imaginative Play of Urban Disadvantaged Kindergarten Children Through Systematic Training." In J. L. Singer (ed.), *The Child's World of Make-Believe: Experimental Studies of Imaginative Play.* New York: Academic Press, 1973.

Gardner, R. A. *Therapeutic Communication with Children: The Mutual Storytelling Technique.* New York: Science House, 1971.

Katz, N. W. "Play Therapy: Uses in Diagnosis and Treatment." Paper presented at the New Mexico Social Services Conference on Child Abuse, Albuquerque, 1979.

Klein, M. *The Psychoanalysis of Children.* (2nd ed.) London: Hogarth Press, 1937.

Lappin, J. "On Becoming a Culturally Conscious Family Therapist." In C. Falicov (ed.), *Cultural Perspectives in Family Therapy.* Rockville, Md.: Aspen, 1983.

Levy, D. M. "Release Therapy." *American Journal of Orthopsychiatry,* 1939, *9*, 713–736.

Martinez, K. J. "Cultural Sensitivity in Family Therapy Gone Awry." Paper presented at the 98th Annual Meeting of the American Psychological Association, Boston, Aug. 1990.

Ramírez, M., and Castañeda, A. *Cultural Democracy, Bicognitive Development, and Education.* New York: Academic Press, 1974.

Rogler, L. H., Malgady, R. G., Costantino, G., and Blumenthal, R. "What Do Culturally Sensitive Mental Health Services Mean?: The Case of Hispanics." *American Psychologist,* 1987, *42*(6), 565–570.

Rogler, L. H., and others. *A Conceptual Framework for Mental Health Research on Hispanic Populations.* Monograph no. 10. New York: Hispanic Research Center, Fordham University, 1983.

Sutton-Smith, B. *Toys as Culture.* New York: Gardner Press, 1986.

Trostle, S. L. "The Effects of Child-Centered Group Play Sessions on Social-Emotional Growth of Three to Six Year Old Bilingual Puerto Rican Children." *Journal of Research in Childhood Education,* 1988, *2*(3), 93–106.

6

~~~~~~

Spirituality and Family Dynamics in Psychotherapy with Latino Children

~~~~~~

JOSEPH M. CERVANTES
OSCAR RAMÍREZ

> In this world, all things are related and of beauty . . . blessings of experience. This beauty enriches our true purposes in life . . . as you know, the physical and spiritual relationship of all living things are tied to each other if we are to survive . . . if we are to see beauty . . . to become beauty.
>
> —*Doña Lencha*, Curandera

The role of spirituality has received increased attention in the psychotherapy literature (Bradford and Spero, 1990; Bergin, 1991; Butler, 1990; Spero, 1985). A recent monograph by Cole (1990) on the spiritual lives of children and their families has highlighted this topic. Conceptual dialogue around what have come to be called "psycho-spiritual themes" in the therapy process by Christian and pastoral counseling groups (Anderson, 1990; Benner, 1987; Malony, 1983) has been useful in clarifying the integration of spirituality into clinical practice. However, this professional literature does not include ethnic minority families, particularly Latino families (those

Special thanks to Leticia De La Torre for her typing and comments on this chapter. Further thanks to Luis A. Vargas, Joan D. Koss-Chioino, and Nancyann N. Cervantes for additional comments on this chapter.

103

from Mexico, Central America, Spanish-speaking Carribean islands, and South America). The purpose of this chapter is to articulate the role that spirituality, as distinct from religious practice
(Elkins, 1988), can play in family therapy with Mexican American
children and families. Historically, religion, particularly Catholicism, has played a significant role in the lives of Mexican American
families (Bach y Rita, 1982; Ramírez and Castañeda, 1974; Trankina, 1983; Falicov and Karrer, 1980). This chapter describes how
family therapy with Mexican American families strongly parallels
the undercurrents of their spirituality and how this awareness can
have a significant impact on the therapeutic relationship.

The concept of spirituality itself has historically been a difficult process to label and clearly grasp. Vaughan (1986) refers to it as
a sense of wholeness, interconnection, inner peace, and reverence for
life. Leon-Portilla (1980), in his review of Mesoamerican spirituality,
describes it as "mystery," "ultimate realities," and contact with a
supernatural process. Elkins (1988) defines spirituality as identifiable
values that characteristically exist outside of traditional religious
practice, including a quest for meaning, a sense of mission and trans-
cendence, and a belief in the sacredness of life. For the present discussion, spirituality will be described as a transcendent level of
consciousness that allows for existential purpose and mission, the
search for harmony and wholeness, and a fundamental belief in the
existence of a greater, all-loving presence in the universe.

Although most Latino cultural groups understand the presence of spirituality in their lives, the present discussion will primarily focus on Mexican American families. While generational,
socioeconomic, and acculturative differences exist within Latino
cultural groups, we believe that these children and families as a
whole demonstrate substantial similarities in most aspects of family
functioning (Falicov and Karrer, 1980; Falicov, 1982; Murillo, 1971;
Ramírez, 1989). Therefore, the ideas generated from this chapter
will also be applicable to the broader range of Latino ethnic groups.

Conceptual View of Mestizo Spirituality
and Family Therapy

A central tenet in this chapter is an understanding of spirituality
within the context of what Ramírez (1983) has referred to as the

"mestizo perspective." *Mestizo* refers to a dynamic, synergistic process developed from the amalgamation of peoples, philosophies, and cultures bridging the European continent and the Americas: the intermingling of physical, psychological, cultural, and spiritual ties between the Spaniard and the Indian. Ramírez viewed this perspective as forged out of several influences: the strong need for survival of the race against European domination and the subsequent development of a spirit of cooperation, the amalgamation of two worldviews and orientations to life, the intersecting of Indian and European religious practices and ideologies, and the struggle to preserve Mexican Indian ideologies with new learnings from European domination. Guerra (1969) spoke of this intermixture of medicine, Catholicism, and its philosophical offspring as a dynamic synergistic process that influenced all aspects of life. Foster (1960) similarly noted this dynamic exchange of cultures and interracial influence and the strong pressures exerted by the Spaniards to usurp Aztec ways of being. In turn, Mexican Indians responded in kind to this tension through dynamic adaptation; however, they did not yield their central core beliefs about spiritual presence.

The pressure and tension forged a congruence of two cultural perspectives on spirituality (Ortiz de Montellano, 1989) that forced a mixture of indigenous, Christian, and Spanish world elements that contributed principally to the development of the character of the mestizo, as noted by Ramírez (1983). Rubert deVentos (1991) further described this creative culmination of "mestizoization" as manifested not just in the struggle between the exploiter and the exploited but in the assimilation of each other's beliefs and values. Thus, the exploiters were involved in their own psycho-spiritual struggle of abandoning European loyalty and converting to the beliefs inherent in the Americas. This context produced internal psychological tension and disequilibrium with their European brothers.

From the historical backdrop of this struggle, a mestizo perspective evolved with the following characteristics:

1. A philosophy that every person has a valuable life story to tell and lesson to learn. A favorite Mexican proverb, *Cada cabeza un mundo,* reflects this idea that each person's life and experience is important and unique.

2. Harmony with the physical and social environment, crucial to psychological adjustment and reflecting a recognition of balance and respect for all living things. Thus, plant, animal, and mineral life are viewed as having cause and purpose.
3. An openness to diversity, fostering a multicultural attitude of mutual respect and acceptance of all peoples.
4. A willingness to learn from diversity and, thus, advance the humanistic agenda of the people.
5. A belief in a theistic cosmology that protects, influences, and engages all of life.

Thus, a mestizo spirituality can be defined as a perspective that allows for an introspective attitude fostering culturally sanctioned inclination toward wholeness, harmony, and balance in one's relationship with self, family, community, and the physical and social environment. This attitude is embedded within a consciousness that understands learning from one's life history, diversity, and multicultural struggle.

Basic family themes emphasized for children growing up in Mexican American households have included a focus on the strength of the family, a respect for the family hierarchy, the development of an interconnected extended family, a genuine respect and trust in interpersonal relationships, and an unquestionable belief in an authoritarian, just God (Ramírez and Castañeda, 1974). Restated within a psycho-spiritual context, Mexican American children are oriented to life with the family and its extended members, as a protective sanctuary houses emotional support, generational wisdom, and a strong belief in the interconnectedness of all life. The family thus enacts family and religious rituals that implicitly bind relationships together toward goals of familial commitment and that build a strong base of community. The following two case examples provide an understanding of familial support and the importance of feeling whole in one's relationships with self and others.

Carlos was a fifteen-year-old Mexican American male initially seen because of a defiant attitude, skipping school, and beginning flirtation with gang life. For the past year, Carlos had been living with his natural mother and very financially successful Anglo stepfather. Carlos's parents divorced approximately four years before the time of the initial interview. His natural father was a narcotics detective who historically had had little or no contact with either Carlos or his younger sister (age thirteen). Carlos presented himself in very *cholo* style dress and personal mannerisms. (*Cholo* is a term whose sociohistorical origins are not clear but that is characteristically associated with Mexican American adolescents who participate in the subculture of the gang.) He manifested poor eye contact and a "tough guy" attitude. He tended to communicate, through his posture, significant nonverbal anger. The therapist supported Carlos's defensive manner and encouraged him to be suspicious of anyone who tried to change him. He was told that he was connecting at a deep level with his roots and that he should be proud of his courage to do so.

Following this seemingly paradoxical intervention, Carlos spoke openly of his need to feel connected to his grandparents and relatives. He further elaborated about how he could not "feel right" about living with his stepfather because he was unable to understand loyalty and commitment to family. In that context, Carlos added that his stepfather and possibly his own mother were "God-less" and were not being responsible people as a result. In subsequent visits, Carlos spoke about a strong need to feel that "all things were in their right place" so that he could feel that he was fitting back into the family.

Therapy visits continued with Carlos, his natural mother, and his maternal grandparents intermittently for the next two months. Carlos moved in with his maternal grandparents soon after. His *cholo* presentation disappeared, and participation in his new school setting was consistent. Although misunderstanding and anger were still evident toward his natural mother and stepfather, he was now able to verbalize these feelings and take responsibility for his part.

José, nicknamed Pelón, was a twelve-and-a-half-year-old Mexican American boy who had run away from home during the latter part of his seventh-grade year. He had been seen by his natural father and his girlfriend in the barrio, but neither was able to convince him to go home. Pelón became involved with a local gang, where he began to use drugs and alcohol and took part in two drive-by shootings. Pelón returned unexpectedly to the family home, and because of prior planning with the therapist, he was taken immediately to a psychiatric adolescent inpatient unit for assessment and therapeutic care.

Because hospitalization happened so quickly for Pelón, he met his initial days in the hospital with confusion and passive resistance. The intense pressure of the therapeutic milieu eventually encouraged Pelón to begin participating in the program and thus allowed him to reveal his own history and emotional agenda. He discussed his anger toward his natural father for always being absent and for mistreating him and his older brother on several occasions. Pelón stated that there was no one who cared about him, and he felt that his "insides were at war all the time" because he did not know what he was supposed to do or where he should be. He further spoke of evil and threatening voices "like the devil" that frightened and confused him. Pelón was encouraged into a guided imagery sequence of envisioning the most secure and holy place he could imagine. The image selected by Pelón was that of being a young child surrounded by his parents, grandparents, and cousins. After progress with peers and authority figures on the unit, Pelón was able to use his imagery to deal with the "evil voices" rather than take medication.

Pelón was discharged prematurely after two weeks of hospitalization because his insurance policy would not pay for any additional care. Once he was released, the natural father was unable to hold back his anger toward his son for his runaway behavior and gang involvement. During the initial outpatient visit following the hospital discharge that afternoon, he verbally abused his two sons, causing them to remain silent and noncompliant for the remainder of the session. Pelón ran away again that evening as his father had predicted.

The case of Carlos illustrates the confusion, resentment, and spiritual crisis of an adolescent boy who was struggling with both characteristic identity issues and distress with regard to concepts of order and beauty (for example, correct moral and ethical behavior). As is often the case with Mexican American youth involved in gang activity who take on an aggressive posture through their mode of dress and personal mannerisms, Carlos was struggling for a secure place in his family/social-interpersonal environment. His lack of connection and balance with family resulted in directed anger toward his mother for having lost her "cultural" beliefs and for having abandoned her "Mexican-ness," which was linked with psychospiritual identity and violation of what God intended to be true for him and his family. Therapeutic connection with Carlos was initiated by affirming his ethnic and cultural background, which made his emotional agenda accessible. Carlos's beliefs about the importance of God and the need for "correct moral behavior" were supported and encouraged as he struggled to understand the spiritual-existential meaning of his family's behavior. Intervention by the maternal grandparents was found to provide the needed contextual frame for familial support that validated his view of culturally sanctioned balance.

The case of Pelón examines several issues that are of significance to themes of spirituality. Initially, Pelón's sense of family integrity was seriously questioned, given his perceptions of the family and subsequent pattern of dysfunctional interactions. Pelón showed in his choice of imagery that he had an earlier history of security and perceived affection in his family that at some point was radically changed. Thus, Pelón's sense of family evolved from some level of comfort and familial interconnection to one that became abusive and intolerable. An intense feeling of vulnerability and woundedness developed that subsequently became internalized as his being evil. Rather than considering the "evil voices" pathological, the therapist interpreted them as Pelón's way of making sense of his inner turmoil reflecting emotional abandonment and self-hatred. The job of the therapist was to create a safe environment for Pelón to be able to make his way out of his cycle of fear. He was taught to use a greater "magic," his imagery, to drown out the voices and reestablish himself in a place of safety and wholeness. That Pelón was able to do this suggested that he had healthy ego functioning and an emotional remembrance of familial balance and order. The encouragement of developing positive energy as he aligned with the "goodness" within him prompted quick changes in Pelón's attitudes and behavior. Unfortunately, the therapeutic environment could not be maintained either in the hospital unit or at home.

Mestizo spirituality emphasizes harmony, interdependence, and respect for the sacredness of one's place in the world. It is, therefore, possible to understand both Carlos's and Pelón's gang involvement as an attempt to seek these values, in place of what a cohesive family unit would provide. As highlighted by these case examples, mestizo spirituality underscores themes of adaptation and survival and beliefs in a higher good. It embraces metaphysical notions of "good" and "evil" spirits and their possible impact upon one's behavior. Illustrations of some of these metaphysical roots are found, for example, in cultural beliefs in the Virgen de Guadalupe and in the celebration of Día de los Muertos (Day of the Dead). Carrasco (1990) notes that each of these traditions takes the believers on special journeys or through sacred landscapes in order to promote a healing of mind, body, and soul. Our Lady of Guadalupe is the protective, all-loving mother who perpetually guides and watches over her people. Día de los Muertos honors those who are deceased, joining together both the living and the dead in a spirit of communion and spiritual renewal. Each of these traditional celebrations gives additional conscious and unconscious validation of mestizo roots and an affirmation of the influence that spirituality lends to one's daily existence.

The legend "La Llorona" lends an additional perspective to the correct and moral behavior underlying a mestizo spirituality (Anaya, 1984; Garcia-Kraul and Beatly, 1988; de Aragon, 1980). In folklore, La Llorona is the woman who is punished for eternity to wail over the loss of her children, whom she drowned in the river. Her wailing has often been heard by children (de Aragon, 1980) and signals one's sense of responsibility to others, as well as both a fear and a conviction that there is "goodness" and balance on a broader existential plane.

Supernatural forces thus play a significant role in the lives of the living (Ramírez and Castañeda, 1974; Ramírez, 1983; Gonzales, 1976; Padilla and Salgado de Snyder, 1988). To hear a ten-year-old child speak about her conscious dialogue with her deceased grandmother, descriptions of family visits to the cemetery to communicate with dead relatives, or accounts of strong beliefs in visionary or premonition experiences are frequent observations in clinical practice. The role in achieving wholeness that this type of experience plays in the consciousness of Mexican American families is encouraged and developed through several processes: an interdependent respect for the physical and social environment, prayer, meditation, visionary experience, and general appeals to a supernatural force. Mexican American children generally learn very quickly about the existence of an invisible world made up of both dark and light entities. On the dark side are the demons, "brujos" or "brujas" (witches), and evil spirits that can harm and negatively influence one's behavior in the external world. On the light side are the angels, saints, and holy ones, along with a positive energy, that preserve balance and respect in one's self and relationship to family.

The following case is an example of direct intervention with a reported problem of "brujería" (witchcraft).

Juan was a ten-year-old child of mixed Mexican and Salvadorean background. He was raised by his mother, who is Mexican. Juan was born in the United States and, by report, was not performing well academically at the time of his referral for therapy. Presenting problems also included fear of the dark and recurrent nightmares. Both Juan and his mother held strong Catholic beliefs. The mother further added that she felt disconnected from family support, was angry at her God for her current life circumstances, and had lost her sense of personal connection with her purpose in life. In addition, she believed that her ex-spouse had cast a "spell" on her for the termination of their relationship. It was her belief that it was this evil spell that was causing so much ill fortune.

Juan was a boy who could trust and build rapport easily. He spoke about "monsters in the night" and about feeling tense all the time. He was taught a relaxation exercise as well as how to use guided imagery. This experience allowed him to verbalize and draw both the "demons" and "angelic presences" that helped him to feel protected and powerful. Juan soon identified a "spirit helper" who helped him feel less afraid of the dark.

Alternatively, his mother was encouraged to resolve her misunderstanding with her extended family and to align with those family members with whom she felt bonding and "entendimiento" (an empathic understanding). The therapist taught her a healing prayer incantation to ward off the effects of the reported "evil spell" and allowed her to ventilate her anger toward God. This process helped her to relive and resolve experiences of abandonment by her mother and reach a more mature understanding of her perceived image of God. Both mother and son were discharged from therapy after four months of work.

Juan's case illustrates the use of religious belief systems as a paradigm for therapeutic intervention. Juan's school performance problems as well as his recurrent nightmares resulted from his internalizing of his mother's own anxiety. Juan was encouraged to transform the "monsters of the night" into concrete images that he could then gain mastery over and control. By identifying a powerful "spirit helper" that could protect him, he could now feel secure. In turn, work with his mother was oriented toward helping her to rebond with her family in order to help her resolve feelings of guilt and anger arising from the previous lack of that bond. The healing prayer incantation was the primary means of empowering her to undo the effects of the suspected spell, thereby helping her to realize her own psycho-spiritual strength and to reconnect with God as her source of protection and safety.

Theoretically, family therapy models generally have placed emphasis on the family as a system that explores roles, boundaries, power hierarchies, communication levels, relational alignments, and general movement of the system, often along developmental paths (Goldenberg and Goldenberg, 1985). Without running the risk of stereotyping all of family therapy, systemic models of therapy generally attend to issues of balance, stabilization, relational attunement, life cycle continuity, and hierarchical organization (Carter and McGoldrick, 1980; Minuchin, 1974). Clinical interventions often focus on helping family members to communicate more effectively with each other, to assist in creating a more caring home environment, and to help balance the familial structure made vulnerable by consistent emotional turmoil, developmental growth, or external stressors. With Mexican American families, strong, interconnecting relationship between mestizo spirituality and family therapy allows for a broader framework of transcendent awareness and responsibility, as shown in Figure 2.

Mestizo spirituality encompasses different interrelated levels of interpersonal contact, represented by a series of concentric ovals. Each oval links to a greater whole, thus encompassing a wider perspective in concert with a social and ethical awareness to be responsible to a larger unit of interpersonal contact. Family therapy models tend to view areas of intervention through levels 1 and 2. Levels 3, 4, and 5 present a visual schema for the integration of ethical-moral, psycho-spiritual awareness. The integrity of the family must go beyond the traditional alleviation of symptomatology or stabilization of the family system. Mestizo spirituality within a family systems perspective is the connecting of group balance with transcendent balance, familial responsibility with broader universal awareness, and familial goals with existential purpose.

Role of the Philosophy of Curanderismo

A significant development in the dynamic forces that led to the molding of a mestizo character and a mestizo spirituality (Foster, 1960; Ortiz de Montellano, 1989) was the creation of a specific folk medicine philosophy that, among Mexican and Mexican American families, has come to be known as *curanderismo*. Perrone, Stockel,

Figure 2. Relationship of Mestizo Spirituality and Family Therapy.

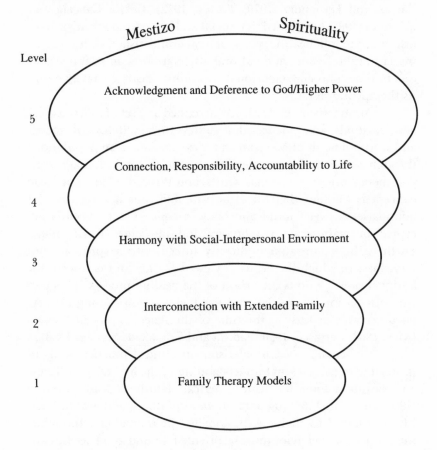

Level

5 — Acknowledgment and Deference to God/Higher Power

4 — Connection, Responsibility, Accountability to Life

3 — Harmony with Social-Interpersonal Environment

2 — Interconnection with Extended Family

1 — Family Therapy Models

and Krueger (1989) have recently discussed the particular psycho-therapeutic aspects of this philosophical perspective.

An exhaustive review of curanderismo will not be presented in this chapter. Rather, the focus will be on understanding the specific tenets in its ideology that are relevant to family work with Mexican American families. The professional literature has extensively reviewed curanderismo, the identified form of folk healing in Mexico and Central and South American countries, with regard to historical origins (Kiev, 1964, 1968), health care (Gonzales, 1976; Keefe, 1981; Castro, Furth, and Karlow, 1984) and folk medicine beliefs (Rubel, 1960, 1964; Martinez and Martin, 1966; Edgerton, Karno, and Fernandez, 1970; Torrey, 1972). De La Cancela and Martinez (1983) have noted that social and behavioral scientists have responded to folk healing, particularly curanderismo, by highlighting cultural relevance and cultural affirmation as an adaptive process in times of social, emotional, or familial distress, and by citing its therapeutic value.

Curanderismo is classically described as a set of folk/medical beliefs, rituals, and practices that address the psychological, social, and spiritual needs of Mexican and Mexican American populations through a system of medicine with its own theoretical, diagnostic, and therapeutic roots (Arenas, Cross, and Willard, 1980). The basic concept is the idea that life is holistic and thus has no artificial boundaries between mind and body, a concept only recently accepted in mainstream psychology and medicine (Rossi, 1986). Further, this connection is directly linked with a spiritual consciousness in which the healer is viewed as only an instrument for a higher power who is the origin of the healing process. This theistic orientation toward healing has had a centuries-long history, documentable at least to the time of the Aztec empire in Mexico (Kiev, 1968; Carrasco, 1990; Padilla and Salgado de Snyder, 1988).

A discussion of curanderismo in clinical practice needs to proceed with a contextual understanding of the backdrop of illness and health among Mexican American families. Both Carrasco (1990) and Kiev (1968) suggest four views of illness and health. First, life is ordained by divine will, namely, the individual's thoughts, intentions, and behavior must be oriented around good deeds. Failure to follow the prescribed rules of belief leads to suffering, sickness, and bad fortune. There is purpose and balance in all things: if one becomes ill, either for physical or emotional reasons, one's purpose and direction in life has been lost and things are no longer in harmony.

Second, illness is perceived as a social-interpersonal matrix rather than just a chance-biological event. Medical problems, psychological concerns, and emotional instability are a direct reflection of the kinds of interpersonal relationships that exist within family and community networks. Thus, issues of guilt, anger, jealousy, envy, and possessiveness are emotions and mind-sets that have a strong interpersonal base, which then assumes that whatever social-emotional-physiological problems erupt are directly related to family life cycle issues, social life events, and, potentially, supernatural forces.

Third, as has been noted previously, supernatural causes play a major role in both health and illness. Some of the basic assumptions made within this metaphysical framework are (1) that the mind can influence social-interpersonal-spiritual events; (2) that wishes and ritual can cause both good and bad fortune; and (3) that communication with the spirit world (for example, the deceased, demons, and angels) is believed to be real and used as part of spiritual favors, healing, and the maintenance of balance. The curandero/curandera is thus consulted in order to advise on specific prayers, incantations, and rituals to bring about the healing process.

Finally, curanderismo views health as a naturalistic process. Similar to the idea of family homeostasis in family therapy, a healthy body is maintained through the balancing of biological needs and social-interpersonal expectations, physical and spiritual harmony, and individual and cultural-familial attachments. Curanderismo incorporates several ideas that relate directly to the understanding of spirituality and family therapy. At a theoretical level, the key idea in curanderismo that mind and body are inextricably linked and consequently influence each other is a concept only recently accepted in mainstream psychology and medicine (Rossi, 1986). At a diagnostic level, curanderismo attributes all dysfunctional areas of physical, mental, and spiritual dimensions to both a faulty and imbalanced family system and spirit possession, spirit loss, and punishment from God (Arenas, Cross, and Willard, 1980). The diagnostic aspect, as in mainstream psychological and medical practice, includes the naming of the disease, the description of its etiology, and the prescribed treatment—all of which strengthen the relationship to the healer and enhance his or her credibility.

At the therapeutic level, curanderismo describes specific cures, sacred words and chants, and ritual prescriptions, including imagery, as therapeutic modes of enacting the healing process. Several authors have addressed therapeutic imagery (Achterberg, 1985; Erickson and Rossi, 1981; Jaffe and Bresler, 1980; Rossman, 1989;

Rossi, 1986); there is, however, little or no published work on the use of imagery with Mexican American families. During the healing process, the curandero/curandera is the master of creative imagery with his or her client, developing an imagery that is culturally appropriate and therapeutically relevant to the presenting problem. In sum, the use of imagery through prayer, ritual, or a directed sequence of thoughts provides the internal contextual rapport that begins the healing process. As described earlier, all healing ultimately is derived from a higher source and the curandero/curandera is merely its agent. A comparison of the curandero/curandera and family therapist is offered below:

Curandero/Curandera	*Family Therapist*
1. Healer	Psychotherapist
2. Intercessor of positive energy through prayer, ritual, and ceremony	Holder of therapeutic intention, consultant on ritual and familial rites of passage
3. Confessor of one's sins, faults, and failings	Empathic and caring professional
4. Restorer of familial/community balance and harmony	Expert on realignment of familial patterns, roles, boundaries toward homeostasis
5. Consultant to the spirit world	Release agent for exorcising familial ghosts and of familial strength and positive energy
6. Teacher of responsible, ethical-moral behavior	Supporter of positive change and responsible social-interpersonal relations
7. Technical consultant on healing plants and herbs	Technical consultant from a social-behavioral sciences framework
8. Creator of healing imagery	Creator of healing imagery

The characteristics of the curandero/curandera and family therapist are remarkably similar and further suggest the dynamic role of spirituality in these functions. The philosophy of curanderismo serves as the connecting bridge between the penitent (client), the confessor/healer, the presenting problem, and the impaired interpersonal functioning in the social and familial system. In brief, we suggest that there is a significant change in mind-set and cultural reorientation of the therapist who sees ethnic minority populations (Sue, 1990) and in our present focus on work with Mexican American families (Cervantes and Romero, 1983; Muñoz, 1981). For the family therapist, this reorientation involves a paradigm shift from a psychology of the self to a psychology of the family/community. Castañeda (1977, p. 357) notes this in his comments, consistent with mestizo spirituality, which reflect the cultural discrepancy between the values of traditionalism and the values of modernism. He articulates this continuum of balance as the following:

- A sacred sense of life where relationships of all living things are viewed as interconnected and spiritually related
- A sense of community where the benefit of others is of utmost importance and identity is linked with the group
- A sense of hierarchy based on age, sex roles, and authoritarian relationships

Thus, the curandero/curandera perspective invites the therapist toward processes of recommitment to self and to one's client, an understanding of the psycho-spiritual forces involved in the therapeutic relationship, and the creation of a dynamic bonding that can become significantly healing for both therapist and client.

Variations of Spirituality in Mexican American Families

In presenting a therapeutic framework within a dimension of mestizo spirituality, we are not suggesting that we have achieved a full integration of the two or that this is even our goal. Rather, this is an initial exploration of how the effectiveness of a traditional therapeutic modality can be enhanced by incorporating a spiritual dimension in working with Mexican American families, a client population in which spirituality has historically played a central role in family functioning. Given this fact, is one then to assume that all Mexican American families can be treated from a perspective of spirituality? The answer, of course, is equivocal. For some families, spirituality is a conscious and ever-present part of their daily lives, which may stem directly from their active involvement with a formal religion (for example, Catholicism) or from multigenerational involvement with the philosophy and practice of curanderismo or some integration of both. For some other families, spirituality is perhaps seen only as some remnant of childhood. Finally, some families completely disavow any influence of spirituality in their lives at any point in their family history.

Our clinical experience with Mexican American families suggests that it is not particularly helpful to attempt to profile certain types that are particularly receptive to a therapeutic intervention that includes a spiritual dimension. For example, socioeconomic status is a factor commonly used to differentiate the Mexican American cultural group into various subgroups. The active presence and role of spirituality in Mexican American family life, however, as clinical experience suggests, seems to cut across all socioeconomic strata, though its expression may differ in subtle ways. The following case example illustrates how spirituality is not bound by typical demographic categories.

The S family was an upper-middle-class Mexican American family with an annual income of well over $200,000. Mr. S was an executive vice president for a major national corporation. The family presented themselves in a spiritual crisis precipitated by their seventeen-year-old daughter (the oldest of five children), who had recently become pregnant. The parents stated that marriage between their daughter and her boyfriend was not something either party wanted. This event seemed to awaken the parents to the fact that their family was no longer a close, loving, interdependent unit. Everyone in the family seemed to be going his or her own way. The parents had prayed for their family situation and had come to a decision (which both described as spiritually inspired) to seek family therapy. They also prayed for a therapist who would understand and appreciate the spiritual nature of their crisis.

At the end of the initial two-hour evaluation by the therapist, the parents stated that they felt their prayers had been answered, as evidenced by the immediate rapport and trust their family had established with the therapist. The therapy itself lasted a little more than two and a half months. It consisted primarily of the usual family therapy types of interventions, focusing on reestablishing open communication among all family members. Beyond these traditional approaches, the entire family was encouraged to go on a spiritual retreat together. This particular experience was critical in reestablishing them as a cohesive family unit. The family was also encouraged to resume praying together as a family once weekly, a practice they had stopped some time prior to coming into therapy. The prayer activity was encouraged because in past experiences following a family prayer session, they had typically discussed how each member in the family was getting along. By the end of therapy, the family had come to see the pregnancy as a blessing; it had reintegrated their family. They resolved to support their daughter and her child in whatever ways all were comfortable with, including taking care of the newborn to allow the daughter to pursue her educational and personal goals.

Spirituality for this family was deeply rooted in their involvement in the charismatic movement within the Catholic church. Family harmony and balance in the relationships among all family members were the critical issues for them. The parents' attribution of spirituality to the therapist, as well as the therapist's own comfort with such a framework, clearly enhanced the therapist's more traditional family therapy interventions.

The following case example involves a family that is at the extreme opposite end of the economic spectrum. Nevertheless, the successful outcome is essentially the same with regard to the family's notions of spirituality, its congruence with the therapist's notion, and the therapist's own comfort with addressing spirituality.

Rosa, a thirty-two-year-old mother who worked as a domestic, brought her eight-year-old son to an outpatient psychiatric clinic, at the urging of his teacher, who complained that she could not manage his constant "hyper" behavior. In the initial evaluation, the mother, who spoke only Spanish, asked the therapist if he believed in curanderismo. Upon hearing that he did, she became tearful, saying that her prayers had been answered. She explained that she had prayed for someone who "knew" God, the power of evil, and also medicine. It turned out that her "son" was in fact her nephew, whom she had legally taken away from his mother (her sister) because of her abusiveness, alcoholism, and life-style as a prostitute. She had had this youngster in her care since age five and had always had behavioral problems with him. She ultimately came to believe that both she and the boy were suffering under evil powers created by her sister's anger at them. Shame had prevented her from seeking spiritual counsel.

Because of the power and authority attributed to the therapist, the mother accepted that her son needed medicine (he was diagnosed with attention-deficit hyperactivity disorder). Also, she was encouraged to seek out spiritual counsel and to continue utilizing prayer, as it seemed to work powerfully for her. In less than a month, the boy's problems had subsided, and work continued for an additional two months focusing on behavioral management skills for use in both the home and school settings. These were easily instituted, giving this youngster the opportunity for optimal response to the medication.

Spirituality and the Family Therapist

Perhaps the most important aspect of an examination of the topic of spirituality in family therapy is the therapist, as is the case in any discussion of psychotherapy. A commitment to spiritual growth and development, to self-awareness, and to a continual self-appraisal of one's values and their priorities in one's life are all inherent in a clinician's responsibility to provide effective and ethically sound therapeutic services. This is heightened, to some extent, when one considers adding a dimension such as spirituality to the repertoire of psychotherapeutic interventions.

Regardless of his or her ethnicity, a therapist who is working with Mexican American families must have a solid understanding of his or her own spiritual values and how they can be manifested in his or her clinical practice. Most psychotherapists have been trained, probably indoctrinated, in mainstream psychotherapeutic models, which inherently carry with them definite belief systems as to how people become ill and how they become healthy. For the therapist who acknowledges a strong spiritual dimension to his or her life, these traditional mental health ideologies can become, at best, more complex and, at worst, at odds with one another. Nonetheless, an integration can occur. However, if such an integration has not yet been achieved, it is essential that we, as therapists, become aware of those spiritual values we bring into our therapy practice. Values can include the belief in "forgiveness" and the belief that a person is basically good at the core or that evil in a person's life can be supplanted by bringing out the good. In the following case example, it becomes exceedingly clear that the mutual impact of the family's and therapist's notions of spirituality can significantly affect both the process and outcome of family therapy. It is worth noting that, in this particular case, both the ethnicity and bilingualism of the therapist were essential in determining the final outcome.

Sergio (age fifteen), Laura (age thirteen), Adam (age twelve) and their parents, Mr. and Mrs. Z, were seen because of the parents' concern about Sergio's "bad temper" and self-destructive behavior, Laura's sexual behavior, and Adam's running with a "bad group of boys" who had introduced him to the smoking of cigarettes. All three did well in school. Mr. Z was forty-five years old and had migrated from Mexico to the United States thirteen years ago. Mrs. Z, thirty-four years old, was born and raised in the United States. All five family members attended the first evaluation session, where it was clear that the father was exclusively Spanish-speaking whereas both the mother and the children were bilingual, even though the children chose to speak only English. The mother and the therapist served as translators for the father.

Mrs. Z reported that Mr. Z had been having increasing difficulty over the past two years as the children reached adolescence and began to assert themselves more, which the father viewed as blatant disrespect. Mr. Z was emotional, articulate, and even philosophical as he complained about his children's exposure to values and standards of morality that were considerably "lower" than he wanted for them and different from those he had learned from his father. Sergio confirmed that he and his siblings held defiant attitudes toward Mr. Z's values and added that they constantly felt torn in opposite directions: On the one hand was his father's "old-world" strict view of family life, where children unquestionably accept the high moral standards set for them; on the other was the constant peer pressure to "go along with the crowd." All three children pleaded with the therapist to help their father understand their emotional conflict and resulting misbehavior, a way of releasing their tension and frustration.

The therapist ended the session by translating for the father what had been said by his children in English and assuring him of their loyalty, their basic acceptance and adherence to the spiritual values he had taught them, and their love and respect for him. The therapist also explained to the father the pressure that his children felt at school to be accepted by their peers and worked toward finding a middle ground. The therapist made three recommendations to the family: first, that all forms of corporal punishment cease immediately; second, that the family members discuss in Spanish how they had been feeling so that the father could understand his children's ongoing emotional dilemma; and finally, that Sergio be allowed to stay temporarily with extended family members in order to reduce immediate tension in the home.

Over the next several sessions, the family improved dramatically, the level of tension decreased significantly, and there were no outbursts of aggression by anyone. The mother, who was more moderate in her views, acted as a mediator when necessary between her husband and the children. Finally, the father was encouraged to express nurturance and support toward his teenagers, whose earlier views of him as playful and affectionate had been replaced by experiences with him as angry and disapproving.

This case illustrates a crisis involving an increasingly widening gap between the parents' spiritual and cultural worldview and that of their three oldest children. They came not only to a mutual understanding but also to a place of forgiveness. In this final case example, one can again see the central, singular importance of harmony within a family as synonymous with spiritual harmony for Mexican American families.

Summary and Clinical Implications

We have suggested in this chapter that spirituality can be used to form a strong therapeutic consciousness in the treatment of Mexican American families. We view family therapy as a natural method with which to integrate spirituality, given its theoretical roots of system balance, family focus, and familial intervention. Mestizo spirituality is a base of knowledge that recognizes a unique perspective and psycho-spiritual themes to guide clinical practice with Mexican American families. Last, we consider the philosophy of curanderismo to be an important mind-set for the therapist/healer who is involved in understanding the intricate, yet natural, connection to the healing process in the family.

Several implications emerge. The family therapist needs a knowledge of cultural themes and behaviors that tend to be epistemologically contained within a framework of spirituality. Thus, relationships and interpersonal attachments, hierarchical organization, and belief in an interconnecting cosmology are vital dimensions of the healing process. Second, the therapist must appreciate and learn the mestizo perspective, understanding the "heart and soul" of Mexican American families and acknowledging familial symbols, patterns, beliefs, and existential postures.

Third, it is important to explore the actual religious and spiritual beliefs of a particular family. A knowledge of psycho-spiritual anchor points will increase the clinician's competence to assess ongoing familial problems and underlying destructive behaviors. Fourth, the therapist must know the role of visionary experience in the family. Aside from ruling out a potential psychotic process, it is more important to know how the experience is affecting family members' relationships to each other and to what degree the experience might be describing the family conflict. Fifth, the family therapist should assess how a child has conceptualized balance and harmony in his or her respective family. Therapeutic understanding of what has occurred before will provide the needed conceptual tools to link behavior, culture, and perspectives about locus of responsibility for problems and solutions to them. Sixth, naming the presenting problem allows the therapist and family to give it concreteness, structure, and boundary and permits the containment of psychic fears. Seventh, prayer, confession, and ritual are powerful therapeutic processes that help bind the healing partnership between the curandero/curandera-therapist and the client. Thus the creation of therapeutic imagery will help to influence the healing process of the family. Last, by describing spirituality in the family therapy process, the therapist is challenged to understand the role of healing and the impact it has on both the family system and his or her own life.

Throughout this chapter, the issue of acculturation and general applicability to other Latino groups has only been peripherally addressed. As a theoretical concept framed within a larger familial-cultural perspective, spirituality in the family therapy process is applicable across generational lines. In clinical practice, mestizo spirituality is a culturally embedded philosophical framework of ancient sociohistorical origin. Further case study and empirical research across socioeconomic levels would help to clarify the impact of acculturation on this area of professional practice that addresses psycho-spiritual themes.

The role of spirituality as a general unifying concept among Latino groups has been previously articulated (De La Cancela and Martinez, 1983; Padilla and Salgado de Snyder, 1988; Perrone, Stockel, and Krueger, 1989; Ramírez, 1983). For example, Cuban and Puerto Rican groups do not share the same sociohistorical origins that gave rise to a mestizo philosophy. However, the widespread practice of *santería,* a Caribbean-Christian-Spanish-influenced system of religious belief, exists alongside mainstream religious practices, and thus spirituality forms a critical element in the behavior and consciousness of these two groups. A mestizo framework, with its influence of Indian traditions and philosophies among Central and Latin American populations, would be applicable.

Trying to discuss concretely and adequately the process of spirituality within family therapy has been difficult. The intended aim has been to initiate dialogue and continuing development of this theme in order to provide optimal treatment interventions with Mexican American families. We regard this present effort as an initial step toward that aim.

References

Achterberg, J. *Imagery and Healing*. Boston: Shambhala Press, 1985.

Anaya, R. *The Legend of La Llorona*. Berkeley, Calif.: Tonatiuh-Quinto Sol International, 1984.

Anderson, R. S. *Christians Who Counsel*. Grand Rapids, Mich.: Zondervan, 1990.

Arenas, S., Cross, H., and Willard, W. "Curanderos and Mental Health Professionals: A Comparative Study on Perceptions of Psychopathology." *Hispanic Journal of Behavioral Sciences*, 1980, *2*(4), 407–421.

Bach y Rita, G. "The Mexican American: Religious and Cultural Influences." In R. M. Becerra, M. Karno, and J. I. Escobar (eds.), *Mental Health and Hispanic Americans: Clinical Perspectives*. New York: Grune & Stratton, 1982.

Benner, D. *Psychotherapy in Christian Perspective*. Grand Rapids, Mich.: Baker, 1987.

Bergin, A. E. "Values and Religious Issues in Psychotherapy and Mental Health." *American Psychologist*, 1991, *46*(4), 394–403.

Bradford, D. T., and Spero, M. H. (eds.). *Psychotherapy: Theory, Research, Practice, Training*, 1990, *27* (entire issue 1).

Butler, K. "Spirituality Reconsidered." *Family Networker*, 1990, *14*(5), 26–37.

Carrasco, D. *Religions of Mesoamerica*. New York: HarperCollins, 1990.

Carter, E., and McGoldrick, M. (eds.). *The Family Life Cycle: A Framework for Family Therapy.* New York: Gardner Press, 1980.

Castañeda, A. "Traditionalism, Modernism and Ethnicity." In J. L. Martinez, Jr. (ed.), *Chicano Psychology.* Orlando, Fla.: Academic Press, 1977.

Castro, F. G., Furth, P., and Karlow, H. "The Health Beliefs of Mexican, Mexican American and Anglo Women." *Hispanic Journal of Behavioral Sciences,* 1984, *6*(4), 365–383.

Cervantes, J. M., and Romero, D. *Hispanic Mental Health Clinicians: Personal and Professional Development Issues.* Paper presented at the annual convention of the American Psychological Association, Anaheim, Calif., 1983.

Cole, R. *The Spiritual Life of Children.* Boston: Houghton Mifflin, 1990.

de Aragon, R. J. *The Legend of La Llorona.* Las Vegas, N.M.: Pan American Publishing, 1980.

De La Cancela, V., and Martinez, I. Z. "An Analysis of Culturalism in Latino Mental Health: Folk Medicine as a Case in Point." *Hispanic Journal of Behavioral Sciences,* 1983, *5*(3), 251–274.

Edgerton, R. B., Karno, M., and Fernandez, I. "Curanderismo in the Metropolis: The Diminishing Role of Folk-Psychiatry Among Los Angeles Mexican-Americans." *American Journal of Psychotherapy,* 1970, *24*(1), 124–134.

Elkins, D. "On Being Spiritual Without Necessarily Being Religious." *Journal of Humanistic Psychology,* 1988, *28*(4), 5–18.

Erickson, M., and Rossi, E. *Experiencing Hypnosis: Therapeutic Approaches to Altered States.* New York: Irvington, 1981.

Falicov, C. "Mexican Families." In M. McGoldrick, J. K. Pearce, and J. Giordano (eds.), *Ethnicity and Family Therapy.* New York: Guilford, 1982.

Falicov, C., and Karrer, B. "Cultural Variations in the Family Life Cycle: The Mexican American Family." In E. Carter and M. McGoldrick (eds.), *The Family Life Cycle and Family Therapy.* New York: Gardner Press, 1980.

Foster, G. M. *Culture and Conquest.* Chicago: Quadrangle Books, 1960.

Garcia-Kraul, E., and Beatly, J. *The Weeping Woman: Encounters with La Llorona.* Santa Fe, N.M.: The Word Process, 1988.

Goldenberg, I., and Goldenberg, H. *Family Therapy: An Overview*. Belmont, Calif.: Wadsworth, 1985.

Gonzales, E. "The Role of Chicano Folk Beliefs and Practices in Mental Health." In C. A. Hernandez, M. J. Haug, and N. N. Wagner (eds.), *Chicanos: Social and Psychological Perspectives*. St. Louis, Mo.: C. V. Mosby, 1976.

Guerra, F. "The Role of Religion in Spanish American Medicine." In F.N.L. Poynter (ed.), *Medicine and Culture*. London: Frank Cottrel, 1969.

Jaffe, D. T., and Bresler, D. E. "The Use of Guided Imagery as an Adjunct to Medical Diagnosis and Treatment." *Journal of Humanistic Psychology*, 1980, *20*(4), 45–59.

Keefe, S. E. "Folk Medicine Among Urban Mexican Americans: Cultural Persistence, Change and Displacement." *Hispanic Journal of Behavioral Sciences*, 1981, *3*(1), 41–58.

Kiev, A. *Magic, Faith and Healing: Studies in Primitive Psychiatry Today*. New York: Free Press, 1964.

Kiev, A. *Curanderismo: Mexican-American Folk Psychiatry*. New York: Free Press, 1968.

Leon-Portilla, M. (ed.) *Native Mesoamerican Spirituality*. New York: Paulist Press, 1980.

Malony, H. N. (ed.). *Wholeness and Holiness: Readings in the Psychology/Theology of Mental Health*. Grand Rapids, Mich.: Baker, 1983.

Martinez, C., and Martin, H. W. "Folk Diseases Among Urban Mexican-Americans." *Journal of the American Medical Association*, 1966, *2*, 161–164.

Martinez, J. L., and Mendoza, R. H. (eds.). *Chicano Psychology*. Orlando, Fla.: Academic Press, 1984.

Minuchin, S. *Families and Family Therapy*. Cambridge, Mass.: Harvard University Press, 1974.

Muñoz, J. "Difficulties of a Hispanic American Psychotherapist in the Treatment of Hispanic American Patients." *American Journal of Orthopsychiatry*, 1981, *51*(4), 646–652.

Murillo, N. "The Mexican American Family." In N. W. Wagner and M. J. Haug (eds.), *Chicanos: Social and Psychological Perspectives*. St. Louis, Mo.: C. V. Mosby, 1971.

Ortiz de Montellano, B. *Syncretism in Mexican and Mexican-American Folk Medicine.* Working Papers no. 5. College Park: Department of Spanish and Portuguese, University of Maryland, 1989.

Padilla, A., and Salgado de Snyder, V. N. "Psychology in Pre-Columbian Mexico." *Hispanic Journal of Behavioral Sciences,* 1988, *10*(1), 55–66.

Perrone, B., Stockel, H. H., and Krueger, V. *Medicine Women, Curanderas, and Women Doctors.* Norman: University of Oklahoma, 1989.

Ramírez, M. *Psychology of the Americas.* Elmsford, N.Y.: Pergamon Press, 1983.

Ramírez, M., and Castañeda, A. *Cultural Democracy, Bicognitive Development and Education.* Orlando, Fla.: Academic Press, 1974.

Ramírez, O. "Mexican American Children and Adolescents." In J. T. Gibbs, L. N. Huang, and Associates (eds.), *Children of Color: Psychological Interventions with Minority Youth.* San Francisco: Jossey-Bass, 1989.

Rossi, E. L. *The Psychobiology of Mind-Body Healing.* New York: Norton, 1986.

Rossman, M. *Healing Yourself.* New York: Pocket Books, 1989.

Rubel, A. J. "Concepts of Disease in Mexican American Culture." *American Anthropologist,* 1960, *62*, 795–814.

Rubel, A. J. "The Epidemiology of a Folk Illness: Susto in Hispanic America." *Ethnology,* 1964, *3*(3), 268–283.

Rubert deVentos, X. *The Hispanic Labyrinth: Tradition and Modernity in the Colonization of the Americas.* New Brunswick, N.J.: Transaction, 1991.

Spero, M. H. "The Reality and the Image of God in Psychotherapy." *American Journal of Psychotherapy,* 1985, *39*(1), 75–85.

Sue, D. W. "Culture-Specific Strategies in Counseling: A Conceptual Framework." *Professional Psychology: Research and Practice,* 1990, *21*(6), 424–433.

Torey, E. F. *The Mind Game: Witch Doctors and Psychiatrists.* New York: Emerson Hall, 1972.

Trankina, F. "Clinical Issues and Techniques in Working with

Hispanic Children and Their Families." In G. Powell, J. Yama-
moto, A. Romero, and A. Morales (eds.), *The Psychological
Development of Minority Group Children*. New York: Brunner/
Mazel, 1983.
Vaughan, F. *The Inward Arc: Healing and Wholeness in Psycho-
therapy and Spirituality*. Boston: Shambhala Press, 1986.

7

Therapy with
Latino Gang Members

ARMANDO T. MORALES

Violent urban gangs are contributing to psychological pain and
trauma, social disorganization, and dysfunction among many
young clients referred for mental health services. Youth gangs and
their violent behavior are a symptom; the members of a community
are indicating that their needs are not being met by the family,
neighborhood, social institutions, and health professions. These
youths have the same rights to service as other clients. Violence in
the United States has become one of the most pervasive issues of our
time, and U.S. ambivalence on violence is historic (Hopps, 1987).
Some mental health professions in recent years have been focusing
on selected aspects of the problem, primarily domestic violence
(family, spousal, and child abuse) and suicide (Kinard, 1987; Ivanoff, 1987; Star, 1987). Including all ages, suicide is the tenth leading
cause of death in the United States and is viewed as a public health
concern.

A comparable leading cause of death in the United States is
homicide, which historically has been a matter of concern for law
enforcement, criminologists, sociologists, and, more recently, the
health profession. *Homicide* may be defined as death due to injuries
purposefully inflicted by another person or persons, not including

deaths caused by law enforcement officers or legal execution by the federal or state government. Homicide is the number one cause of death for Latino youth, ages fifteen to twenty-four. (*Latino* is a generic term designating persons of Latin descent residing in the United States. This may include persons of Mexican, Cuban, Puerto Rican, Guatemalan, Nicaraguan, Salvadoran, or other Latin country descent.) Aside from occasional brief epidemiological data related to forensic populations, suicide, or domestic violence, this subject is by and large ignored in the mental health literature. As is the case with suicide, many mental health practitioners deal daily with people suffering the effects of social, psychological, economic, and political oppression and dehumanization who eventually become homicide perpetrators or victims.

In contrast to psychiatry, psychology, and nursing, social work has had a history of working with the social problem of gangs. During the Great Depression in the late 1920s and 1930s, for example, in urban areas such as Chicago, social workers armed with social group work skills were deployed from settlement houses to work directly with youth gangs. Social workers also made their presence known as gang group workers in Los Angeles following massive violent confrontations between U.S. servicemen and Latino gang youths in the early 1940s. These intergroup conflict situations were called the "zoot suit riots." Working with gangs in various parts of the country continued to be an area of interest for social work in the 1950s and into the 1960s with the federally funded Office of Economic Opportunity programs.

Since the 1960s there has been a growing public apathy toward the poor in the United States, particularly the immense needs of inner-city youth. Group work, anchored in social work's longstanding values of social reform and concern for oppressed people, dwindled as a practice interest as it was replaced by a shift to the clinical, intrapsychic functioning of individuals and families (Middleman and Goldberg, 1987). Fox (1985) points out that the quality of life in U.S. cities has continued to decline and that social workers and other mental health practitioners have paid little attention to the urban youth gang, symptomatic of what is feared most concerning the consequences of human and environmental neglect. Fox's article was only the second of four articles to date in a social work journal since June 1984, confirming that gangs are no longer a social work practice interest (Spergel, 1984); even less interest in gangs is seen in psychiatric and psychological journals.

The "gang" label has a negative connotation and has been applied to what is generally considered a unique lower-class phenomenon. Rarely are middle-class adolescent groups referred to as gangs, irrespective of the similarity of their criminal behavior to their lower-economic-class counterparts. For example, the white, middle-class youths involved in the killing of a black in 1986 at Howard Beach in New York were not referred to as a "gang." The author therefore proposes the following more general definition of gang group behavior, which incorporates destructive harm as a key factor (Morales, 1978). A gang is a peer group of persons in a lower-, middle-, or upper-class community who participate in activities that are harmful to themselves and/or others in society (p. 133). This definition is similar to a definition proposed by law enforcement gang experts Jackson and McBride seven years later (1985). They define a gang as "a group of people that form an allegiance for a common purpose, and engage in unlawful or criminal activity" (p. 20). These definitions remove the potential bias of viewing this group criminal activity as primarily a lower-class, adolescent, ethnic/cultural, or inner-city phenomenon, as it is often perceived by the media, general public, and some social scientists. (Richard Nixon's Watergate episode could have conformed to these definitions of gang activity, as it involved a group of people who formed an allegiance and conspired to commit a crime that had the result of being harmful to society. Some of the participants were convicted and sentenced to prison.) The focus of this paper, however, will be more on lower-socioeconomic-class Latino adolescents and young adults belonging to some groups who have some members who commit and are convicted of crimes.

Urban gangs are a growing health and mental health crisis; their antisocial behavior results in thousands of homicides and assaults each year and their involvement with drugs, as both consumers and dealers, causes untold human destruction in central-city communities, particularly as it concerns poor families. At a recent public hearing conducted by the California State Task Force on Youth Gang Violence, a victimized parent who had lost two sons stated (California Council on Criminal Justice, 1986): "When I lost my second son I was depressed and in shock. I couldn't believe that this happened to me, not twice. After this, I thought I was the only mother who had lost two sons. Since then, I have met other mothers who have lost a couple of sons to gang violence" (p. 4).

Gangs are not a unique U.S. phenomenon and do not originate from Anglo American or Latino culture, as most countries have gangs. In Japan they are called "Mambos," in Germany "Halbstarke," in Italy "Vitelloni," in South Africa "Tsotsio," in France "Blousons Noir," and in England "Teddys" (O'Hagan, 1976). In Japan in 1983, approximately 12 percent (713) of 5,787 juveniles entering detention facilities were gang members (Ministry of Justice, 1984).

The History of Gangs

Gangs have been with us since the beginning of civilization, but the concept was first reported in the literature by a former gang member, Saint Augustine (A.D. 354–430), over 1,600 years ago (Saint Augustine, 1949). His father was a pagan who lived a "loose life" and his mother, whom he loved dearly, was a pious Christian who had difficulty controlling St. Augustine during his adolescent years. In his book *Confessions,* he demonstrates an astute understanding of the psychology of adolescent gangs with his discovery that committing a crime in the company of others further enhances the gratifications derived from it. Through his autobiographical psychoanalytical method, he discovered that peoples' actions are determined by more than a single motive, stating: "I loved then in it also the company of the accomplices with whom I did it . . . for had I then loved the pears I stole and wished to enjoy them I might have done it alone, had the bare commission of the theft sufficed to attain my pleasure; nor needed I have inflamed the itching of my desires by the excitement of accomplices. But since my pleasure was not in those pears, it was in the offense itself, which the company of fellow-sinners occasioned" (p. 34).

The first youth gangs in the United States made their appearance in the national turf-oriented atmosphere of "manifest destiny" (the rationale justifying the forceful takeover of the Mexican-owned greater Southwest) in the mid 1800s. These gangs did much more than steal pears from neighbors. They were first seen in Philadelphia in the 1840s, having evolved from volunteer fire companies. Volunteer fire companies provided status and recognition to young, white, lower-class adult males who were competitive with other companies in trying to be first in extinguishing a fire. The intense competition at times developed into physical conflict and even killing when a company extinguished a fire on the rival company's "turf." The tough firemen—the Super Bowl heroes of that era—were the idols of neighborhood adolescents, who looked upon them with awe. These early gangs had names such as the "Rats," the "Bouncers," and the "Skinners." They defaced walls, fences, and buildings with graffiti, as gangs do today in urban areas. The Philadelphia *Public Ledger*, on August 13, 1846, described them as "armed to the teeth with slug shots, pistols, and knives" (Davis and Haller, 1973).

During the pre-Civil War period, intense conflict was also seen in New York among white adolescent and young adult gangs forcibly attempting to establish dominance over a particular neighborhood. Asbury (1927) writes in *The Gangs of New York*: "The greatest gang conflicts of the early nineteenth century were fought by these groups (the Bowery Boys and the Dead Rabbits) . . . sometimes the battles raged for two or three days without cessation, while the streets of the gang area were barricaded with carts and paving stones, and the gangsters blazed away at each other with musket and pistol, or engaged in close work with knives, brickbats, bludgeons, teeth, and fists" (p. 29).

Police did not intervene during these two- to three-day gang wars. Gangs comprising latency-age children, eight to twelve years of age, such as the "Little Plug Uglies" or the "Little Daybreak Boys," were almost as ferocious as the older gangs whose names they adopted and whose crimes they tried hard to imitate. Such intense, prolonged conflict is not seen today; rather, "drive-by" shootings characteristic of the 1920s Al Capone era are the most common expressions of violence between gangs.

The Prevalence of Gangs

Attempting to estimate how many gangs there are in any given community is as complex as defining gangs. The smaller a given community, the less difficult this process becomes. For example, in a small community of 20,000 to 50,000 people, law enforcement would not have much difficulty in identifying the poorest areas of the community with corresponding predelinquent or delinquent youth groups, more commonly identified as "gangs" by law enforcement when they are minority group persons. Peer pressure to conform to clothing, walking, talking, music, and hair style (youth culture) is a powerful, universal, adolescent developmental need and is not different for poor, minority youth. Many youths might unknowingly incorporate a "culture" that law enforcement or schools might define as pertaining to gang membership. The counting of gangs and gang members, therefore, becomes largely a subjective exercise. Perhaps the most important factor to consider is whether those youth groups identified as "gangs" have actually committed the violent crimes for which they have been convicted.

In a 1989 gang-related homicide in Watsonville, California, for example, the author, appointed as a gang expert for the Superior Court of Santa Cruz County, discovered through community and law enforcement records analysis that the county had not had one gang homicide since 1979, a period of ten years, in spite of the presence of some thirty gangs in the community for almost forty years ("Watsonville or East L.A.?", 1990). Literally thousands of gang hand signals, taunts, fist fights and nonlethal assaults, flashing of gang colors, turf boundaries defined by graffiti with retaliatory "cross-outs," and other gang-type activities between rivals had occurred in that county during those ten years. This example illustrates that *some* youths may knowingly or unknowingly adopt and internalize the gang *culture* but not serious criminal behavior such as homicide. Many persons in law enforcement, the courts, schools, mental health, the media, and the general public continue to fail to make this distinction, concluding instead that gang membership automatically translates into criminal and/or violent behavior for *all* members.

Thrasher (1963), in his classic 1920s studies of youth gangs in Chicago, discovered 1,313 gangs in that city alone, made up mostly of whites. This represented approximately sixty-five gangs per 100,000 persons in the general population, a far greater ratio than Los Angeles's 70,000 gang members in 700 gangs in 1987, representing seven gangs per 100,000 persons in the general population (Morales and Sheafor, 1989). In October 1990, Captain Gott of the Los Angeles County Sheriff's Department stated to the author that the Los Angeles gang problem had increased to 900 gangs with 100,000 members. Los Angeles has a population of 8,000,000 persons, so this would only increase the ratio of gangs per 100,000 population to 11.25, still far short of Thrasher's large volume of gangs. Law enforcement gang membership lists leave much to be desired, as they are related to how gang members and gang groups are identified, how current the lists are, how often they are updated, and for how long they are kept. Once placed on the list, when is a person dropped? Gang members do not have formal membership lists or carry membership cards. Given these imprecise accounting procedures, it would be possible for law enforcement to carry a gang member on the list for many years even after he or she had decided to stop associating with the gang. Are we to believe that once a gang member, always a gang member? Or, as many gang members have told the author, "I'm still from the neighborhood [still identify with the gang], but I stopped gang-banging [fighting]."

Causes of Gangs

Related to the complexities of defining a gang and the actual members of gangs in communities, it is also difficult to arrive at a theory or set of theories to explain this group phenomenon with a high degree of confidence. Nevertheless, there are at least five common theories explaining the underlying causes of gangs. These will be briefly touched on, and the reader may refer to the original sources for much greater depth. Thrasher (1963) sees the gang as a natural progression from, and the consequence of, a youth's search for excitement in a frustrating and limiting environment. Gangs are usually a result of a general breakdown of social controls, and they are characterized by young persons with few social ties—such as immigrants, the mentally ill, the destitute—and a corresponding lack of parental control over them.

A second causal factor has been proposed by Miller (1958), who studied lower-class gangs in Boston. He describes gang members as males who usually were reared in female-dominated

Working with Culture

households and consequently, in adolescence, the gang provided the first opportunity to have male role models among peers facing similar difficulties in sex role identification. This theory does not account for the fact that even though 68 percent of black and 67 percent of Latino poor families were headed by a woman, according to a 1983 U.S. Commission on Civil Rights report, approximately 95 percent of the youths were *not* gang members or delinquents (*Los Angeles Times,* 1983).

The third perspective is suggested by social scientists such as Cohen (1955) and Cloward and Ohlin (1960). They maintain that the gang is the collective solution of young, lower-class males placed in a situation of stress, where opportunities for the attainment of wealth and/or status through legitimate channels are blocked. In response, the gang develops a subculture or "contraculture." The gang, therefore, must be explained in terms of social conditions in which lower-class youths are placed by the dominant society, which would account for the continued existence of minority group gangs in Chicago since 1918 and the existence of few white ethnic gangs.

A fourth theory is advanced by Matza (1964), who challenges the "blocked-out" subculture theory, stating that it explains too much delinquency. He believes that gangs exist because adolescents are in a state of suspension between childhood and adulthood; hence, they spend most of their time with peers and are anxious about both their identity as males and their acceptance by the peer group (gang). They conform to the norms of the gang because not to do so would threaten their status. This theory is limited in explaining the continued involvement of some adult and middle-aged *veterano* (veteran) gang members found in some Latino *barrios,* who are responsible family providers yet occasionally participate in some gang activities, usually in a consultive, nonviolent role.

The author proposes a fifth theoretical causal factor related to the family. In a study of East Los Angeles Latino gang and nongang juvenile probation camp graduates, the author (Morales, 1963) found that gang members, significantly more often than nongang members, come from families exhibiting more family breakdown, greater poverty, poorer housing, more alcoholism, more drug addiction, and more major chronic illness and have more family members involved with law enforcement and correctional agencies. In the face of these overwhelming problems, the youngster turns to the gang as a surrogate family. In subsequent work with gangs, this observation was again confirmed (Morales, 1978, 1982; Morales and Sheafor, 1989). In 1988, Vigil arrived at a similar conclusion (Vigil, 1988). In the gang surrogate family, the gang member receives affection, understanding, recognition, loyalty, and emotional and physical protection. In this respect the gang is psychologically adaptive rather than maladaptive. It would not appear to be a coincidence that one of the largest Latino gangs in California is called "Nuestra Familia" (Our Family). Latino gang members call themselves "homeboys" or "homegirls," labels again consistent with a family and home orientation. Black gang members often refer to themselves as "brothers" or "sisters." Indeed, close friends *can* be good medicine. On the other hand, many gang members often die or kill rival gang members for their gang or turf in the neighborhood, and when this occurs, membership then becomes maladaptive.

Types of Gangs

Most social scientists investigating gangs (Cohen, 1955; Cloward and Ohlin, 1960; Morales, 1982) agree that there are at least three types of gangs: the *criminal*, the *conflict*, and the *retreatist*. The author suggests that a fourth type has been emerging in recent years, which could be called the *cult/occult* gang.

The criminal gang has as its primary goal the acquisition of material gain through criminal activities—the theft of property from premises or persons, extortion, fencing, and obtaining and selling illegal substances such as drugs. In the 1920s, Thrasher (1963) discovered that some of the wealthiest youth gangs—which he called "beer gangs"—were involved in the illegal liquor business during Prohibition. Today some gang members are making their money selling drugs.

Asian gangs are similar to other racial/ethnic gangs, as they developed out of a need to protect their communities. However, according to law enforcement authorities (Attorney General's Youth Gang Task Force, 1981), contemporary Asian gangs are the criminal type, as they are more concerned with generating profits from illegal activities (extortion, gambling, prostitution) within their communities than with protecting their turf. The newest Asian gangs are composed of Korean and Vietnamese youth.

The conflict gang is very turf oriented and will at times engage in violent battle with individuals or rival groups that invade their neighborhood or commit acts that they consider insulting or degrading. Respect is very much valued and defended. Latino gangs, in most cities, are usually conflict gangs. Their mores, values, rituals, and codes are quite consistent in various neighborhoods and cities throughout the nation and have existed in some areas for almost seventy years. As Father Terrance A. Sweeney (Sweeney, 1980, p. 86) learned in his work with conflict gangs: "The Code of the *Barrio* means watching out for your neighborhood. This entails protecting your homeboys (and family) as the area designated as your 'neighborhood.' The Code demands absolute loyalty; every gang member must be willing to die for his *neighborhood* (homeboys and turf)."

The predominant feature of the retreatist gang is the pursuit of getting "loaded" or "high" on alcohol, marijuana, heroin, acid, cocaine, or another drug substance. Retreatism is seen by Cloward and Ohlin (1960) as an isolated adaptation, characterized by a breakdown in relationships with other persons. The drug user has a need to become affiliated with other retreatist users to secure access to a steady supply of drugs. What distinguishes the criminal gang involved in drugs from the retreatist gang is that the former is primarily involved in drugs for financial profit; the retreatist gang's involvement with drugs is primarily for consumption.

The fourth type of adolescent delinquent group is the cult/ occult gang (Attorney General's Youth Gang Task Force, 1981). "Cult" pertains to a religious system of faddish worshiping. In the cult gangs, the target of worship is often the Devil or evil. "Occult" means keeping something hidden or secret, or a belief in mysterious or supernatural powers. Not all cult/occult Devil or evil worship groups are involved in criminal activity or ritualistic crime. The Ku Klux Klan, for example, may be seen as a cult group and some chapters, in spite of their hate rhetoric, are law-abiding, whereas other chapters have committed criminal acts. The Charles Manson

Family is perhaps one of the better known cult/occult criminal groups. Some of the occult groups place a great deal of emphasis on sexuality and violence, believing that by sexually violating a virgin or innocent child, they have defiled Christianity. Eleven members of one occult group called "OTO" (Ordo Templi Orientis) were convicted of felony child abuse in Riverside County in California (Kerfoot, 1985).

The majority of occult groups, whether criminal or law abiding, are composed of adults. However, some juvenile groups are becoming interested in some of these satanic and black magic practices and are using them for their own gratification of sadistic, sexual, and antisocial behavior. Their knowledge and application of rigid, ritualistic occult practices, however, is often haphazard. Los Angeles has perhaps the largest number of these adolescent cult/occult-type gangs, about thirty-two in 1982 (Poirier, 1982)—in 1991, Captain Gott of the Los Angeles County Sheriff's Department stated to the author that there were about forty.

These gangs are composed predominantly of white, non-Latino, middle-class youths and a few middle-class Latinos. They are not turf oriented like conflict gangs but are found in several middle-class locations. These gangs call themselves "Stoners"; examples are the "Alhambra Stoners" or the "Whittier Stoners." Stoners from one location are allied with Stoners of other locations. They originally named themselves after the Rolling Stones and valued "getting stoned." Their philosophy is based on "Do what you will. The end is soon; live for today." Heavy metal music is very popular and among their heroes are Adolf Hitler, Charles Manson, and Aleister Crowley (a leading occultist in the United States in the early 1900s who advocated violation of every moral law from sexual perversion to homicide). Some of the self-destructive activities in which Stoners participate, in addition to substance abuse, include sadism, masochism, and suicide. Their antisocial crimes are violence for violence's sake, ritual rape, ritual child abuse, and ritual homicide. Some examples of the graffiti of these groups are "666" (biblical sign of the beast), "KKK," "FTW" (Fuck the World), and "SWP" (Supreme White People). In some areas of the country, these gang groups may call themselves "Skinheads."

Age Levels in Gangs

There is an age level consistency among the four types of gangs discussed above, which seems to be related to maturational and natural developmental stages of growth. Thrasher (1963) in the 1920s described four general "gang-age types" as follows:

Gang child	six to twelve (child)
Gang boy	eleven to seventeen (early adolescent)
Gang boy	fifteen to twenty-five (later adolescent)
Gang man	twenty-one to fifty (adult)

In contemporary conflict and criminal gangs, a similar natural age-group phenomenon may be observed, however, with more specific age categories required by the gang. Small gangs may range in size from ten to twenty members, but in larger gangs with 200 to 300 members, the age categories in Latino gangs are more obvious (Morales, 1982):

Pee Wees	eight to twelve
Tinys	twelve to fourteen
Dukes	fourteen to sixteen
Cutdowns	sixteen to eighteen
Veteranos	eighteen to twenty
Locos (the "crazies")	mixed ages

The age levels of retreatist and cult/occult gangs are less formal and female participation is minimal. The cult/occult gang age categories are more consistent with school grade levels, such as fifth and sixth grade, junior high, and high school. Older adolescent and young adult members, predominantly male, are often found in juvenile and adult correctional facilities.

The involvement of girls in gangs has been an evolving issue. For example, Thrasher (1963) found that out of 1,313 predominantly white gangs in Chicago in the 1920s, only six were female gangs. From the author's experience, it appears that about 10 percent of Latino adolescent gangs are female gangs. The female adolescent gangs have incorporated some of the gang culture as it pertains to dress, language, music, art, and graffiti. However, with few exceptions, they have not adopted the violent behavior of adolescent male gang members.

Predisposition Related to Gang Behavior

Psychiatrists Good and Nelson (1984) outline childhood predisposition factors (which spell the acronym VACUUM) that they believe are related to later adolescent and adult antisocial behavior. The "V" pertains to the *violence* often present in the family of a child who has committed an antisocial act. "A" identifies *alcoholism*, which is common. The "C" stands for *child abuse*, which is frequently found in the future adolescent or adult perpetrator. The first "U" relates to *unempathic parenting*. The second "U" considers *underprivileged class*, which, they admit, does not of itself cause antisocial behavior; but children can learn violent behavior from their social environment as well as from their family. Finally, "M" pertains to *maternal deprivation*. Good and Nelson believe that, generally, inadequately cared for children grow up feeling angry about this deprivation and vent their anger in a variety of areas, including antisocial acts. Maternal deprivation may be a sexist term because it places more blame on the mother than the father and the father in this context is not perceived as also having an important nurturing role. The author therefore suggests the term *nurturing deprivation*.

Assessment and Treatment of Gang Members

One of the first factors to consider in the counseling/treatment of a Latino gang member is the therapist's own countertransference stance (conscious or unconscious, positive or negative feelings, biases, and attitudes) toward the client, who may be either a voluntary or involuntary participant. Countertransference issues can be quite numerous, but a few of the more common ones are as follows:

1. The belief that antisocial personality disorders and/or gang members are untreatable
2. The therapist's fear of violent persons and/or gang members
3. The belief in the lack of psychological capacity for insight of poor and uneducated people.
4. Do-gooder" bias, that is, that *all* gang members can be treated
5. "Policeman's mentality," that is, that gang members are all manipulative and will be caught in lies by the therapist
6. The belief that the therapist has the power and hence will control the interview

The gang member entering treatment may also have some conscious and unconscious transference issues, such as:

1. A distrust/dislike of authority figures, often the result of prior negative experiences with parents, teachers, and police
2. A strong resentment of being forced into treatment (involuntary client) as the result of a probation, court, board or parole officer mandate
3. A feeling of discomfort with the therapist, who might be of a different ethnic/racial group
4. A sense of a generational, cultural, and perhaps language gap with the therapist
5. Looking forward to winning yet another power struggle with another social control agent (Freudian cop)

Often these transference and countertransference issues on the part of the client and therapist can result in treatment resistance.

In an earlier article (Morales, 1982), the author described in-depth ways in which a therapist can reduce clients' resistance by giving involuntary clients the power to decide whether or not they wish to be in treatment. In those cases where there is a mandate for treatment, they can at least decide if they wish to see a different therapist. If they decide to remain with the original therapist, an effort is made to negotiate two, four, or six initial sessions with the understanding that they have the authority to discuss whatever they want in these sessions. At the end of the contracted number of sessions, clients can either terminate (without negative sanctions previously agreed to by the referring agent) or renegotiate additional sessions. When involuntary clients agree to participate in a certain number of sessions, they in fact transform themselves into voluntary clients, which may reduce the resistance often present in forensic populations.

Factors such as self-admission, gang-type tattoos, gang-type arrests with convictions (assault, group conflict, and other violent offenses) reinforced by law enforcement and probation/parole files should be sufficient to establish gang membership and level of involvement, such as leader, hard-core, regular, or periphery member. This is of secondary value and not as important as it would be in a case where establishing gang membership may have legal consequences. The primary emphasis in a treatment context should be on viewing the gang member as a person who potentially might need help. Consider the following first interviews of parolees referred involuntarily for treatment.

Martian

"Martian," a large-headed, sixteen-year-old Latino gang member, released three weeks previously from the institution where he had spent four years for burglary, "gang-banging," and dealing cocaine, responded to the therapist's innocent, neutral question in the first interview as to where he was currently living.

Client: I'm living with my older brother.

Therapist: Why didn't they let you live with your parents?

Client: My father died when I was eleven and my mother died when I was thirteen.

Therapist: Oh, my. I'm really sorry. That really must have been painful.

Client: No, I was glad my father died because he used to beat me a lot. See my scars [lips and lower leg]?

Therapist: What about your mother's death [cancer]? Was that difficult?

Client: I refuse to talk about that and I've never talked about it.

Therapist: Was it about that time after your mother's death that you got into gangs?

Client: Yeah, and taking drugs, too. The homeboys in the gang gave me a lot of help, like a family.

The focus could be on the anger and unresolved guilt and grief that he was suffering as a result of the loss of his parents. He had already established the "rules of the game," which were that he did not want to talk about his mother. This should not be challenged in order to permit him to maintain control over the interviews and also because moving too swiftly clinically could overwhelm this vulnerable young man. He was also a battered child, and subsequent interviews should focus on ruling out posttraumatic stress disorder (PTSD) symptoms and/or a major depression. In the spirit of keeping control of the interview with the parolee (actually, clients really always have control, as at any time they can decide to leave or become incommunicative or passive), the interview proceeded as follows:

Therapist: How can I help you?

Client: You can help me by getting me another place to live. Since I've been out, I've been shot at four times from cars and three times I've had to run to keep from getting jumped by gang-bangers.

Therapist: That is frightening. Let me see—what can *we* do?

By stating "we," the therapist began to immediately assume an empathic stance, which provided the youngster with a feeling that he was being understood, that someone was sharing his concerns and attempting to find a solution to the problems *with* him. It also provided the therapist a rare opportunity to put himself in the client's place and view the world from that difficult position. A discussion then followed concerning his "average day and night" and which hours, streets, and locations placed him at higher risk for visibility and victimization, including changed walking patterns that always positioned him in the direction of facing traffic in order to run away in the opposite direction from any possible danger. The therapist also suggested survival strategies such as not "hanging out" in front of friends' houses. However, when the therapist pointed out how proudly the client displayed his gang colors and how that targeted him for police or rival gang attention, the client replied that he had a right to dress any way he wished even if it increased the likelihood of arrest or gang retaliation.

Given his history of being battered and orphaned in the first year of adolescence and subsequent substance abuse that eased the emotional pain, along with his gang that served as a surrogate family, the severity of these overwhelming cumulative critical life events no doubt contributed to a severe depression and possibly PTSD. His insistence, however, on continuing to be a target for rivals (an apparent subintentional suicidal act) while at the same time maintaining a walking pattern that enabled him to run away from potential death indicated his unconscious ambivalence of not knowing whether he really wanted to live or die. Rather than flushing out the unconscious "death wish," which would have been premature in this first interview, the therapist focused on the client's need to be punished rather than killed.

Therapist: By flying your colors, it's almost like asking to be picked up by the police and returned to the institution.

Client: I'd really rather be there than out here. I already smoked some PCP and will be giving my parole officer a dirty test—so maybe he can send me back.

This youngster was well on his way to manipulating the system as a means of protecting himself by participating in behavior that would ensure his return to the institution. As a result, the benefit of therapy was limited. Had this young man been seen by the therapist during the first week that he was out of the institution, perhaps, with his approval, the therapist could have served as his advocate with the parole department in attempting to work out an alternative living placement as compared to the gang-infested environment to which he returned. In other words, the therapist might have had greater impact in preventing this youngster from getting involved with the gang again. As it turned out, he did give the therapist permission to speak to his parole officer about trying to find a different area in which to live.

Flaco

"Flaco" was a handsome, sharp-looking, tall, hard-core, eighteen-year-old Latino gang member with a long history of gang-related arrests, convictions, and substance abuse. He began his gang involvement at age ten when he was stabbed with an ice pick in the stomach; he suffered a second stab wound at age thirteen. He had been using various drugs and alcohol since approximately twelve years of age, with his preferred drug in recent years being PCP. He was seen for therapy under parole mandate the second week after release from the institution where he had been for three years due to a parole revocation (dirty PCP test) and subsequently being absent without leave (AWOL) with accompanying vehicle theft. While being chased by the police, his companion lost control of the vehicle, which flipped over, killing the companion and seriously injuring the parolee.

For the first interview, Flaco appeared well groomed, neatly dressed and pressed in proud gang attire. He was polite and attentive. His tattoos were of gang origin, with the most recent being a teardrop at the corner of his eyelid. When asked why he had violated parole and returned to the institution, he gave the circumstances of his AWOL. Rather than pursuing the substance abuse track, the therapist followed the accident episode as a more urgent matter in order to explore the possibility and/or extent of any permanent physical effects and/or psychological trauma.

Therapist: What was the extent of your injuries?

Client: I was hospitalized and in a coma for one week. My upper body was paralyzed. I wanted to die because I thought I would always be in a wheelchair. I thought I was facing thirty to forty years in prison. I was in the hospital six months getting therapy.

Therapist: Do you have any physical limitations now?

Client: No, only my knee. I hurt my knee playing ball in the institution a few months ago. I can't jog or play handball.

He denied having headaches or feeling any remorse over the incident but did state: "If I had been the driver, it wouldn't have happened," indicating survivor's guilt that is often seen in PTSD. The remainder of the interview focused on gathering data to determine whether or not the parolee was suffering from PTSD. He was, and the symptoms were more chronic than acute.

Many "tough" male adolescents and young adults find it difficult to verbalize, admit, or identify feelings related to depression. Often they will make a permanent impression on their body with a tattoo to symbolize pain or a critical life event they never want to forget, such as the name of a sister who unexpectedly died while they were incarcerated. At the third interview, the therapist's inquiry about the tattoo teardrop by his eye resulted in the parolee commenting that he had done this while hospitalized and at a time when he wanted to die. He was only able to admit that he was feeling "bad." The interview then focused on any history of suicide in the family, suicidal ideation, or prior attempts on his part, all of which were negative. He was not sure if he had a history of depression because he was not quite sure how depression "felt." He recalled having a lot of anger and being in several fights, coupled with significant alcohol and drug use. These behaviors are consistent with the manner in which many adolescent and adult males express depression, as compared to females, who more often cry and feel sad, isolated, and withdrawn, with accompanying weight and sleep loss—all symptoms found in the *DSM-III-R* criteria for dysthymia and major depression. The parolee wanted help with his sleeping problems, nightmares, and fear of leaving the house— symptoms indicative of PTSD.

In the initial interviews with Martian and Flaco, it was not necessary to enter into a contract for a specific number of sessions. Even though both were involuntary clients, they participated relatively freely—in effect, made themselves voluntary clients. Perhaps they sensed the therapist's genuine concern about their difficult, complicated lives and desire to be of practical help to them. Both were hard-core gang members of average intelligence. Gang involvement was not the main focus of discussion. Rather, the interviews focused on more immediate issues related to their physical and psychosocial well-being and home and community adjustment.

In both cases there is a comorbidity of substance abuse with a mental disorder, for example, a history of cocaine, alcohol, or PCP use *and* a diagnosis of conduct or personality disorder. A recent psychiatric epidemiological study involving a national random sample reported by the National Institute of Mental Health (NIMH) revealed that in the adult general population, 79 percent of cocaine abusers had at least one comorbid psychiatric disorder (26 percent affective disorder, 28 percent anxiety disorder, 18 percent antisocial personality disorder, and 7 percent schizophrenia) (American Psychiatric Association, 1990). Thirty-seven percent of alcohol abusers had a comorbid psychiatric disorder. More startling was the fact that in prison populations, 81 percent of inmates with addictive disorders also had another mental disorder. Among those inmates diagnosed with antisocial personality disorder, affective disorder, or schizophrenia, 90 percent had substance abuse comorbidity.

The implication of these findings is that, when attempting to treat juvenile or adult gang populations on an outpatient basis, there is a high likelihood of a substance abuse problem (either a history of, in remission, or active). Mandatory random drug testing, therefore, is extremely important as an ally to treatment. "Dirty tests" can also provide rich clinical material once the therapist goes beneath the client's usual "I don't know why I did it" response. The "dirty test" may communicate that the client wants emotional distance in a conflicted marital relationship, wants to be returned to the institution, wants to return to an old life-style, wants to be punished, wants to feel less depressed, or wants to "get back" at someone, usually parents. The therapist can then begin to help the client identify circumstances prior to use that eventually led to the act. Often substance-abusing clients were capable initially of saying "no" when they were completely sober; however, after a few drinks they "mellowed out" and it was harder to say "no." Clients can also be helped to verbalize their needs ("I want to live elsewhere") rather than forcing changes through negative behavior (getting dirty tests so they can return to the institution).

Cyco Ike

"Cyco Ike" was an eighteen-year-old parolee who had the least going for him yet had made an outstanding adjustment in the community since his institutional release fifteen months previously. (Demonstrating excellent psychiatric assessment skills, gang members will often provide a peer a nickname consistent with their personality profile.) He spent five years in a state juvenile corrections institution for attempted homicide. He had no prior arrest record. At age thirteen, while he was drinking with his "homeboys," they became involved in an argument with two nongang adults in a liquor store. Later, in the parking lot, Cyco Ike shot one of the adults three times. Due to problems of adjustment in the institution for several years (fighting and breaking rules and regulations), in his last year he finally was assigned to a specialized treatment unit for very disturbed inmates.

Perhaps due to marked psychological changes during his adolescent years in the institution, it was difficult to evaluate him with precision. Initially he was diagnosed as "conduct disorder of adolescence." A few years later, he was diagnosed as "schizotypal personality disorder" and placed on bimonthly injected Prolixin (antipsychotic medication) and Cogentin (antiparkinsonean agent). He remained on these drugs by order of the parole board and physician when released on parole.

Cyco Ike returned to live with his fifty-year-old Mexican mother, who was permanently disabled with an arthritic condition, his twenty-six-year-old sister and her boyfriend, and their three children. His father had died in an accident when he was six years old. They resided in a small, crowded house in a poor, gang-infested neighborhood. Because he had grown up in this neighborhood, he was automatically accepted into the gang (like his older brothers); hence, he did not have to be initiated ("jumped").

Since his release, he had not had one dirty test and had missed only one of his approximately sixty psychotherapy visits. Upon his release, the therapist urged the parole officer to assist the parolee to apply for a psychiatric disability pension because it was the therapist's opinion that he suffered from a schizophrenic disorder. Six months later, following extensive evaluations, independent psychiatric examiners concurred in the diagnosis and a Social Security disability pension of $700 per month was approved. This immediately raised his self-esteem and status at home, as he was now the main wage earner.

The focus of therapy has been on making sure he keeps his medication appointments, twice-a-month phone conversations by his therapist with his mother in his presence concerning his behavior at home, monitoring his psychological state with occasional mini mental status exams, and helping him deal with the daily problems of living, such as how to get from one place to another using public transportation.

When he first received his pension, he was very popular in the neighborhood, as he was purchasing his "homeboys" gifts and "booze." He would become angry at his mother when she would not give him "his" money because he was spending large amounts. The therapist helped the parolee and his mother establish a weekly budget of $50 per week for all of his spending, and he learned to stretch out his allowance. His mother deducts money for food and other household expenses and saves the remainder for him. He has been stopped by police on seven occasions on suspicion of being either a gang member or under the influence of drugs, but they have not found drugs on his person. He carries a letter from his therapist outlining the medications he is taking, and he simply tells the police that he is taking prescribed medication for his "nerves." He denies hallucinations but often is seen at home, in the parole office, or in the therapist's office laughing to himself inappropriately for no apparent reason. He states that he laughs by himself because he is happy.

He is valued by his mother, the parole staff, and the therapist and carries in his mind three therapeutic instructions: (1) no alcohol; (2) no drugs; and (3) be careful with the "homeboys." He has less than one year before being discharged from parole.

Conclusion

In summary, most youngsters join and/or associate with gangs largely to have some of their basic emotional, social, and physical needs met in a gang culture milieu that also provides excitement, a feeling of empowerment, and an escape from boredom and at times depression. These needs are often not met by the family, extended family, church, school, and other socializing groups. It is not uncommon to observe that frequently these groups initially rejected these youths, causing them to seek out other alternatives, such as the gang. For some gang members, too, being in the gang and being raised in a gang neighborhood was simply the norm, as their parents, older siblings, and relatives were also gang members.

Youths thus join gangs for many different reasons (violence, companionship, crime for profit, substance abuse, and so on), though the gang may or may not participate in violent activities. Even when they join a violent gang, they, as well as the majority of the members, may not participate in violent homicidal behavior. For example, in Los Angeles, known as the "gang capital of the world," 100,000 gang members representing 900 gangs committed approximately 450 homicides in one year, which translates into one-half homicide for each gang—a figure that may not necessarily conform to the media's and public's image of seeing *all* gang members as "killers."

In addition to assessing the criminal profile of the youth's gang (for example, number of annual felony crimes, assaults, and homicides), it is equally important to assess the gang member's actual, objective criminal history (convictions rather than arrests). Has he or she primarily internalized the gang culture rather than violent behavior, or both?

Suggestions were provided on how to transform an involuntary into a voluntary client through contracting and initially focusing on topics of interest to him or her. Even this intervention technique, accompanied by all of the therapist's charm and charisma, may not be sufficient to break down resistance. Thirty-eight years of experience in working with juvenile and adult male and female gang members from Latino (Mexican, Cuban, Puerto Rican, Guatemalan, Salvadoran), African American, Asian (Japanese, Chinese, Vietnamese, Filipino), and Anglo American heritage has taught the author that the most important variable related to treatment success—even considering class, race, ethnicity, and culture—is *readiness* for change. The point of readiness, however, is highly subjective and can occur at any time during the career of a gang member—from the date of the first arrest at age seven for glue sniffing to age thirty-five or forty after numerous state prison incarcerations for felony convictions. A few may never achieve a point of readiness because the gang life-style, criminal offenses accompanied with incarceration, is meeting their needs.

All that one can really offer a gang member through therapy—even a hard-core one such as those discussed in this chapter—is a new, unique, and emotionally corrective relationship with an adult whom he or she can learn to trust and who can provide some support, guidance, nonjudgmental listening, and advocacy at home and with law enforcement, parole, school, employers, and other community persons. If the therapist is successful in doing this *and* the gang member is ready for change, the gang violence-homicide victim/perpetrator cycle will be stopped at least for this one family. If one hundred mental health practitioners in private practice in a given city each adopted one similar pro bono (free service) gang case, the reduction of gang violence and homicide would be impressive.

References

American Psychiatric Association. "Comorbidity Rates of Substance Abuse, Mental Illness Found to Be Surprisingly High." *Psychiatric News*, Dec. 21, 1990, p. 2.
Asbury, H. *The Gangs of New York: An Informational History of the Underworld*. New York: Knopf, 1927.
Attorney General's Youth Gang Task Force. *Report of Youth Gang Violence in California*. Sacramento, Calif.: June 1981, pp. 16-20.
Augustine, Saint. *Confessions*. New York: Modern Library, 1949.
California Council on Criminal Justice. *State Task Force on Youth Gang Violence: Final Report*. Sacramento, Calif.: Jan. 1986.
Cloward, R. A., and Ohlin, L. E. *Delinquency and Opportunity*. New York: Free Press, 1960.
Cohen, A. K. *Delinquent Boys: The Culture of the Gang*. New York: Free Press, 1955.
Davis, A., and Haller, M. (eds.). *The People of Philadelphia*. Philadelphia: Temple University Press, 1973.

Fox, J. R. "Mission Impossible? Social Work Practice with Black Urban Youth Gangs." *Social Work*, 1985, *30*, 25.

Good, W. V., and Nelson, J. E. *Psychiatry Made Ridiculously Simple*. Miami, Fla.: Med Master, 1984.

Hopps, J. G. "Violence—A Personal and Societal Challenge." *Social Work*, 1987, *32*, 467–468.

Ivanoff, A. M. "Suicide." In *Encyclopedia of Social Work*. (18th ed.) Vol. II. Silver Springs, Md.: National Association of Social Work, 1987.

Jackson, R. K., and McBride, W. D. *Understanding Street Gangs*. Sacramento, Calif.: Custom, 1985.

Kerfoot, T. "Crime and the Occult." *Peace Officers Association of Los Angeles County*, Oct. 1985, p. 23.

Kinard, M. E. "Child Abuse and Neglect." In *Encyclopedia of Social Work*. (18th ed.) Vol. I. Silver Springs, Md.: National Association of Social Work, 1987.

Los Angeles Times, Part I, Apr. 12, 1983, p. 6.

Matza, D. *Delinquency and Drift*. New York: Wiley, 1964.

Middleman, R. R., and Goldberg, G. "Social Work Practice with Groups." In *Encyclopedia of Social Work*. (18th ed.) Vol. II. Silver Springs, Md.: National Association of Social Work, 1987.

Miller, W. B. "Lower Class Culture as a Generating Milieu of Gang Delinquency." *Journal of Social Issues*, 1958, *14*, 15–19.

Ministry of Justice. *White Paper on Crime, 1983*. Tokyo: Foreign Press Center, 1984.

Morales, A. *A Study of Recidivism of Mexican-American Junior Forestry Camp Graduates*. Unpublished master's thesis. Los Angeles: School of Social Work, University of Southern California, 1963.

Morales, A. "The Need for Nontraditional Mental Health Programs in the Barrio." In J. M. Casas and S. E. Keefe (eds.), *Family and Mental Health in the Mexican American Community*. Monograph no. 7. Los Angeles: Spanish-Speaking Mental Health Research Center, University of California, Los Angeles, 1978.

Morales, A. "The Mexican American Gang Member: Evaluation and Treatment." In R. M. Becerra, M. Karno, and J. Escobar (eds.), *Mental Health and Hispanic Americans: Clinical Perspectives*. New York: Grune & Stratton, 1982.

Morales, A., and Sheafor, B. W. *Social Work: A Profession of Many Faces.* (5th ed.) Boston: Allyn & Bacon, 1989.

O'Hagan, F. J. "Gang Characteristics—An Empirical Survey." *Journal of Child Psychology and Psychiatry,* 1976, *17,* 306–314.

Poirier, M. *Street Gangs of Los Angeles County.* Unpublished pamphlet, 1982.

Spergel, I. A. "Violent Gangs in Chicago: In Search of Social Policy." *Social Service Review,* 1984, *58,* 199–226.

Star, B. "Domestic Violence." In *Encyclopedia of Social Work.* (18th ed.) Vol. I. Silver Springs, Md.: National Association of Social Work, 1987.

Sweeney, T. A. *Streets of Anger: Streets of Hope.* Glendale, Calif.: Great Western, 1980.

Thrasher, F. M. *The Gang: A Study of 1,313 Gangs in Chicago.* Chicago: University of Chicago Press, 1963.

Vigil, J. D. *Barrio Gangs.* Austin: University of Texas Press, 1988.

"Watsonville or East L.A.?" *Santa Cruz Sentinel,* Jan. 24, 1990, p. A-2.

PART THREE

Working with Asian American Children and Adolescents

8

The Inner Heart:
Therapy with
Southeast Asian Families

CHRISTINE M. CHAO

"We Do Not Even Eat Rice the Same"

We embark on a therapeutic journey with Southeast Asian children with little to guide us (Williams, 1987). In our clinical training as mental health professionals, in the research projects we undertake, and in the theoretical courses we take, the needs, development, and problems of minority children (much less Southeast Asian children) are not adequately addressed. Furthermore, the dynamics involved in understanding Southeast Asian children are different from those of third-, fourth-, and fifth-generation Asian American children, that is, children born in the United States whose parents and grandparents are also U.S. born. These children are different from the children of Asian immigrants from countries such as Korea, Taiwan, Hong Kong, or Japan. In turn, these groups are different from

The author wishes to acknowledge a deep debt of gratitude to all the clinicians with whom she has worked at the Asian Pacific Center for Human Development. It is to these teachers that this chapter is dedicated: Jae Wha Ahn, Onechanch Inthamanivong, Kham Ko Ly, Maysy Martin, Chuong K. Nguyen, Duyen Nguyen, Lourni Nourn, Soeuth Nun, Vangmoua Sayaovong, Marilyn Ung, Hue Ngoc Vo, and Yoshiko Wang.

Asian-born children adopted into non-Asian families, who are different from children who are the offspring of Asian-born mothers and U.S. servicemen. Biracial children, where one parent has "outmarried" from his or her group, are also different. Moreover, we know little of the dynamics involved with children from the Pacific Islands, for example, Guam and Samoa.

It is crucial to also understand that even the loose term *Southeast Asian child* will connote vast differences in the ethnic and cultural background of a child. Hence the title to this section, "We do not even eat rice the same," a comment made during a luncheon conversation with the pan-Asian staff of the Asian Pacific Center for Human Development, a community mental health center in Denver, Colorado. We were sitting in a makeshift kitchen where the staff crowded in for lunch. The speaker was Laotian. A H'Mong coworker placed a straw basket packed with "sticky rice" in the center of the table; a Japanese counselor added short-grained rice from a rice cooker; a Chinese American clinician added a bowl of long-grained rice. The different varieties of rice silently spoke to the different philosophical, ethnic, cultural, historical, and religious traditions represented around that table. And yet we were all considered to be "Asian." Both viewpoints contain aspects of truth. As soon as you think you know the similarities among Asian groups, you must leave room to understand the vast differences that can and do occur. And just when the differences among the various Asian cultures leave the clinician in despair of ever achieving any real understanding of a particular group or client, certain principles of Asian culture and thought can be called upon to help the therapist arrive at an understanding as to what might be occurring in the client's life and psyche.

This chapter then will present some of the generalities and particulars of Asian culture as a whole and the dynamics operating in various subgroups to more effectively work with Southeast Asian children, adolescents, and their families.

The Psychologist as Expert of the Inner Heart

Much has been written about the reluctance of Asians to seek out mental health professionals (Tsui and Schultz, 1985; Kitano and

Natsushima, 1981; Sue and McKinney, 1975). In part, the explanations offered have referred to the strength of the family unit and the
bonds between members, so that going outside of the family threatens to bring shame to the other members as well as to oneself and
to cause them to "lose face." Many clients feel that they do not even
have the luxury of deciding for themselves, that the gains to be made
from seeking therapy might make it worthwhile to lose a little face.

At the root of the whole issue of shame or honor or loss of
face is the concept of "filial piety." To explain filial piety accurately
is a bit like trying to explain a concept like "Yankee ingenuity";
there are the broad strokes and then the vast array of subtleties.
Broadly defined, however, filial piety is the honor, reverence, obedience, loyalty, and love owed to those who are hierarchically above
you. It sets the parameters for behavior of children toward parents,
adult children toward parents, younger siblings toward older siblings, students toward teachers, employees toward bosses, patients
toward doctors. It is the intricately fashioned web that undergirds
much of Asian social as well as familial interaction. Therefore, to
come into therapy and talk about or complain about other family
members or even one's teachers or supervisors puts the person peri-
lously close to violating the whole meaning of filial piety. From this
perspective it is easy to understand why college counseling offices
complain that their Asian therapists are underutilized or that legis-
latures do not fund specialized Asian services. They point to the
statistics on utilization patterns that might lead one to think that
the Asian population has no struggles with mental illness, no difficulties with their teenagers engaging in acting-out behaviors,
and/or no desire to explore intrapsychic issues that may be curtail-
ing one's functioning in interpersonal relationships, the family, or
the work world.

Filial piety is a fundamental concept that any clinician working with Asian clients needs to understand (Shon and Ja, 1982).
However, it is the feeling of this author that too often these caution-
ary warnings may lead to Asians not being offered psychological
help of any real substance. If you look at what has been written in
the United States about the more dynamic schools of therapy, you
find almost nothing written about Asian clients. This may be due,
in part, to projections that non-Asian clinicians cast onto their

Asian clients. These clinicians have some sense that an Asian client will probably not delve into his or her innermost feelings. This resonates with the cultural stereotype of the Asian as "inscrutable" that often leads to the treatment of choice being short-term directed therapy.

We need to rethink this premise. Understanding the literal translation of the word "psychologist" in a number of Asian languages provides an insight that I have found helpful in educating both Asian and non-Asian clients about the nature of psychotherapy. The Chinese characters for psychologist read, "expert of the inner heart" (xinlixuejia, Pinyin system of romanization). In Vietnamese a psychologist is "tâm lý gia" or "expert of the heart, or soul" or the "expert who helps one understand the heart." "Tâm" also means "the bull's-eye," the center of things. So when I meet clients I will often discuss with them what consulting an "expert of the inner heart" means.

While acknowledging that Asian culture on one level does not look kindly on a person going outside the family to discuss problems, we also examine what it means to understand "heart" issues. I discuss with my client that it may take a while before he or she feels completely comfortable with me. That is understandable; one does not delve into the heart lightly. In addition (and this is a reminder more for the clinician, since the Asian client already knows it both consciously and unconsciously), heart issues encompass both the mind and the body. In Asian culture, there is no notion of duality or split between psyche and soma. Muecke (1983) suggests that Asian clients present their psychological distress as somatization. The problem with this is that it tends to have a pejorative ring to it suggesting a deficient level of psychological-mindedness. The issue needs to be reframed for clinicians so that we understand that a person suffering from depression, post-traumatic stress disorder, an anxiety disorder, or even adjustment disorder, as defined by *DSM-III-R* criteria, will most likely have headaches, aches in joints and limbs, and general feelings of fatigue. We must respect these symptoms and understand them, as well as help our clients understand them as manifestations of things going on in the heart. I tell my clients that if your heart is aching or overburdened or about to break, of course your head will pound and your stomach will ache; your muscles will be sore or weak. These symptoms must be honored, and it is important to spend time with them. Has the client sought Western medical help, sought traditional Asian healers, consulted family elders, or tried coining, cupping, moxibustion, or acupuncture? Perhaps one or more of the aforementioned avenues needs to be explored. This does not mean that the psychologist is practicing beyond his or her realm of expertise; it does mean that he or she is being aware of the whole person.

A brief word should be said here about coining, mainly because Southeast Asian families are still being reported to social service agencies and accused of abusing their children when the marks from coining are seen by teachers or physicians who have not taken the time to understand what has occurred. Coining involves rubbing a coin or sometimes the edge of the bowl of a spoon along various muscle groupings of the body, including the back, chest, neck, arms, and legs. Usually a cream, lotion, oil, or even the juice of a lemon is used to reduce friction, add to the suppleness of the skin, and make one feel good. The coin is rhythmically rubbed in short strokes that are often along the same meridians used in acupuncture and acupressure. Coining is done for a variety of reasons: achiness, tight muscles, an overall run-down feeling, and sometimes as a preventive measure when someone "feels a cold coming on," in short, for many of those instances when someone from the West would "pop a couple of aspirin." Because blood is brought to the surface of the skin, coining leaves red markings that disappear within a day or two.

Not only is the process painless and very soothing, to which I and members of my family can attest, but the fact that it involves two people can point to a loving cohesiveness within a family. A parent does coining for a child; a child does coining for a grandparent, aunt, or uncle; a sibling does coining for another sibling. Coining is an act of caring and healing and should be seen as such.

Cupping and moxibustion are also remedies that are sought and usually performed by people skilled in this form of traditional healing. I can offer only the barest outline of these practices and do so mainly to alert the Western reader to the vast number of healing practices of which we are woefully ignorant. Cupping will leave a red circular patch because a glass container evacuated by heat draws blood to the surface of the body. Bamboo tubes are sometimes used. In moxibustion, a cone of medicinal herbs is made, which is often placed along the points used in acupuncture. The top of the cone is lit and allowed to smolder. In some instances it is removed before it burns down to the surface of the skin and in other instances it is allowed to touch the skin.

To sum up, understanding the therapist as "expert of the inner heart" means that you and the client have the potential to enter into a dialogue that will go deep into the heart. Things that touch the heart can be anything that is current in the life of the client or issues from the past, a dream, or a stomachache. Being a heart expert gives the therapist enormous latitude. It means that he or she can visit the family in their home for tea or a meal so that the whole family can meet and feel comfortable with the therapist before entrusting themselves to his or her care. It makes the whole arena of accepting gifts not quite so problematic—a true gift is offered from the heart and must be accepted by the heart (Sue and Zane, 1987). It is not that issues of transference and countertransference do not come up. They do. However, if a client cooks you some special food, eat and enjoy it. It is of therapeutic significance that a client who has been depressed can now cook something special, and it says something about a family's trust in the therapist when a mother gives her child something she has cooked to bring.

In the past, when attempting to educate parents about the potential benefits of therapy for their child, I often appealed to their desire to have their child succeed in school. I would stress that therapy might remove psychological impediments to the child's ability to do well in school. I used a stereotype of Asians and capitalized on the positive value of education. Now, I still talk about this problem of psychological impediments to successful education, but I talk much more about heart issues. What troubles the heart of a Southeast Asian teen desperately wanting to be accepted by his or her U.S.-born peers? What fears lie deep and often unspoken in the heart of the collective family that whispers, "Maybe our son or our daughter is no longer really Vietnamese [or Cambodian, H'Mong, or Lao]?"

A Good Doctor Is a Good Mother

In Vietnamese "Lương Y Như Từ Mẫu" means "A good doctor is a good mother." This was first said to me by a Vietnamese physician who confided that it was a saying originally attributed to Ho Chi Minh, but she felt the authorship should not be widely publicized for fear of offending American political sensibilities. This pediatrician went on to say, "Asian people work with their hearts, not with their minds. The patient will look at the doctor and demand the doctor nurture them and take care of them. They will be very obedient and be very disappointed if the doctor is more concerned with money than with helping. They will be confident about all of the decisions the doctor makes and rely on the advice of the doctor, ask no questions and never question decisions of the doctor" (Hue Ngoc Vo, personal communication, 1989). The same attitudes apply to psychologists, social workers, and psychiatrists. Although the axiom most probably reflects a universal wish to be cared for when we are sick, there are important cultural components to examine.

Asian culture is exquisitely hierarchical. As mentioned previously, this hierarchy orchestrates how one's obligations under filial piety are to be fulfilled. As a psychologist, you are placed near the top and are owed certain things due to your position; for example, what you say may not be overtly challenged. However, Ho Chi Minh's pronouncement makes clear your obligations and duties toward your client. You do not just enter into a business proposition but a familial relationship, which contains the flip side of all that is implied by the concept of filial piety. It is what the parent must do for the child, the teacher for the pupil, the king for his subject, and the therapist for his or her client. It is a weighty responsibility. For the psychologist, it entails many of the qualities of the good mother. Some might argue that this will encourage a transference relationship that could easily lead the client into being too passive or too dependent on the therapist; however, building an empathic bond between the therapist and client is crucial. It is out of this bond that the therapist demonstrates what has been called "achieved" credibility (Sue and Zane, 1987). Moreover, problems in a therapeutic relationship usually do not arise out of a positive transference but from unexamined countertransference issues on the part of the therapist. This chapter cannot go into depth with this aspect of working with Southeast Asian clients, but it is important for the therapist to know him- or herself well in terms of his or her own perceptions of refugee and Asian clients and of past involvement or feelings regarding the wars in the various countries of Southeast Asia. This holds true both for Asian American therapists and American therapists whose ancestry is not Asian.

A good mother knows when to step in and when to step back; there are no hard and fast rules here. However, advocacy for the client, and by extension the client's family, is something the therapist should not shirk. Again, in Asia, mind and body are not split and neither are the issues pertaining to each. You will lose both your credibility and opportunities to know and understand your client if, for example, you say to the mother of a child with whom you are working: "Oh, no, it's not appropriate for me to help you fill out this application for citizenship. Here is the address for the immigration office," or, "I'm sorry. I can't take the time from your daughter's session to fill out this food stamp application. Let me get you the telephone number of social services. You need to see your caseworker." As a result, the family may soon decide you are not the person they need. It is usually the personal or professional insecurity of the therapist (often involving some sort of pecking order) that causes him or her to decide that certain behaviors are "not what we were trained for." What is the correct response? You help fill out the applications. You take the initiative and make whatever calls might ease the family's way through the maze of American bureaucracy. These actions can be as therapeutic as the best-constructed interpretation you could offer.

Birthdays

Many American therapists in social service agencies and medical personnel have been frustrated when trying to ascertain the exact age of an Asian child. Children appear to be older or younger than their stated age as determined by the dates of their alien registration cards. Sometimes Southeast Asian adolescents will complain that they have been placed in the wrong grade in school and that the birth date on their papers is not correct. What is going on? Many Southeast Asian refugees who are now in this country were born at home, in rural areas of their own countries, far from big cities or hospitals, where official documentation of the birth may not have occurred. Even those people born in the capital cities may also have been born at home and again do not have an official registration of their birth or do not remember it. Birth certificates may have been lost in the person's flight to safety. As a result, a person's "birth date" is what they orally told an official assigned to process people in a refugee camp.

Parents have, at times, altered their children's birth dates along lines that they perceived would help the child. Thus, if there was a rumor that parents might get more food for their family if there were younger children, birth dates were adjusted accordingly. Some families with developmentally disabled children also altered their birth dates, feeling that once they got to a host country they would need as much help as possible. A younger child might have a better chance to be eligible for services.

Sometimes a person is truly unsure of the birth date and it appears to the therapist that it would be beneficial to have an exact date, at least in terms of a year. One way to ascertain the date is to ask them the animal of the year they were born. Many Asian people are very aware of this zodiac that follows the Chinese lunar calendar. A cycle takes sixty years to complete; there are five simple cycles of twelve years each, each year bearing the name of a different animal that is said to influence a person's life. This idea is much like the Western zodiac where certain characteristics are thought to be descriptive of the people born under that sign. Many persons have heard throughout their life how they seem to embody a particular sign, such as "You truly are a tiger" or "That part of you is the ox," so if you ask for their year they will usually know it. Therefore if a person does not know his or her age or child's age but knows the animal sign under which they were born, based on a cycle of twelve years one can figure out the age. How the years came to be named for each particular animal is told in the following legend: "The Lord Buddha summoned all the animals to come to him before he departed from Earth. Only twelve came to bid him farewell. As a reward he named a year after each one in the order that it arrived. First came the Rat, then the Ox, the Tiger, Rabbit, Dragon, Snake, Horse, Sheep, Monkey, Rooster, Dog and Boar" (Lau, 1979).

Names, Ancestor Altars, and Religion

In all Asian languages dozens of words translate into familial designations. There is, for example, no one word that translates "sister" in Putonghua (Mandarin Chinese)—it is either *jie jie* for an older sister or *mei mei* for a younger sister. Immediately on hearing the word "sister," everyone knows where everyone stands. In part because of this ordering of people and the roles they occupy, I always use my title with first-generation adult clients and I use "Mr. and Mrs." when addressing them. With children and most adolescents I address them using their first name and they use my title and last name. Of course, there are always exceptions. With the majority of adult third-, fourth-, and fifth-generation Asian American clients, I am on a first-name basis, as with young adult, first-generation Southeast Asian clients.

Here, however, the question of how we will address each other has often proved a rich entry point into discussions of the struggles of acculturation, what it means to be "Asian" or "American," and how it feels when you locate yourself in one dimension as opposed to the other. This issue is too lengthy to do it justice in this chapter, but it is an especially salient topic for Southeast Asian adolescents, who struggle with their identity on many levels. Many feel they are scorned by their school peers because they are "too Asian" and taunted by labels of "FOB" (Fresh Off the Boat). Yet at home, their parents and other family members berate them for becoming "too American" and worry when they listen to American popular music or want to date outside their ethnic group, even someone from another Southeast Asian country. A young Vietnamese girl bitterly reported being teased by classmates for "wearing pajamas" to school. She had recently been reunited with her mother, who had been in a reeducation camp in Vietnam for ten years. When the mother saw the tight jeans her daughter was wearing, she declared that only "a prostitute from the streets of Saigon would wear such clothing." Her daughter, like many young people, struggled with what she perceived to be the "old-fashioned" Asian world and her new American world.

In this respect, how names are used and what names are used can also be diagnostically informative. First-generation children, who want to anglicize a first name or a family name because their own names seem too difficult for their teachers to pronounce and they do not know how to deal with taunts or racial slurs from peers, can be at odds with parents, who fear their children are losing their Asian identity and heritage in this new country. How this dilemma is resolved and what fears, fantasies, and conflicts underlie the viewpoints of the different family members are all issues about which the therapist needs to be sensitive. What is also implied is that the therapist will take the time to learn the correct pronunciation of his or her clients' names. He or she may never achieve a great Vietnamese or Laotian or Cambodian accent but should keep trying.

It should also be remembered that in most Asian countries, women keep their own family surname when they marry, even though they may often be referred to as the "mother of X" or the "wife of X" in their mother tongue. Do not assume, therefore, that the wife of Mr. "X" will be Mrs. "X." You will also find that some women have encountered so much confusion on the part of U.S. government agencies or other social agencies that they have started using their husbands' last names. And even if an Asian woman does use her husband's name, the therapist should find out if it is a true choice or just a way of avoiding lengthy explanations to agency personnel. For example, you could say, "I know you use Mrs. "X" with your son's teachers but that your own name is Mrs. "Y." Which would you prefer me to use?"

Why focus on names? There are two reasons. First, in Asian culture your name links you to your family and your clan, in some cultures denoting your generation, and your name will ultimately link you to your ancestors. A person's name usually is not given lightly. In most instances, the name has a meaning that is important to the family, and many times a new baby's name will be chosen by the paternal grandparents. Many young H'Mong males will be given a new name when they assume the responsibilities of adult life, marry, and father children. For the H'Mong, two people who share the same last name are assumed to belong to the same clan, and each must afford the other the hospitality due to extended family members. Similarly, a marriage between two people with the same last name is considered to be incestuous. In a number of instances, there has been great conflict when, for example, a young woman from California with the name of Vang wanted to marry a young man from Minnesota also named Vang. They may appeal to U.S. law, which says they are not even distant cousins and will grant them a marriage license, but for both families there will be tremendous consternation and rifts that sometimes do not heal.

The second reason why one's name is so important is simply that who you are should itself be honored. Refugees, for example, have given up everything they once knew; unless it is their choice, they should not be made to give up their names.

Often therapists will hear a child client refer to a sister(s) or a brother(s), check their intake notes, and become mystified when they cannot find the name. Sometimes this is an indication that there has been a sibling who either had to be left behind or chose to stay behind when the family fled their country of origin. In other cases, the child is referring to one of the members of the extended family. The use of the term *sister* or *brother* for what Westerners would consider a distant cousin underscores the bond that family membership creates. Reflecting this dynamic, the therapist may also hear of an "aunty" or an "uncle" who may not have any blood ties to the family but may rather be an old friend who carries the status of a family member and to whom the child owes all the loyalties that filial piety dictates. It may be important for the therapist to know of these persons because sometimes they may be asked to be go-betweens for children and their parents and helpful allies to which the therapist can turn.

Eventually, death will elevate each person to the important status of an ancestor of the family. Thus, it is not sufficient to just take into account a child's extended family consisting of grandparents, aunts, uncles, and cousins. Although this chapter cannot present an in-depth discussion of Asian religions and spirituality or in any way do justice to this subject, a few things will be mentioned that may prove helpful for the therapist working with Southeast Asian children and their families.

Many, though not all, Southeast Asian families have an altar to their ancestors. By inquiring about it the therapist can better understand the family with whom he or she is working. An ancestor altar may be made by anyone or it can be kept by the eldest son of a family. It can be elaborate or plain. It can hold a wide variety of things or very few things—objects might include incense, a vase of flowers, a statue of the Buddha, pictures of family members who have died, and offerings of food and fruit. A particular family's devotion in caring for its altar and praying at ritually prescribed times varies tremendously. For some families, whether or not to erect an altar has caused conflict. In some cases, clients have said to me that they are embarrassed to put up an altar in their homes because it invites too many questions. Some families erect their altar in a private part of the house. One client told me: "I have come to a new country. I throw away my old gods and take new gods, your gods." Some tell of deep existential despair and feelings that their ancestors could not intercede and protect them from the horrors of war, so they no longer see any value in maintaining an altar or teaching their children how to pray. Many other families, however, will tell you that they owe their survival to the agency of their ancestors protecting them.

Though a sizable minority of Vietnamese have always been Roman Catholic, stemming from the days of French control of Vietnam, many other Southeast Asians have become Christian since coming to the United States. Sometimes they have joined the denominational group of the church that sponsored them. Of course, the meaning attributed to such membership varies with families and individuals. For some, it is an expression of politeness and/or gratitude. Some people can fuse together different religious aspects into a new hybrid with which they feel quite comfortable. Thus, it would not be unusual to see a statue of Jesus next to a statue of the Buddha. In one H'Mong family, the father and mother had their daughter baptized in a local church and then went home and conducted a traditional H'Mong ceremony calling in beneficent spirits of health and happiness, which were "caught" in string bracelets tied around her wrists (*khi tes* or *tie hand*).

Some families, however, have been torn apart because of religious dissension. For example, some members who have converted, usually to a fundamentalist Christian denomination, refuse to participate in offerings of food that have been placed in front of the ancestors and then shared by the family members. Often they are pained by this but feel compelled to tell the other family members that their pastor has forbidden them to take part in such practices anymore and that food offered to the ancestors must be considered "devil food." Of course, to the other relatives, this is the height of disrespect. Deep divisions and bitterness have also occurred around how to conduct rituals for those who have died. How these dynamics are played out in the family and resulting repercussions involving the children is something to which therapists need to pay attention.

There is no right course of resolution. Each family must find its own way, with the therapist helping in making that journey. An example concerns a Laotian family.

A young mother of two children was suffering from a post-traumatic stress disorder. As we talked about her dreams she presented a particularly poignant, recurring dream in which a young boy floated in a river with his pockets pulled out as if to show, the woman said, that he had no gold or money. She revealed that just before escaping from Laos, her youngest son, a baby boy, had died. In the frantic rush to escape she had left his ashes on the home altar and felt that she had never had the proper rituals and prayers performed for him. After escaping and enduring a number of years in a refugee camp, the family came to the United States, sponsored by the husband's father, who had gotten out of Laos earlier and converted to Christianity. In deference to his father and to honor the father's religion, the husband, who was the only surviving son, declared that he and his whole family were now to be Christian. He told his wife she was not to go to the Buddhist temple or seek out any monks to perform ceremonies for their dead son, or to erect any ancestor altars in their home.

This was a significant stressor in her life and its resolution took some time, involving meetings with various family members (alone and in pairs) and with the Christian pastor and church members who originally sponsored the father. Eventually a Christian altar was placed in the living room with a framed picture from the New Testament, a vase of flowers, and a copy of the Bible, and in a side room she erected a small traditional ancestor altar. After a tacit agreement between the husband and the wife, she quietly went to a Buddhist monk to have ceremonies performed for the baby who had died. She felt content that she had done what had not been done, and she stopped having the dream of the little boy in the river.

Traditional Healers and Spirits

Exploring how a family has used a traditional healer, when to call one, or whether or not to consult one are questions the Western psychotherapist has only recently learned to be of value (Tobin and Friedman, 1983; Lemoine, 1986). As in the area of religion, a complete discussion of the different traditional healers of each Southeast Asian group would go beyond the scope of this chapter (Conquergood, Thao, and Thao, 1989; Bliatout, 1982). Bringing up the subject of traditional healers with a family probably reveals more about the therapist than anything else. Western therapists often appear to be very turf conscious when it comes to other professionals who can act in a healing capacity. Lest our "hubris" prove to be our downfall, however, we would probably do well to note that before there were social workers, psychologists, psychiatrists, and marriage and family counselors, there were H'Mong shamans (*Txiv Neeb*), Cambodian *Kru Khmer* (traditional healers), and Vietnamese herbalists and seers. Furthermore, it is important to realize that these traditional healers are very much present and active within the Southeast Asian community. It is probably not by accident that the wording we employ for these healers is only slightly better than the archaic and pejorative term *witch doctor.*

The dynamics involved in the discussion of whether or not a family has sought help from a traditional healer, who has made that decision, how it has worked out, and how they would like the therapist to be involved is very similar to the subject of ancestor altars. Once the therapist views it as a legitimate subject for discussion, it can prove extremely beneficial in understanding a child, the parents, and the entire family. The therapist needs to be aware of and explore the widely differing opinions on whether a traditional healer should be employed, otherwise resistance can quietly but effectively scuttle the case. Families are often caught between the conflicting pulls of traditional practices of their own cultural groups and the cultural practices employed by twentieth-century U.S. psychologists.

At a conference, a teacher once asked what she should do when more than one Southeast Asian pupil came in talking about ghosts. My reply was that she might ask them who the ghost was and what the ghost had to say or what it wanted. My Western training in Freudian and Jungian psychology has taught me to believe in the existence of an unconscious and to respect its manifestations in the form of the id, the ego, the superego, and the collective unconscious. Most Southeast Asian clients and friends will relate either a personal experience or that of a close friend or relative with a spirit. Our job is to listen and understand. If a client and I together cannot understand the meaning of a visitation by a spirit or if a client is frightened and our work together is not easing this, I suggest that I may not be the most expert person in this matter. I will explore with the client who or what might help.

The following is a composite example, which is based in part on clinical cases and personal accounts told to me, presented to illustrate a number of the dynamics that have been discussed. This is not a perfect case by an expert in H'Mong psychology. It is an attempt to show the slow and at times confusing process of working on the inner-heart issues of family members.

A seven-year-old H'Mong boy, born in the United States to refugee parents from Laos, had been in a car accident with his mother. Shortly afterward, the boy said he did not want to go to school, even though he previously had enjoyed school and had good grades. He could not articulate why he balked at leaving home, but each morning became a struggle.

His teacher could think of nothing occurring in school to account for the problem and related that once the boy was in the classroom he did well. The school psychologist identified it as a case of "school phobia" and felt the accident was the precipitant. She surmised that the behavior was probably motivated by some elements of a post-traumatic stress reaction—the little boy feared to leave the security of his mother lest something happen to her. Perhaps, also, he had magical feelings concerning his own omnipotence and wish to take care of her. The psychologist speculated that the boy might be unconsciously tuning into certain family dynamics whereby the parental relationship was strained and the wife felt unsupported by her husband, who in turn felt shut out by the strength of the mother-son bond.

The psychologist called for a meeting with the parents and the boy. They came with two older children and the husband's mother. On an intuitive hunch, the psychologist decided to meet with everyone, even though it was evident that the grandmother spoke only minimal English. The psychologist got everyone coffee and wished tea had been available. She hoped it would be a hospitable gesture to put everyone a little more at ease. It also gave her a few spare minutes to think about how to conduct the meeting.

First the psychologist asked the father for his opinion of the situation. He replied with a short speech. He said he was grateful for the help of his son's teacher and wanted the psychologist to thank the teacher for him. He spoke of the value of education and of his desire that his sons graduate from high school, something he had not been able to do in Laos. He also thanked this country for taking his family in; he and his wife were not yet citizens, but he was proud that his son was. The speech had taken a fairly long time and the psychologist wanted the mother's opinion. The mother said that since the accident she as well as her son were listless and easily fatigued. Though the doctors at the hospital clinic found nothing wrong, both had been having headaches.

The psychologist felt frustrated and unsure of how to proceed. Out of politeness she asked the grandmother her opinion. (The father served as translator.) She gave a long and animated reply. While the grandmother spoke, the boy's mother looked embarrassed. When asked to translate, the father replied in vague terms that his mother loved her grandson, wanted him to do well in school, and felt he had not been himself lately. The psychologist decided that the translation was too bland for the affect just displayed and gently asked for a fuller explanation. The grandmother indeed had definite ideas. She felt that the accident caused the souls of her daughter-in-law and grandson to be frightened out of their bodies. Not only were their souls wandering lost but they themselves were vulnerable to attacks by other harmful spirits.

At first, the father assured the psychologist that these were "old people's beliefs" and, even if there were harmful spirits, they were left in Laos and did not have the strength to come to the United States. The psychologist admitted to not having much experience in such matters but said that maybe the grandmother was on to something and wanted to hear more. She was beginning to sense this was where the action lay; everyone seemed to become more attentive when the spirits were discussed.

They then spoke of many discussions with numerous members of their large extended family, some of whom advised seeing a highly respected shaman in another city. The boy's mother was not so sure whether she believed in the efficacy of shamans anymore. Beginning to cry, she told the psychologist she wished she could consult with her parents, but her father was killed in the war and she had to leave behind her mother, who is now old and sick and may soon die. She then voiced that she was reluctant to take off any more time from her job, afraid her supervisor at work would think she was malingering. She also worried about expenses, since her husband had just been laid off from his job. She knew that sometimes a shaman needs a live chicken or perhaps even a pig. The mother concluded that she thought it best to just keep taking the medicine the American doctor gave her and maybe give some of her pills to her son and hope for the best.

The psychologist strongly discouraged giving the pills to the son but told the family that the discussion about whether or not to consult with the shaman seemed very valid, especially because the family had already verified the reputation of the shaman. In fact, it was clear that there was a strong pull for the family to make this trip. The psychologist then called the mother's union representative, who got her a two-day mental health leave; called the family physician to enlist her aid in coordinating the mother's treatment; and had the boy and his siblings excused from school. The psychologist reassured the parents that the school would not call social services with a "dependency and neglect" report or a child abuse charge. The parents looked relieved. They told the psychologist that they had heard that American courts often took children from their parents because schools reported child abuse charges. The parents thanked the psychologist and said their worries about making the trip had been greatly alleviated. The children were both solemn and excited. The psychologist followed up with a call the next day and learned that the trip to the shaman would commence that afternoon.

Monday morning the boy was back in school. His teacher reported that he had even come a bit early and that there had been no signs of the earlier reluctance. He had a twine necklace and two strings tied around his wrist. The boy tried to describe the ceremony: the shaman shook a lot; there was a gong and a bowl of water; the shaman tied on the strings. The boy no longer felt worried about coming to school. He said the shaman did some things for his mother and she felt stronger.

The next week the psychologist visited the home and learned more about the family, their escape from Laos, and the hardships they had endured. An infant had died during the escape and the parents felt very guilty. The family had escaped through the jungle with groups of people. All had to be extremely wary of being found by soldiers, who regularly combed the area. Opium was often used to make the infants sleepy so they would not cry and disclose the presence of the group. The parents thought their baby's death was due to an accidental opium overdose. The husband thought his wife had accepted this loss, but after the accident she had recurrent nightmares of soldiers shooting at them and of a little baby crying. The husband admitted that he, too, often became depressed and wondered why he had not been killed as had so many of his friends. The loss of his job had placed stress on the whole family, and he regretted that his wife might be becoming "too Americanized" because of working outside the home. The father said that for the first time in a long while the whole family had been talking about what occurred in Laos, during the escape, and in the refugee camps. The boy who had been school-phobic had not known about this other sibling who had died. He had started asking his grandmother many questions about Laos. An older sister said she had asked her mother and grandmother to teach her to do traditional embroidery (pandau), which could depict her family's life in Laos and their escape.

The psychologist told the father of a job-training agency and, with his permission, offered to call them and enlist their aid. She remained frustrated, however, about how to deal with the other problems. What about the father's survivor guilt? She also wondered about the mother's situation, whether a future ceremony by the shaman would heal the pain and guilt she carried. Should she refer her to the local community health center and would the mother even consider it? She could see the mother nodding in agreement and then never going. The American psychologist wished there were a H'Mong psychologist with whom to consult.

Self-Disclosure and the Therapeutic Relationship

The above sections described how the psychologist deals with matters of the heart and how his or her actions should be those of a "good mother." The hierarchical nature of Asian culture has also been discussed. Now, I want to briefly reverse this order and discuss the use of self-disclosure to balance the relationship between the therapist and the client, especially when dealing with the father of a child you are seeing.

When a family seeks help with an identified problem or "problem child," they are already dealing with issues of shame and guilt. Stepping into your office can be an act of losing face. A passage from *The Analects of Confucius* applies to every Asian family I have ever met. "What is meant by 'In order to rightly govern the state it is necessary first to regulate the family,' is this: It is not possible for one to teach others while he cannot teach his own family. Therefore, the ruler, without going beyond his family, completes the lessons for the state." Basically, every father is the king or "ruler" of his family. If there are problems that necessitate his going outside the family for help, the father of a family often suffers a terrible blow to his feelings of self-worth. How can he claim "kingship" in any other area of his life if there is unrest within his kingdom? The family has been referred to therapy by a social service agency or the courts, and the father experiences this as a direct assault on his authority and quite naturally resists the therapist's interventions.

For these reasons it is important to reach out to the father. I meet fathers the way one head of state meets another head of state; the ruler has been forced to seek help and must be treated with respect and dignity. These are delicate negotiations. Should this ruler trust you with the problems occurring in the kingdom or should he look elsewhere for help? How a therapist creates the trust that enables construction of a therapeutic container wherein everyone feels secure is up to each individual therapist, but there are some guidelines. I give clients information about my education, training, and clinical experience. (In some states, including the one in which I reside, there are mandatory disclosure laws regarding the therapist's education, mode of practice, fee schedule, the right to a second opinion, and the address of the grievance board.)

I tell the father something about the families of which I am a member, including my nuclear family, my family of origin, and my extended family. I tell him where I obtained my degree, what my training was, where I have worked. Without breaching confidentiality, I speak of other Asian families with whom I have worked. All clinicians are familiar with these concepts of "reframing" and "normalizing." While the family may look at me as the expert, I let the father know that *he* is the expert in terms of his culture and his country of origin. I explain that my "Americanness" will at times be so close to me that I will make mistakes with regard to his culture and not even realize it. I say he must point these mistakes out, even if it looks like I do not want to know about it or he fears it will be too impolite.

Basically I try to treat the father as a "head of state." Granted, his kingdom is in trouble—perhaps his subjects are rebelling—but he is still "king," and that position, with all of its responsibilities and stresses, must be acknowledged. I am an ambassador with whom he can consult for possible solutions. I am the guest in his kingdom.

The next issue is whom to meet with first and whom to include. It will vary with each situation. It may only be at the third meeting that you actually meet the child who is the reason for the referral; sometimes, the first appointment will be set by the school or by the courts and the child will come with the parent(s). It may be most advantageous to leave the child in the waiting room with crayons and paper while you talk with the parent(s). Certainly, at the first meeting, you need to minimize the likelihood that the parents will lose face in front of their child or children.

Countertransference

If a psychotherapist deals with issues of the inner heart of the client, the therapist must also be in touch with issues that will arise in her or his own heart or psyche or unconscious when working with clients. The topic of countertransference is enormously complex, and a few things should be mentioned in regard to working with Southeast Asian clients. Many American therapists remember being involved politically in antiwar efforts during the years of conflict in Southeast Asia and have unresolved guilt about our country's actions. Or the therapist may have served in the armed forces during that time in one of the Southeast Asian countries where the client is from. Even if the therapist was not involved directly in the conflict, he or she may have had loved ones who died or for whom the war left deep and unhealed scars. The therapist's unresolved psychological issues may be expressed in a number of ways over the course of therapy. Pity over what a client has endured may cause a therapist not to push a client or delve deeply into issues that need to be explored. Unconscious anger may activate certain stereotypes, with the therapist viewing the client as exotic and not quite human.

It is unlikely that a therapist will be able to become an expert in Vietnamese, Laotian, H'Mong, Lao Lu, or Cambodian culture, to name but a few of the Southeast Asian cultural groups. What is more detrimental than making a cultural faux pas is assuming one knows all there is to know about a particular Asian culture. Southeast Asian clients are very tolerant and patient with American therapists who can admit that they need to learn about a culture different from their own. Unfortunately, often the opposite occurs and the clients sense that the therapist views Asian family dynamics as archaic, primitive, or, at best, sexist and unenlightened. The result will be that the family leaves therapy, albeit the leave-taking will be quiet and polite. The therapist then will talk about the "resistance" of the family and conclude that Asians are not able to engage in in-depth psychological work. If nothing else, I hope this chapter has refuted these latter fallacies.

American therapists who are Hispanic, American Indian, or African American may share with the Southeast Asian client their own cultural backgrounds and experiences, including such things as parenting by a large extended family, respect for spiritual values, and the importance of the unity of the group. It is also important for therapists of color to remember that most Southeast Asians will not know the history of minorities in the United States, including various Asian American groups. The therapist might be perplexed, shocked, or angered when the client is ignorant of the dynamics of prejudice and racism occurring in the United States. Finally, members of minority groups can hold deeply ingrained stereotypes of each other, with tragic consequences, as is being shown in a number of cities across the United States where there is terrible tension between African American communities and newly arrived Korean immigrants who open small businesses.

While Asian American therapists are somewhat at an advantage when working with Southeast Asian clients because of certain broadly shared experiences, there are countertransference issues of which to be aware. For example, often Asian American therapists will not be fluent in the language of their group, such as Japanese or Chinese. Many Japanese grandparents who faced the horrors of the internment camps during World War II both consciously and unconsciously discouraged their children and by extension their grandchildren from speaking Japanese in an effort to be "more American." The third-generation (*sansei*) Japanese American therapist may regret deeply not being able to speak the language of the ancestors. Faced with Southeast Asian clients who are able to converse in both English and their own mother tongue, countertransference issues of jealousy can arise.

A concomitant issue that may arise with the Asian American therapist is feelings of authenticity or "Am I really Asian?" Where the Asian American clinician will feel a bond of racial camaraderie with a Southeast Asian client, the client will regard the therapist as "just another American," who speaks perfect English and has all the power. Or the clients, depressed, frustrated, and disillusioned over experiences in a country they hoped would solve all their problems, will let the therapist know that they do not really regard him or her as "truly Asian" because he or she was born in the United States or acts "too American" and is "too loud" or "too forward and aggressive." This can be a very discomfiting experience for the

Asian American therapist who has experienced racism and prejudice, despite being born here and speaking "perfect English."

Countertransference issues remind us that when we do psychotherapy it is not just the inner heart of the client that is engaged but our own heart as well. When these issues arise it is important that they be addressed for our own sake as well as the welfare of our clients. They can be dealt with in our own therapy, in supervision, or in consultation with someone knowledgeable about Asian culture and the dynamics of therapy with Asian clients.

This Chapter Should Have Been Written by a H'Mong Psychologist

Though this chapter is about therapy with Southeast Asians, the author is not from a Southeast Asian country. Southeast Asians are not an overwhelming presence at the graduate or professional schools in the various fields of mental health, and because this chapter was not written by a H'Mong psychologist or a Vietnamese social worker or a Cambodian psychiatrist, the reader will be shortchanged.

Therefore, a final conclusion that I hope has emerged is the need to have Vietnamese, Cambodian, H'Mong, and Laotian psychologists, social workers, and psychiatrists trained at and graduated from American schools. It is curious that hundreds of thousands of dollars have been spent on needs assessment studies of Southeast Asians and agencies have been created with coordinator jobs and director jobs and assistant-to-the-director jobs but these never seem to be filled with Southeast Asian persons, who are too often relegated to the job of translator, mental health aide, "bilingual consultant," or author placed last on a research project or publication. Although nothing is intrinsically wrong with the job of translator or mental health aide, this often perpetuates a closed and racist system in fields that purportedly exist to heal the heart. Even more important, it eliminates the richness of insight and variety of experiences and ways of knowing that Southeast Asian persons bring to the knowledge and understanding of how the human heart operates.

These issues must also be addressed in the Asian American

community. What are we doing professionally to identify promising Southeast Asian persons who would excel in the field of mental health and then mentor them, encourage them to go on for a professional degree, lobby for them, financially support them? We who are American by birth and Asian by ancestry cannot say, "I am Chinese or Japanese or Filipino American; they will have to struggle the way my parents and grandparents and great-grandparents struggled." This "benign neglect" can be as lethal in its consequences as any internment camp or exclusion act.

Conclusion

This chapter touches on certain psychological dynamics that a therapist should keep in mind when dealing with Southeast Asian refugee families. It is vitally important for a positive therapeutic outcome that the particulars of a family's specific culture be explored and understood by the person undertaking therapy.

At times the statements may seem a bit sweeping and the discussion perhaps too far ranging. In fact, what is needed are separate chapters on Vietnamese families, Laotian families, Lao Lu families, Cambodian families, H'Mong families, Chinese-Vietnamese families, Chinese-Cambodian families. The hope is that the reader will want to delve deeper into each culture and develop an increasingly more sophisticated understanding of what is involved in therapy with Southeast Asian families.

References

Bliatout, B. T. *H'Mong Sudden Unexpected Nocturnal Death Syndrome: A Cultural Study.* Portland, Oreg.: Sparkle, 1982.

Concise Columbia Encyclopedia. New York: Columbia University Press, 1983.

Confucius. *The Analects.* (D. C. Lau, trans.) New York: Dorset Press, 1979.

Conquergood, D., Thao, P., and Thao, X. *I Am a Shaman: A H'Mong Life Story with Ethnographic Commentary.* Minneapolis: Southeast Asian Refugee Studies Project, Center for Urban and Regional Affairs, University of Minnesota, 1989.

Kitano, H.H.L., and Natsushima, N. "Counseling Asian Americans." In P. B. Pedersen, J. G. Draguns, W. J. Lonner, and J. E. Trimble (eds.), *Counseling Across Cultures.* (rev. ed.) Honolulu, Hawaii: East-West Center, 1981.

Lau, T. *The Handbook of Chinese Horoscopes.* New York: Harper-Collins, 1979.

Lemoine, J. "Shamanism in the Context of H'Mong Resettlement." In G. L. Hendricks, B. T. Downing, and A. S. Deinard (eds.), *The H'Mong in Transition.* New York: Center for Migration Studies, 1986.

Livo, N. J., and Cha, D. *Folk Stories of the H'Mong: Peoples of Laos, Thailand, and Vietnam.* Englewood, Colo.: Libraries Unlimited, 1991.

Muecke, M. A. "In Search of Healers—Southeast Asian Refugees in the American Health Care System." *Western Journal of Medicine,* 1983, *139,* 835–840.

Shon, S. P., and Ja, D. "Asian Families." In M. McGoldrick, J. K. Pearce, and J. Giordano (eds.), *Ethnicity and Family Therapy.* New York: Guilford, 1982.

Sue, S., and McKinney, H. "Asian Americans in the Community Mental Health Care System." *American Journal of Orthopsychiatry,* 1975, *45,* 111–118.

Sue, S., and Zane, N. "The Role of Culture and Cultural Techniques in Psychotherapy: A Critique and Reformulation." *American Psychologist,* 1987, *42*(1), 37–45.

Tobin, J. J., and Friedman, J. "Spirits, Shamans, and Nightmare Death: Survivor Stress in a H'Mong Refugee." *American Journal of Orthopsychiatry,* 1983, *54,* 439–448.

Tsui, P., and Schultz, G. L. "Failure of Rapport: Why Psychotherapeutic Engagement Fails in the Treatment of Asian Clients." *American Journal of Orthopsychiatry,* 1985, *55,* 561–569.

Webster's Seventh New Collegiate Dictionary. Springfield, Mass.: Merriam-Webster, 1967.

Williams, C. L. *An Annotated Bibliography on Refugee Mental Health.* Washington, D.C.: U.S. Department of Health and Human Services, Public Health Service, Alcohol, Drug Abuse, and Mental Health Administration, National Institute of Mental Health (DHHS Publication no. (ADM) 87-1517), 1987.

9

~~~~~~

Differential Application
of Treatment Modalities
with Asian American Youth

~~~~~~

MAN KEUNG HO

The increased acceptance of the ecological approach to working with ethnic minority children and youth has generated many treatment theories and modalities. The philosophical orientations and the techniques employed by some of these modalities, such as individual, family, and group treatment, may diametrically oppose the indigenous cultural values, individual preference, and family structures of an ethnic minority child (Mizio and Delaney, 1981). Tseng and McDermott (1975) warn that the minority child's orientation to the process of help seeking and the fit between traditional paradigms and those utilized by providers may be critical to successful process and outcome. Judging by the overwhelming underutilization of mental health services and high dropout rate of ethnic minority clients (Jones, 1977; Fujii, 1976; Barrera, 1978; Jackson, 1973), a wide gap clearly exists between the unmet treatment needs of ethnic minority children and families and the therapist's ability to meet these needs successfully (Mokuan, 1987). It is also clear that therapy with ethnic minority children requires an organized, culturally sensitive, theoretical framework, from which different treatment modalities can be applied to meet the specific needs of individual ethnic minority children and youth.

This chapter represents a pioneering effort in focusing on the differential application of treatment modalities within a conceptual framework for therapy with Asian American children. This ecological approach considers the Asian American child's reality, culture, biculturalism, family tradition and structure, degree of acculturation, language, and help-seeking behavior. It does not consider an Asian American child's problem as a disease but as a result of a lack in the environment, dysfunctional transitions between systems, or interrupted growth and development. Hence, assessment and intervention efforts are directed to multivariable systems, and a variety of means can produce a single effect. Although a therapist may try to relate intervention strategies that are universal or Western middle-class American oriented, innovative strategies of change based on the Asian American child's specific cultural background and life space (the emic approach) also are encouraged.

Asian Americans are often perceived as sharing the same or similar characteristics, but they actually comprise many diverse groups: Chinese, Japanese, Koreans, Filipinos, Samoans, Guamanians, Hawaiians, and other Pacific Islanders. Other groups include recent immigrants and refugees from Vietnam, Thailand, Cambodia, Laos, and Indonesia; persons from India, Pakistan, and Ceylon; and children of mixed marriages in which one parent is Asian. There are obvious language, historical, social, and economic differences. Generational status (new immigrants versus third and fourth generations) among groups and individuals should not be overlooked.

In this chapter, Asian Americans' traditional responses to different treatment modalities will be discussed. The therapist's modification of traditional techniques and skills in the application of treatment modalities with Asian American children and youth will be illustrated by a case example.

Characteristics and Advantages of Selected Treatment Modalities

It is generally recognized that effective service to Asian American children and their families should be multidimensional, that is, directed at the various components of the child's environment. Treatment should be multidisciplinary, involving professionals and workers from a variety of disciplines, and multimodal, offering a combination of individual, family, and/or group treatment (Gibbs, Huang, and Associates, 1989; Ho, 1989).

Individual treatment involving one-to-one therapist-client contact is the most frequently used modality (Korchin, 1980). It can be used with a wide spectrum of children and can be flexibly provided in myriad ways, including crisis intervention, short-term, long-term, ego-supportive, intensive or ego-modifying, educative, and cognitive-behavioral approaches. Individual treatment is also useful in combination with a variety of other types of supportive and concrete services. Advantages of individual treatment include the provision of optimal safety, support, privacy, and confidentiality for the client and a corrective, transferential growth process that allows the child to develop.

Family therapy emerged from the idea of conjoint treatment where the entire family or a relevant subunit (parents or siblings) of the family is seen together, as contrasted with the traditional approach, in which family members are seen individually by the same or different therapists. Family therapy, however, can be defined by its approach and focus rather than by the number of people seen together (Johnson, 1986). For the purpose of delineating and contrasting different treatment modalities, family therapy here is defined as an approach in which parents and children are seen simultaneously, with an explicit focus on family interactions. The advantages include (1) the opportunity for accurate assessment of family interaction and dynamics; (2) direct and open communication among family members; (3) opportunity for family members to problem solve jointly; (4) opportunity for sharing, learning, and experimenting with effective modes of communication; and (5) reduction of family members' and the therapist's tendency to polarize, split, blame, or scapegoat members of the family system. Employment of family therapy as a treatment modality in work with Asian American children also has been documented (Shon and Ja, 1982; Kim, 1985).

Group therapy refers to an alliance of people who are brought together to work on a common task, to use the group experience for support and mutual aid, for educational purposes, or to effect personality change. Group therapy can provide different members, who are not related to each other but share similar backgrounds, powerful experiences in being accepted and supported and can lead to the development of better communication and other interpersonal skills (McKinley, 1991). It can also provide an atmosphere in which to develop increased empathy for others, new values, attitudes, and behavior, and the control of strong and often unacceptable impulses (Yamaguchi, 1986). Group therapy can provide and serve as an important support network and diminish an individual's sense of isolation, thus enhancing his or her ability to receive or offer help.

A therapist should review each treatment modality and consider the advantages of each. The next step is to decide which to use to best meet the specific needs of an Asian American child or adolescent.

Guidelines in Selecting a Treatment Modality

Determining which treatment modality to use to achieve certain treatment goals largely depends on how the therapist and client define the client's problem. The ecological perspective has been very useful in assessing an Asian American child's problem (Ho, 1987). Many theories of therapy with children are directed at the process of conflicts, anxiety, and defense systems within the individual. The ecological perspective, as proposed by Bronfenbrenner (1979), maintains that imbalance and conflict may arise from any locus in the interlocking transactional systems, ranging from the microsystems of the individual, family, and school to the macrosystem of governmental, social, and economic policies. The degree of emphasis on each of these systems, in turn, depends on the specific nature of the child's problem.

At the individual level, the focus is on the biopsychological endowment of each child, including physical appearance, personality strengths, level of psychosocial development, cognition, perception, problem-solving skills, emotional temperament, level of acculturation, habit formation, and interpersonal competence and language skills. At the family level, the focus is on the life-style, immigration history, culture, family organization, sex-role structure, division of labor, affective styles, traditions, rituals, and management of internal and external stress. At the cultural level, the focus should be on understanding the value systems, beliefs, and social norms of the host culture and the original or native culture. An Asian American child in a predominantly white school soon learns that many of his or her reference group values are in conflict with the cultural values being practiced at home. Such a conflict in values may hinder the child's development of self-identity and self-concept. At the environmental level, the focus should be on understanding the economic, social, and political structure of American society, which frequently discriminates against and oppresses individuals in minority groups.

The ecological perspective is quite helpful to the therapist, who must determine the kind of data that are needed to gain a full understanding of the Asian American child's problem in order to plan treatment. In organizing the data, the therapist needs to consider to what extent the child's problem is a function of

1. Stresses imposed by immigration and acculturation, current life roles, developmental tasks, or a past traumatic reaction experienced by many Asian American children. Two physiological systems, respiratory and digestive, have been found to be primary somatic targets for Asian children experiencing immigrational stress (Holmes and Masuda, 1974).
2. The child's idiosyncratic characteristics or problems
3. The child's home environment and family conflict
4. The child's school environment, including the attitudes of the teachers and staff
5. A lack of fit between the child's or family's needs and essential knowledge and/or resources
6. The child's native culture and background

To formulate a treatment plan and to select treatment modalities, the therapist also needs to consider the following three questions:

1. What individual and/or family capacities and strengths and environmental resources can be mobilized to prevent further problems and to improve the child's situation?

2. Given the child's level of acculturation, language proficiency, expectation and motivation, attitude toward therapy, and past experiences with helping agencies, what treatment modality and strategy would best engage the child at this time? (Literature on psychotherapy and social services indicates that Western modes of therapy have not been effective [Mokuan, 1987]. Low utilization and early termination of services by Asian Americans support this premise [Sue, 1981].)
3. What treatment modalities and strategies would fit best with this particular child in order to achieve long-term results?

These global guidelines can assist the therapist in selecting treatment modalities to use with children *in general.* However, they need to be augmented to ensure that the treatment modality selected is relevant and responsive to the particular minority client. Following is a discussion of ethnic-specific factors that a therapist should explore.

Consideration of Ethnicity Factors in Selecting a Treatment Modality

Five ethnicity-related factors can profoundly affect the therapist's appropriate or inappropriate choice of a treatment modality: (1) native culture, (2) the child's and family's level of acculturation, (3) speech and language, (4) the child's and family's conceptualization of problem and help-seeking behaviors, and (5) the degree of pathology and motivation of the child and his or her family. Let us look at the case of the Asian American child and how each of the above factors must be carefully considered by the therapist in order to provide the best possible help to this client.

Native Culture

Asian American culture, which emphasizes filial piety, shame as a behavioral influence, self-control, the virtue of taking the middle position, a sense of obligation, awareness of social milieu, fatalism, and inconspicuousness (Ho, 1976) can affect the Asian child's (and family's) preference or responsiveness to different treatment modalities. These cultural values can inhibit the child from participating openly in family therapy. The family is the control unit of social organization for Asian Americans. Their cultural orientation, English-language limitations, separation from friends and extended family, and other isolating environmental factors sometimes make the family itself the only means of interaction, socialization, validation, and stabilization. The continued underutilization of mental health services reflects the strong reliance on Asian American tradition that personal/interpersonal problems or issues should be kept within the family and solved there. To the therapist who is not culturally sensitive, family therapy, on the one hand, may appear to be an appropriate problem-solving approach and modality for Asian American clients. Taking a deeper look, however, shows that due to the Asian culture's emphasis on filial piety, self-control, shaming, inconspicuousness, and vertical hierarchical interaction between adults and children, most children and parents will find conjoint family therapy threatening, inhibiting, and unwelcome.

Additionally, studies have indicated that Asian American children and youth are more emotionally restrained and nonexpressive than white American youth (Han, 1985; Jourard, 1971). Emotional displays are discouraged in the home because of the formal relationship between parents and children. Asian American parents may feel they are losing face or feel shame that they have to solicit outside help for their own personal and family problems.

A therapist might next consider the group treatment modality. Asian children are taught at an early age that there is pervasive awareness of mutual interdependence, and an Asian child who values interdependence and cooperation can gain significantly from the power and strength of collective group feedback. The group atmosphere can be less threatening than individual treatment. Rather than being constantly pressured to talk, the Asian child in group sessions can choose when to interact. In individual treatment, the pressure of attention focused on the child maximizes conspicuousness and heightens the awareness of the social milieu, which can be an inhibiting factor in and of itself. Individual treatment typically is a more one-sided relationship in which the therapist does the giving and the client the receiving. In the group therapy setting, the Asian child is not only the recipient but also the helper.

The problems that render the Asian child an unwilling participant in family therapy can apply also in group therapy, however. Because of cultural upbringing, including the reluctant public display of affective behavior, an Asian child may be inhibited in talking and in expressing deep feelings in a group. The child's feeling of shame about failures in school or in life may be difficult to bring to light. An Asian child may also be reluctant to share with the group information about family members because he or she does not wish to be disrespectful and disloyal to his or her family. The child may feel it is rude to interrupt other group members, or that it is the height of narcissism and egomania to "monopolize" a session with his or her problem.

Just this brief look at how significantly a client's native culture affects his or her behavior in therapy illustrates the difficulties that a therapist confronts in selecting a treatment modality. It is important to devote sufficient time and care to finding the best possible treatment method for an ethnic minority child.

Level of Acculturation

In an attempt to combat social isolation and gain a feeling of belonging and acceptance, an Asian American child is forced to find reference groups in the United States. The child may identify entirely with traditional Asian culture or reject Asian culture as old-fashioned and dysfunctional. He or she may adopt U.S. values exclusively or become bicultural. Unfortunately, regardless of which value system a child adopts, there are potential adjustment problems.

Lee (1982) has suggested four criteria to determine a child's degree of acculturation: (1) years in the United States (the longer the child lives in the United States, the more he or she is acculturated); (2) age at time of immigration (an eight-year-old is more easily acculturated than an eighteen-year-old); (3) country of origin and political, economic, and educational background (a Chinese student from Hong Kong, which is a British colony, is more easily acculturated than a young adult from mainland China); and (4) professional background of the parents (a child of an English-speaking parent who is a medical doctor is more easily acculturated than a child whose parents work in a Chinese restaurant). The family's immigration history also is important in the assessment of the child's acculturation level. If the child was born in this country and is a third-generation family member who speaks fluent English, ethnicity and acculturation will be less an issue in the selection of a treatment modality.

Speech and Language

Care must be taken to assess the client's degree of fluency in English and in the native language when selecting a treatment modality. This can deeply affect the therapeutic process and outcome. Asian American children seem to have a special problem involving the use of a different language. According to the Human Education and Welfare Office of Special Concerns (1974), about 70 percent of Asian American children under the age of fourteen still speak their native language in their home. More recent needs assessment surveys (Kim, 1978; Wang and Louie, 1979) also reported that the lack of English proficiency seemed to exacerbate virtually every problem area perceived by Asian Americans, and it also tended to limit the availability of problem-solving strategies.

Asian Americans' general lack of proficiency in the English language is further complicated by the Asian culture's de-emphasis of verbal skills in meaningful interpersonal exchanges. Indeed, among the Japanese there is a distrust of verbal skills as connoting glibness, possible dishonesty, or lack of trustworthiness (Lebra, 1976).

Although the acculturation level of Asian American children varies, most of them are bilingual, which can drastically reverse the hierarchical role if their parents are monolingual. The children's rejection of their parents' culture can also be manifested in their unwillingness to speak their native language. The language differential between children and their parents and grandparents widens the generational and cultural rift within many Asian American families, especially among those in which the parents are immigrants and the children are American born.

The treatment modality selected should always be contingent upon the child's, the parents', and the therapist's fluency in English and in the client's native Asian language. If the child is bilingual, the parents are monolingual, and the therapist is monolingual in English only, family therapy should not be employed, especially not until a trusting relationship has been established between the therapist and the parents. If the child is bilingual, the parents are monolingual, and the therapist is bilingual, individual and family therapy can be used differentially depending on the special needs of the child or the family. If family therapy is employed, the bilingual therapist should use exclusively the family's native language to maintain respect and the hierarchical role of the parents. Finally, a bilingual child who speaks limited English should not be placed in a group with other English-speaking children, regardless of their race and ethnicity.

Conceptualization of Problem and Help-Seeking Behaviors

To apply a treatment modality successfully, a therapist must understand an Asian American child's traditional values and attitudes toward dysfunctional behavior. The process of acculturation may have altered a child's or a family's cultural values, but as Mass (1978) indicates, the influence exerted by the value patterns that were acquired throughout childhood is often considerable, even among those whose behavior is highly Westernized. Asian Americans feel a stigma and shame in talking about personal problems. Most of them do not seek psychiatric dynamics and psychological theories to account for behavioral difficulty (Lapuz, 1973); instead, social, moral, and organic explanations are used. When an individual behaves dysfunctionally, he or she commonly identifies the reason as some external event such as physical illness, death of a loved one, or loss of a job. The individual, therefore, is not to blame. Interpersonal duties and loyalties are held sacred by many Asian Americans. The dysfunction or suffering of an Asian American individual may be attributed to his or her violation of some duty, such as filial piety. Community elders or family members may be expected to exhort the individual to improve. In a survey of a sample of Asian Americans in Los Angeles regarding their attitudes toward mental health, ministers, relatives, friends, and family doctors were mentioned as resources more frequently than professional mental health workers (Okano, 1977). Over one-half the sample indicated they would prefer to work out emotional problems on their own.

Asian Americans' conceptualization of their problems and their solutions clearly indicates the need of the therapist to frame the client's presenting problem according to the client's conceptualization. This process also can provide important cues as to how a therapist should approach the client about selecting the best treatment modality.

Since most Asian Americans, especially those from immigrant families, find it difficult to admit they have emotional or psychological difficulties, the therapist may need to reframe the presenting problem relative to their practical and concrete needs. For example, a therapist will have a difficult time convincing the parents of an Asian American child who has psychological problems to assume the client role regardless of the treatment modality need. Nevertheless, they most likely will be cooperative in treatment if the therapist approaches them about their involvement, explaining that it will assist in enhancing the child's school achievement. Similarly, if the therapist wishes to conduct conjoint couple therapy with the parents, whose unresolved conflicts contribute to the child's psychological adjustment and school performance, the therapist needs to appeal to the parents for assistance to work collaboratively for the sake of improving their child's well-being rather than focus on reconstruction or improvement of the couple's marital relationship. Working collaboratively may entail involving the child individually, or the couple conjointly, or the family or extended family as a unit.

Should the therapist decide that a group treatment modality can best meet the needs of a particular Asian American child, group size and group context must be properly balanced. A structured group content, such as assertiveness training that is concrete and relevant to the needs of the child to succeed in school, is recommended. Such a group could be fairly large. The largeness of a group may allow the child to feel safer, and it also may convince him or her that group therapy must be valuable if so many children wish to become members. As the group gets deeper into content, it should break down into smaller components or subgroups.

Degree of Pathology and Motivation of the Child and Family

Generally, a child who displays extreme paranoia and poor impulse control and demands the therapist's total attention should not be included in family or group therapy. Similarly, treatment of the family in a joint therapeutic approach is feasible and sound when the "children are old enough, the family sufficiently articulate, and the level of anger in it not too high" (Kempe and Kempe, 1978, p. 80). Also, for treatment to be effective, individual and family members must recognize difficulties and express willingness to participate in a treatment program on a regular basis.

Because culture dictates an individual's conception of stress and the impression of defense mechanisms, it is important that the therapist's assessment of an Asian American child's and his family's pathology not be culturally biased. Due to situational stresses, cultural conflicts, language difficulty, and past negative experiences that some Asian American parents have had with the U.S. health and social service agencies, it is to be expected that an Asian American family may initially display reluctance for treatment. Such behavior should not be misconstrued as a lack of motivation and willingness to seek and benefit from therapeutic services.

Case Example

The differential application of treatment modalities is further illustrated by the following case example involving family violence.

Family immigration history	The Tran family was brought to the attention of the Transcultural Family Institute by a complaint from Mrs. Tran that their fourteen-year-old son, Fen, had been missing for more than three days. The intake interview with Mrs. Tran revealed that the family immigrated to the United States in 1975 after the fall of Saigon. The Tran family resides in a run-down neighborhood in Oklahoma

City, where there are about thirty
Asian families. Most of them are refugees, some Cambodians, a few Lao-
tians. Before the refugees moved in,
the neighborhood was heavily popu-
lated with blacks and a few
Hispanics.

Father's degree of accul-
turation and stress

Mr. Tran is fifty-one years old,
trained as a dentist in Saigon, and
speaks fairly good English. Because
he received his professional training
in Vietnam, he has been unable to
obtain a license to practice dentistry
in Oklahoma City. Mr. Tran works
as a clerk in a neighborhood Asian
food store.

Mother's degree of accul-
turation and role change

Mrs. Tran was a housewife and
never worked outside the home in
Saigon. She is now employed in a
day-care center serving mainly Vietnamese preschoolers. She has attended several English classes offered
at her church.

Family dynamics

The Trans have three children: a
twenty-two-year-old daughter, who is
married and lives with her Vietnamese husband in Dallas, Texas; a nine-
year-old daughter, whom Mrs. Tran
described as "very nice"; and Fen.
"Our son Fen is just the opposite of
our nine-year-old. He gets into fights
all the time at school and with the
neighborhood kids, especially the

Child's level of
acculturation

black kids," volunteered Mrs. Tran.
Both Fen and his younger sister were
born in Texas. The Trans moved to
Oklahoma City two years ago when
Mr. Tran got his present job. Mrs.

Family violence

Motivation of mother for
treatment

Use of individual treat-
ment to help father save
face

Conveying of therapist's
respect to father

Natural resistance to
treatment

Meeting client where he is

Client's need for privacy

Showing respect to client

Establishing mutuality

Tran also fears that Fen and his family "may hurt each other. The men
in our family are of a violent type."

One day after the interview, Mrs.
Tran called to inform me that Fen
had returned home voluntarily and
that her husband and Fen had gotten
into a "big physical fight." Mrs.
Tran was asked if I could talk with
her and her family before "something terrible" happened. I replied
that I would assist the family and I
indicated to Mrs. Tran that I would
like to see Mr. Tran alone for the
first meeting. I also suggested to Mrs.
Tran that I would telephone Mr.
Tran for the appointment.

When I telephoned him for an appointment the next day, he expressed
appreciation of my willingness to
help. However, he said he doubted he
could get off work and that he did
not know where my agency was located. I volunteered to meet with him
at a Vietnamese restaurant two
blocks from where he worked. He accepted my invitation.

Mr. Tran, a frail but gentle-looking
man, was early for the appointment,
and he graciously ushered
me to a corner table that was quiet. I
expressed to him regret that I
couldn't speak Vietnamese. Mr. Tran
reciprocated by informing me that
despite his Chinese/Vietnamese ancestry, he could speak only a few
words of Chinese. (Perhaps his wife
had informed him that I was Chi-

	nese.) As Mr. Tran was relating his background to me, he avoided eye contact by helping me with tea.
Engaging the client	I asked Mr. Tran if his work at the store kept him busy. He immediately played down the importance of his present job. I empathized by letting
Showing empathy	him know that he must feel frustrated at not being able to practice his profession. Mr. Tran sighed that
Showing sensitivity toward client's pain and need for inconspicuousness	"my best years are over—they have been for quite some time." I remained silent but at the same time helped Mr. Tran with tea.
Encouraging and appreciating client's self-disclosure	Mr. Tran continued to relate to me his immigration experiences, his love for his lost home and country, information about his extended family members who were left in Vietnam, and finally a description of his beloved vocation as a dentist in Vietnam.
Focusing on purpose of interview	"I am happy for you that you still have your immediate family with you," I commented. "That's my greatest problem now," complained Mr. Tran. Mr. Tran then proceeded to tell about the difficulty he was experiencing with his son, Fen, who
Stress caused by family role change and father-son conflict	was fluent in English but doing marginal work at school, not getting along with neighborhood kids, and refusing to defer to him as father. Mr. Tran also complained that his wife had not been treating him with respect. He attributed this to his wife's
Somatization	"Americanization" and financial independence. Mr. Tran disclosed that

recently he had developed a colitis problem and that medication prescribed by the doctor did not help.

Importance of family to client

Before my interview with Mr. Tran ended, I summarized my understanding of his personal and family problems. Mr. Tran quickly told me his personal problems did not matter; it was his family problems he needed

Therapist's use of directness

help with. I respected and supported his views and explained to him the manner in which I could assist the family, especially his son.

Son's lack of motivation for therapy

Mr. Tran then related to me that his son had told him he would "never see no shrink" or social worker. I comforted Mr. Tran by letting him know that Fen's behavior could change without his actually seeing me. I emphasized that since

Restoration of client's position in family

Mr. Tran was the head of the family, I would need his help the most in order to help the family. Mr. Tran responded very positively and assured me he would do whatever was needed in order to restore family harmony.

Individual treatment for role restoration and stress management

Over the following two weeks, I saw Mr. Tran individually four times at my office. Our conversations centered around four major issues: (1) his immigration and relocation experiences, (2) his father role and relationship with his son, (3) his role and relationship with his wife, and (4) his activities in the workplace, neighborhood, and home.

From ventilation to insight to role restoration

Having an opportunity to ventilate the loss associated with immigration and relocation, Mr. Tran realized he had a great deal of grief and unexpressed anger. Mr. Tran admitted: "I have been a walking time bomb for some time." His pent-up feelings coupled with his disappointment with his present job and his wife's lack of deference toward him made him especially eager to assume the authoritarian, disciplinary father role toward his teenage son.

Reframing technique

Mr. Tran was helped to realize that he had been displacing all his disappointment and frustration onto his son. To support Mr. Tran and to help him understand adolescent characteristics, I reframed the situation by saying to him that he must have done a good job for his son to be adult enough to say "no" to him. Mr. Tran began to realize that Fen also was having a difficult time adjusting to family, school, friends, and the "American way of life." As I encouraged Mr. Tran to list the positive features about Fen, he relaxed more and commented: "But I cannot allow Fen to say 'no' to me. If I had done that as a child, my father would have knocked my head off." I responded by agreeing that some Asian parents felt violence was the only way to control their children. I suggested that such disciplinary action may be antithetical to the love and care we originally intended to provide for our children. I later provided Mr. Tran with some other ideas and ways

Indirect means to reaffirm client's worth and success as father

Intergenerational transmission

Promoting filial piety, obligation and self-control

Conjoint session to pay respect to therapist and to affirm family stability

Termination ritual

to discipline. I challenged him to exercise self-control in order for these new disciplinary ideas to work. Mr. Tran accepted my challenge.

At our last session, Mr. Tran invited his wife to come with him. Mrs. Tran was elated and volunteered that Fen was getting along well at home and at school. Fen and her husband had had no fights at all, and she and her husband also got along much better. The Trans invited me to their home for dinner as a way of expressing their appreciation. I accepted the invitation and had a wonderful dinner. As the evening ended, Mr. Tran told me he no longer had "stomach problems." As I was departing, Fen shook my hand firmly with an uneasy smile, uttering, "You're O.K.! May I come by your office sometime?" "Sure," I replied.

This case illustrates the strategic use of the individual treatment modality in helping an Asian American family to resolve a family violence problem. Because of the volatile nature of the family problem and the acculturation level of the client (immigrant father) and the family (immigrant parents and American-born son), and the alleged lack of motivation for therapy on the part of the son, conjoint family therapy, which normally should be conducted in family assessment, was not the treatment modality of choice. The important role of an Asian father as well as the father's stress level caused by unsuccessful acculturation adjustment, occupational role disappointment, and familial role failure were factors that would have made inviting the family for conjoint therapy at this juncture insensitive. The suggestion would also have been met with great resistance, especially by the father. Realizing the father's overwhelming stress and need for dignity, privacy, and emotional relief,

the therapist reached out to him. By telephoning the father personally instead of requesting his wife to arrange for the appointment,
the therapist conveyed respect, empathy, and hope that the father
desperately needed and therefore accepted.

After seeing the father individually, the therapist realized the
father-son conflict was caused mainly by the father's acculturation
difficulties, including different child-rearing practices, different
cultural values, and family life cycle crisis. The father's allegation
that his son was unwilling to seek help from mental health professionals also reflected his own discomfort and uncertainty in engaging in conjoint therapy with his son. The father's self-disclosure of
feelings of low self-worth explained his overwhelming need to control his rebellious teenage son. Conjoint therapy involving father
and son at this juncture would have been too volatile, antagonistic,
and therefore unproductive. If conjoint therapy had been initiated
and failed, both the father and son would probably have refused to
return for future sessions.

Some family violence cases involve a connection between
mother and son, which isolates the father in the periphery. Conjoint
couple therapy and later family therapy may be in order to repair
the father-mother couple subsystem relationship. However, in
working with Asian American families, prior to seeing the couple
conjointly a therapist needs to interview them separately. If the
couple is acculturated and motivated, then conjoint therapy can be
arranged.

Mr. Tran did bring his wife in voluntarily for the last therapy
session. Mr. Tran's objective was to pay his respect to the therapist
and to show the therapist that his family relationship had improved
and that he had fulfilled his family obligation. Hence, the specific
focus of a particular treatment session should also influence the
number of family members present. As trust develops between the
therapist and the family, more confrontative issues can be addressed.

Conclusions

Asian American children and families can benefit from various
treatment modalities. Whatever the treatment method, it is very important for the therapist to consider the Asian American child's

culture, family structure, level of acculturation, proficiency in the English language, and level of difficulty and motivation.

This case illustrates the differential application of treatment modalities with an immigrant Vietnamese family. Other Asian American families of different nationalities who are not first-generation immigrants and who are more acculturated and can speak fluent English may respond to different treatment modalities with greater ease and lesser modification. However, a therapist needs to realize that even when Asian American children and families are acculturated and are members of a higher social class, Asian ethnicity and culture still play an important role in their lives. As Mass (1978) indicates, the influence exerted by the value patterns that were acquired throughout childhood is often considerable even among those whose behavior is highly Westernized.

As the population and service needs of Asian American children have continued to mount, treatment resources available to them have dwindled because of cutbacks in federally funded programs. Because of language difficulties and cultural value conflicts, Asian American clients will need more competent service workers and therapists who can apply different culturally sensitive treatment modalities to meet their needs.

References

Barrera, M. "Mexican-American Mental Health Service Utilization: A Critical Examination of Some Proposed Variables." *Community Mental Health Journal*, 1978, *14*, 33–45.

Bronfenbrenner, U. *The Ecology of Human Development: Experiments by Nature and Design.* Cambridge, Mass.: Harvard University Press, 1979.

Fujii, S. "Elderly Asian-Americans and Use of Public Service." *Social Casework*, 1976, *57*, 202–207.

Gibbs, J. T., Huang, L. N., and Associates (eds.). *Children of Color: Psychological Interventions with Minority Youth.* San Francisco: Jossey-Bass, 1989.

Han, Y. "Discriminant Analysis of Self-Disclosing Behavior and Locus of Control Among Korean American and Caucasian

American Adolescents." *Pacific/Asian Mental Health Research Review*, 1985, *4*, 20–22.

Ho, M. "Social Work with Asian/Americans." *Social Casework*, 1976, *57*, 195–201.

Ho, M. *Family Therapy with Ethnic Minorities.* Newbury Park, Calif.: Sage, 1987.

Ho, M. "Application of Family Therapy Theories to Asian Americans." *Contemporary Family Therapy*, 1989, *11*, 61–70.

Holmes, T., and Masuda, M. "Life Change and Illness Susceptibility." In B. Dohrenwend (ed.), *Stressful Life Events: Their Nature and Effects.* New York: Wiley, 1974.

Human Education and Welfare Office of Special Concerns. *A Study of Selected Socioeconomic Characteristics of Ethnic Minorities.* Vol. II: *Asian-Americans.* Washington, D.C.: Human Education and Welfare Office of Special Concerns, 1974.

Jackson, J. "Family Organization and Ideology." In D. Miller (ed.), *Comparative Studies of Blacks and Whites in the United States.* New York: Seminar Press, 1973.

Johnson, H. "Emerging Concerns in Family Therapy." *Social Work*, 1986, *31*, 199–206.

Jones, D. "The Mystique of Expertise in the Social Service." *Journal of Sociology and Social Welfare*, 1977, *3*, 332–346.

Jourard, S. *Self-Disclosure: An Experimental Analysis of the Transparent Self.* New York: Wiley, 1971.

Kempe, R., and Kempe, C. *The Developing Child.* Cambridge, Mass.: Harvard University Press, 1978.

Kim, B. *The Asian-Americans: Changing Patterns, Changing Needs.* Montclair, N.J.: Association of Korean Christian Scholars in North America, 1978.

Kim, S. "Family Therapy for Asian Americans: A Strategic Structural Framework." *Psychotherapy*, 1985, *22*, 342–348.

Korchin, L. "Clinical Psychology and Minority Problems." *American Psychologist*, 1980, *35*, 262–269.

Lapuz, L. *A Study of Psychopathology.* Quezon City: University of the Philippines Press, 1973.

Lebra, T. *Japanese Patterns of Behavior.* Honolulu: University Press of Hawaii, 1976.

Lee, E. "A Social System Approach to Assessment and Treatment for Chinese American Families." In M. McGoldrick, J. Pearce, and J. Giordano (eds.), *Ethnicity and Family Therapy.* New York: Guilford, 1982.

McKinley, V. "Group Therapy as a Treatment Modality of Special Value for Asian Clients." *Social Work with Groups,* 1991, *13,* 255-266.

Mass, A. "Asians as Individuals: The Japanese Community." *Social Casework,* 1978, *57,* 160-164.

Mizio, E., and Delaney, A. (eds.). *Training for Service Delivery to Minority Clients.* New York: Family Service Association of America, 1981.

Mokuan, N. "Social Worker's Perceptions of Counseling Effectiveness for Asian American Clients." *Social Work,* 1987, *32,* 331-335.

Okano, Y. *Japanese Americans and Mental Health.* Los Angeles: Coalition for Mental Health, 1977.

Shon, S., and Ja, D. "Asian Families." In M. McGoldrick, J. Pearce, and J. Giordano (eds.), *Ethnicity and Family Therapy.* New York: Guilford, 1982.

Sue, D. *Counseling the Culturally Different: Theory and Practice.* New York: Wiley, 1981.

Tseng, W., and McDermott, J. "Psychotherapy: Historical Roots, Universal Elements and Cultural Variations." *American Journal of Psychiatry,* 1975, *132,* 378-384.

Wang, L., and Louie, N. "The Chinatown Aftercare Program: A Report on a Selected Group of Chinese Patients and Their State Hospital Experience." Unpublished paper, 1979.

Yamaguchi, T. "Group Psychotherapy in Japan Today." *International Journal of Group Psychotherapy,* 1986, *19,* 45-49.

10

Living Between Two Cultures:
Treating First-Generation
Asian Americans

NGA ANH NGUYEN

The interactive interface between cultural and developmental processes underlies both psychological health and psychopathology in first-generation Asian American children and adolescents. This interaction may also be used as a guidepost to formulate therapeutic strategies for this population.

Before elaborating further on the above concept, a clarification of the term *Asian American*—as it will be used here—is in order. Vietnamese Americans and Chinese Americans will be the focus of this chapter, as these ethnic cultures have been shaped by the same Confucian philosophy. The author's own experience as a refugee from Vietnam adds experiential depth to the insight a child therapist must have in working with first-generation Vietnamese American and Chinese American children and adolescents.

Cultural beliefs and values are the bedrock of child development principles that aim at endowing the adult with psychological means to function optimally within the expectations and sanctions

The author wishes to express her appreciation to Povl W. Toussieng, John F. McDermott, Jr., Howard F. Stein, and Walter H. Slote for their assistance with the preparation of this manuscript.

of a particular society. From an early age, American child rearing fosters autonomy and independence to help the child mature into a self-sufficient adult adept at competing successfully in a progress-driven society. Vietnamese and Chinese child rearing, on the other hand, places emphasis on interdependence, familial affiliation, and relatedness over individuality in order to prepare the child for a lifelong harmonious existence within an intricate system of extended family.

In light of the fundamental differences between Western and Eastern cultures, some first-generation Chinese American and Vietnamese American youths suffer from major intergenerational conflicts and deep identity struggles resulting in intense emotional turmoil (Ganesan, Fine, and Lin, 1989; Tobin and Friedman, 1984; Bourne, 1975; Sommers, 1960; Sue and Frank, 1973; Nguyen, 1986; Nguyen and Williams, 1989).

Because polarization is at the core of the conflict in these "living-between-two-cultures" youths, psychotherapeutic interventions with them should be aimed at integration rather than further dichotomization of the cultural differences. In order to integrate the paradoxes of the two poles, one must first analyze the strengths and liabilities inherent in the psychological makeup of individuals raised in each of these two cultures.

Programmed toward self-actualization, the American strong "I-self" (Roland, 1988), with its self-assertiveness, maximizes the individual's chance to succeed in the Western race toward productivity. However, this upward mobility struggle often involves moves away from extended families, as well as frequent shifts in residences, jobs, schools, and social support networks. Gains in progress and wealth are sometimes achieved at the expense of losses in the emotional quality of relationships, resulting in self-alienation and self-fragmentation (Roland, 1988). The increase in self-psychopathologies in the modern Western world, such as borderline and narcissistic personality disorders, gives credence to this speculation.

Geared toward interdependent and harmonious living with extended family members, the Asian "I-self" is underemphasized in favor of a strong "familial-self" (Roland, 1988). A warm sense of familial affiliation and interpersonal relatedness often serves as a robust fortress to shield the individual from the self-estrangement that plagues some Americans. However, the psychological price paid for the overemphasis on self-negation is a suppression of ambivalence and anger, which often finds relief in somatization, a common form of psychopathology among Asians (Marsella, Kinzie, and Gordon, 1971; Sue and Sue, 1971; Wong, 1988). Because self-negation requires the relinquishment of one's own wishes in order to abide by the exacting ego-ideals of the parents, Asian Americans can be burdened by a harsh superego, intense self-criticism, and a false self-structure (Roland, 1988).

In this chapter, I attempt to show that a reconciliation of the paradoxes posed by both Eastern and Western cultures can be achieved by a selective integration of their unique psychological potentials, thus minimizing their individual liabilities. The feasibility and adaptiveness of such an approach are supported by the research findings of Ching and others (unpublished manuscript) in their longitudinal study of American adolescents of Japanese and European ancestries in a Hawaiian community sample. Adolescent girls from both groups (who are more oriented than their male counterparts toward familial affiliation, support, and guidance) experience more success in the integration of family relationships and job roles in the outside world. In contrast, male adolescents of both heritages, who prefer to struggle for separation-individuation outside the family, experience less success in conflict resolution within the family and in the outside world. In this case, the seemingly polarized "familial-self" and "I-self" are successfully integrated to enhance psychological health in female adolescents, regardless of their ethnicities.

Therapeutic work usually benefits from having a successful model of health as a guide. Thus, I propose to use the separation-individuation concept from object-relations theory as a framework for understanding Asian American child development, and as a backdrop to psychotherapeutic work with the Asian American child and his or her family. Elaboration of this formulation, and its illustration through case vignettes about Vietnamese American and Chinese American children and adolescents, will be the focus of this chapter, which will be organized along the following themes: (1) object-relations theory and developmental norms and deviations, (2) description of an integrative therapeutic model, (3) identity conflict from an object-relations perspective, (4) cultural loss and adolescence, and (5) therapist ethnicity.

Object-Relations Theory and Developmental
Norms and Deviations

Adaptability of the Object-Relations Model

A number of authors (Kakar, 1985; Pande, 1968) who reject the use of Western classical drive theory for non-Western people do advocate, nevertheless, the use of Western object-relations models—such as those of Mahler, Winnicott, Kernberg, Kohut, and Erikson—as developmental models least likely to be contaminated by cultural biases (Kakar, 1985; NG, 1985). The prolonged biopsychological dependence of the human infant on the mother is a universal condition that differentiates the human species from all others. In turn, this specifically human, prolonged mother-infant symbiosis is not only crucial to the biological survival of the human infant but also to the development of his or her intrapsychic structure. The universal "mother of symbiosis" (Mahler, Pine, and Bergman, 1975) not only regulates her infant's biological homeostasis but also decodes every perception, cognition, and insight for her infant, as has been suggested by Spitz (1965). For instance, by accurately differentiating their infants' hunger cry from their wet cry, Western and Asian mothers alike interpret reality testing for their infants and consequently enable themselves to respond appropriately to their infants' needs. Thus, in all cultures, the universal "mother of symbiosis," by her ministrations, helps her infant build the rudiments of his or her intrapsychic structure, such as reality testing, frustration tolerance, ego boundaries, and impulse control. Emphasis on the particular details of these ministrations may vary from culture to culture. For instance, to comfort a fussy baby, a traditional Asian mother may hold the baby while singing; a modern Western mother may instead use a musical swing. However, the quality of the mother's ministrations—namely, the degree of empathy and appropriateness of her responsiveness to the infant's needs—seems to depend mostly on her own personal dynamics.

The next phase, the "postsymbiotic" phase, made up of

"practicing," "rapprochement crisis," and "separation-individuation" subphases (Mahler, Pine, and Bergman, 1975), is an equally
critical development phase, because it involves the formation of the
sense of self, self-esteem, and self-worth for children of any cultural
background. Again, the developmental process in this phase is universal, while the culture provides only variations in form. In congruence with the Western culture's emphasis on autonomy,
independence, and self-sufficiency, Western mothers will likely encourage their toddlers to engage in independent motor exploration
and thus reflect back to them their individual sense of self, self-
worth, and self-esteem. Mahler called this function "communicative
matching." On the other hand, Eastern mothers are less inclined to
support their toddlers' aggressive moves toward independence and,
in synchrony with their cultural background, will likely praise their
toddlers' success in using proper etiquette toward family elders,
their willingness to set aside their own wishes to share their toys
with a bully-cousin, and so on. Thus Asian mothers use a different
route (namely, respect for elders and negation of one's desire for the
sake of family harmony) to reflect back to their children their sense
of self, self-worth, and self-esteem. Both Eastern and Western
"mothers of postsymbiosis" perform the same important "communicative matching" function to bring about the "psychological
birth" of their infants.

        In summary, because of the universality of the human in-
fant's long journey from total biopsychological dependence on the
"mother of symbiosis" to the final achievement of "psychological
birth" via the universal ministrations of the "mother of separation-
individuation," this Western relational theory of human development seems to be equally useful for understanding developmental
norms and deviations in relation to the Asian child.

Object-Relations-Based Family
Dynamics and Narcissistic Vulnerability

For a number of reasons, including overriding needs of her own,
any mother, Western or Eastern, may unwittingly place unrealisti-
cally high expectations on her child. Her faulty "communicative
matching" will likely fail to reflect to her child his or her sense of

self, and a strong inhibition of the child's direct self-assertion and the development of a narcissistically vulnerable self may ensue. Investigations of this principle with regard to Vietnamese American and Chinese American children have not yet been carried out; however, the literature does report the applicability to Japanese children. For instance, internalized high maternal expectations in terms of achievement and success have been reported to be frequently experienced by Japanese children and adults as being tailored more to the mother's needs than their own. Thus, they may feel that there is a big gap between their actual performance and the internalized maternal expectations "in a context of lack of maternal empathy and sensitivity, or lack of sufficient nurturance" (Roland, 1983, p. 503).

Feelings of Powerlessness and Helplessness

Feelings of powerlessness and helplessness—not uncommonly found in children of any culture—seem to be inherent in the child's status itself, which subjects the child to a more or less strict submission to parental dominance. The Vietnamese and Chinese (and other Asians with a Confucian heritage) carry these feelings well into adulthood because of the early internalization of cultural ethics of a lifelong, unquestioned obedience to the absolute authority of the parents (Slote, 1972, 1986). Such feelings combined with narcissistic vulnerability may explain the similar attributes and attitudes that Asian and white children bring into therapy. Indeed, the transcultural literature reports that adult Asian American patients display high emotional inhibition and low verbal expressiveness; they demonstrate a propensity for somatizing or acting out their feelings rather than talking them out; more often than not, they are brought to the therapist against their will and are loaded with self-blame for having brought shame to their families. Because of a lifelong dependence on parents' approval, they feel awkward if not totally confused at being forced to discuss their most private feelings with a total stranger. This awkwardness can be easily transformed into a frightening sense of disloyalty, if the feelings happen to be negative feelings, such as anger, directed at family members or parents. In my view, these so-called "deficiencies," ascribed uniquely to adult Asian American patients, are in fact common occurrences in white as well as Asian American child-patients.

Metaphoric Styles of Communication

The obvious frustration that white psychiatric residents experience in their first encounter with an English-speaking white child who refuses to respond to their verbal inquiries is reminiscent of white therapists' feelings of frustration and estrangement at *their* inability to make effective use of verbal communication with Asian American adults. The reported insistence of Tatara, a Japanese psychoanalyst, on the frugal use of verbal communication with Japanese adult patients (Roland, 1983) seems applicable to the average white or Asian child-patient. Metaphors and symbols, such as somatization, symbolic play, and behavioral acting out, seem to be the preferred modalities of communication for most persons suffering from narcissistic vulnerability and/or a sense of powerlessness and helplessness. A Chinese psychiatrist, Wong (1988), reported the case of a ten-year-old Chinese boy who used fourteen months of vomiting as symbolic tears expressing the sadness of losing his mother.

The following vignette illustrates how the grasp of the transcultural language of metaphor is more crucial to the understanding of children's communication than overt language.

Long, a six-year-old Vietnamese American boy, was referred by his English teacher because of his aggressive behavior toward his white friends and his inability, after one year, to learn a single English word (in spite of average intelligence). Three years prior to that time, Long had been tricked into coming to the United States with his father. The father had told Long to say goodbye to his mother and their little South Vietnamese rural town before a short trip to Saigon. In the mental status examination, it became obvious to the therapist that Long was still very attached to his mother and felt very angry and sad because of his traumatic loss of her. Significantly, Long preserved his mother's rural South Vietnamese dialect in its purest form, in spite of his constant exposure to his father's North Vietnamese accent over the last three years. His stubborn holding on to his mother's South Vietnamese dialect coupled with his reluctance (or even unwillingness?) to pick up either his father's North Vietnamese accent or English, and his aggression toward American children, created a metaphoric picture aimed at conveying Long's feelings of anger at his father and at America for having traumatically severed him from his mother. In this case, the therapist's ability to read the transcultural metaphoric communication of this Vietnamese boy was far more vital to the understanding of his symptoms than her knowledge of the Vietnamese language.

An Integrative Therapeutic Model

The following case description illustrates the implementation of this model in the treatment of a Chinese American boy with symptoms of "identity confusion," which manifested via a conflicting relationship with his mother.

Dien Wong, a seven-year-old Chinese American boy born to Taiwanese immigrant parents, was evaluated for "identity confusion." Although fluent in both Chinese and English like his parents, Dien refused to speak Chinese with his mother. Dien also "talked back" to his mother and became, as she said, "as disobedient and selfish as the American kids." He defied his mother's order to play piano for Chinese relatives, although he enthusiastically performed piano recitals for American audiences. The onset of Dien's symptoms had coincided with his father's departure from home to attend law school in a nearby state six months earlier. Since then, Dien's father had not been home except during his monthly weekend visits. At the same time, Dien's mother started working full time while attending a graduate night class.

In her psychotherapeutic work with Dien, a white child fellow (supervised by the author) lent herself as a "mother of symbiosis," by helping him to accurately identify the inner source of his identity confusion and to uncover why his mother was chosen to be the target of his power struggle around cultural issues. Through play and talk therapy, Dien became aware that his own needs for attention and love were thwarted by what he perceived as a physically and emotionally unavailable father and an altogether too busy mother. Thus, Dien's behavioral transgression of Chinese ethics was his unconscious revenge on his mother, the only parent physically available as a target for his anger. He also reported his reluctance to face and to direct his anger at his father "because Dad may leave me for real." Like a good "mother of postsymbiosis," the child therapist conveyed to Dien her congenial acceptance of his individual needs for love and attention from his parents (and from herself, via transference, within the therapeutic boundaries). She also used "communicative matching" to praise the courage he exemplified in exploring the threatening and painful feelings of ambivalence he felt toward his parents.

Relieved by the therapist's empathetic understanding and acceptance, Dien became freer to explore more adaptive ways to get his parents to meet his needs; for instance, he "nicely and politely" (as well-behaved

Chinese children do) asked his mother to take him for a walk to the park one day. This accomplishment represented the first step toward the therapeutic goal of restoring the sense of familial affiliation between Dien and his parents. This goal was also achieved through casework with the parents. The child therapist encouraged Mr. Wong to rearrange his schedule to make more frequent home visits and thus to spend more time with Dien. She advised Mrs. Wong to decrease her night school hours and to give her son more quality time. She also taught Mrs. Wong to emphasize positive rewards for Dien's adaptive behavior, while de-emphasizing the mother-child power struggle over cultural issues.

While object-relations-based individual therapy helped to bolster Dien's individual self, casework with the parents restored Dien's sense of familial affiliation and relatedness. Dien's "I-self" could grow stronger because it was reconnected with the "familial-self."

Identity Conflict: An Object-Relations Perspective

Migration and resettlement, uprooting and rerooting, cultural loss and acculturation are often accurately pictured as human experiences of cataclysmic proportions. Yet from a different perspective, they may merely represent macroscopic magnifiers of the microscopic (too often taken for granted) experiences of the universal, human life cycle. As Stein (1984, p. 271) has aptly described, "migrations and relocations, expulsions and uprootings are part of the fabric of human history." To illustrate Stein's view, let us consider the following. School-aged children must separate from the familiar security of mother and home to venture into the unfamiliar world of socialization with contemporaries at school. Young adults have to leave—at least emotionally—the coziness of the families of their childhoods to establish new families of their own. And middle-aged parents must let go of their grown-up children and find new foci of procreation, such as investment in church or pagoda activities.

Parallel to the extraordinary experience of cultural uprooting and acculturation, these more "regular" life events tap into universal human ambivalence about oneness and separation, dependence and independence. With such ambivalence, the reconciliation of the polarized ends of holding on and letting go, detaching and reattaching, uprooting and taking root, separating and individuating becomes a horrendous task. Because of the great ego strength required, unfinished resolutions of these tasks of separation and individuation, mourning and integration seem to be the natural parts and parcels of the human condition.

Such unfinished emotional business is usually reactivated by uprooting experiences (Stein, 1984). The immigrant, for example, is then confronted with a double task: integrating the emotional experience of cultural uprooting and acculturation and renegotiating new solutions for the recapitulated, unfinished issues of separation and individuation. This task will burden the immigrant with painful internal struggles that are often unconsciously externalized to take on the artificial facade of cultural conflict. In the case of Asian American child-patients, this externalization is often well hidden from the awareness of both the patients themselves and their therapists.

What we must question is how the adult Asian Americans' defensive posture affects their offspring. Vietnamese American and Chinese American child-patients not uncommonly identify with their parents' externalization of conflictual feelings by presenting a superficial picture of cultural identity crisis. The latter camouflages the resurfacing of unresolved separation-individuation issues triggered by a new experience of object loss. Ideally, therapists must not only help Asian American children work through those two layers of psychopathology but also encourage the children's parents to work on coming to terms with their double loss: cultural loss and the revived early object loss.

Additional information about Dien Wong and his family will illustrate this issue.

Dien's parents were strikingly polarized between Americanization and Chinese traditionalism. Mrs. Wong bitterly complained of her son's adoption of the American children's "decadent code of conduct," while Mr. Wong advocated his son's need to adapt to the American way of life. Thus, this appeared to be a classic case of parental cultural conflict that filtered down to their son, creating in him an "identity confusion."

However, during the course of marital therapy instituted to alleviate the parents' cultural conflict, the following dynamics started to unfold. It became obvious that underneath the cultural conflict lay a severe, long-term marital discord, due to the parents' unresolved separation-individuation from their families of origin.

Mrs. Wong angrily blamed Mr. Wong for having always sided with his mother against her, for instance, by preventing Mrs. Wong from visiting her own mother back in Taiwan. A year ago, when Mrs. Wong's mother died, Mr. Wong had not allowed her to send enough money to Taiwan to provide her mother with a big funeral. Mrs. Wong also expressed rage at discovering, through friends and relatives, that Mr. Wong had secretly smuggled his mother out of Taiwan. Mr. Wong's side of the story was as follows: Mrs. Wong had always looked down on his mother and his family because his family was poorer than hers. He had sent some money to Taiwan for Mrs. Wong's mother's funeral, but not as much as his wife had requested because of the couple's financial constraints. He had hidden his mother's arrival in the United States from his wife because he had known all along that his mother's presence would infuriate Mrs. Wong.

The marital therapy helped Mr. and Mrs. Wong to understand how these earlier unresolved developmental issues were reactivated by the couple's immigration to the United States and, inflamed by recent stressors, resurfaced under the more culturally acceptable pretense of cultural discord. Thus, the process of the marital therapy paralleled the process of Dien's individual therapy—both addressed the superficial layer of cultural conflict and the deeper layer of intrapsychic conflict.

Object-Relations Theory, Cultural Loss, and Adolescence

Although the universality of puberty with its hormonal upsurge and growth spurt is well established, that of its psychological counterpart, adolescence, has been an ongoing subject of controversy. For some, adolescence is a mere by-product of Western cultures' discontinuity; therefore, it does not exist as such in Eastern cultures typified by continuity. However, for the Asian American families who resettle in America, the existence of a developmental phase between childhood and adulthood—whether it is named adolescence or not—undoubtedly becomes a harsh reality. While living in the United States, Vietnamese American, Chinese American, and white adolescents alike must sooner or later resolve the issue of emotional separation and individuation from their parents. In their farewell to childhood, they all must loosen up dependency ties to their parents in order to gradually move into a mature type of relationship (of reciprocity) that includes both intrafamilial and extrafamilial "objects." They have to soften their rigid old identifications with parental values, goals, and beliefs and integrate them with new extrafamilial identifications, in order to function successfully outside the family within a competitive and mobile Western society.

The enormous amount of grief work (as well as integrative work) required of adolescents to complete those tasks has been abundantly addressed in the literature (Blos, 1967; Jacobson, 1961), but their parents' parallel mourning has often been overlooked. As adolescents prepare themselves to enter adulthood, their parents must painfully confront the emptiness of the family nest and the end of emotional gratification derived from the feeling of being needed. Parents' degree of resolution of their own separation and loss issues will either greatly enhance or impede their adolescents' emotional separation and individuation.

Especially for Vietnamese American and Chinese American adolescents and their parents, grief work is much more intensified by the issue of cultural loss. Indeed, separation and loss are at the core of the parents' immigration and exodus experience. With impending separation from their adolescents, parents' unresolved mourning over cultural loss can forcefully push itself to the forefront (Tobin and Friedman, 1984). Under the threat of being abandoned by their adolescents (physical and/or emotional removal from parents in order to immerse themselves in college, work, or romantic love), Vietnamese American and Chinese American parents' suppressed feelings of sorrow and guilt at having themselves abandoned their own parents, villages, and ancestors' tombs will likely reemerge with a renewed intensity. Any dim awareness of their own transgression of the sacred cultural norms of filial piety is likely to flood them with anxiety. To deal with the latter, they may unconsciously strive to redeem themselves and become fanatic defenders of these same traditions against potential transgressors, namely their adolescents. Through persuasion, cajolery, coercion, and guilt-producing strategies, they forcefully make their adolescents observe the sacred tradition of filial piety that dictates that adolescents show an unquestioned obedience to parental domination regarding careers, dates, marriage, and so on. Caught up in their own emotional struggle, Vietnamese American and Chinese American parents are often unable to lend support to their adolescents' work on emotional separation-individuation. Instead they cling to their adolescents to solicit their support for their own emotional turmoil.

Because of the extra load posed by parental unresolved mourning over cultural loss, intergenerational conflict in the Vietnamese American and Chinese American families can at times take on catastrophic proportions, to a degree one seldom witnesses in the white population. Ideally, therapeutic work should target both the adolescents and their parents. Therapeutic work with the adolescents should include the issue of their emotional entanglement with their parents' unresolved cultural loss in addition to that of their developmental task of separation-individuation. Therapeutic work with the parents should aim at helping them work through their unresolved mourning over cultural loss and at preventing their unfinished grief from spilling over into the parental issue of emotional separation from their adolescents. However, because the parents grew up in a culture that fosters beliefs in a symbiotic reunion with "lost objects"—as evidenced by ancestor worship (Stein, 1984)—the therapeutic goal of helping the parents come to terms with their cultural loss is obviously a very difficult undertaking.

Kim, a seventeen-year-old Vietnamese female refugee, was referred to me because of a sudden psychotic break following Dung's (her fantasized lover) departure to California. Kim ran naked from her bathtub to the street, screaming at the top of her lungs, "Ha, ha, I am making love with Dung!" and then hit her mother as the latter attempted to drag her back into the house. Prior to this psychotic break, Kim had been subjected to the strictest Vietnamese ethical standards for adolescent girls, such as no phone calls from boys, no dates, and no "frivolous" parties. Kim was ordered to go straight from school to home and had only one Vietnamese girlfriend and no male friends.

Recently, when Kim asked her parents for permission to go to a movie with her brother and his male friends, she was spanked by her father, who furiously scolded her for betraying the Vietnamese tradition of filial piety by breaking the rule of unquestioned obedience to parents. It was interesting to note that her father had himself broken the sacred code of filial piety when he had defied his own parents' injunction of not leaving them, the ancestral tombs, and Vietnam, and had been harboring severe guilt about his own transgression. However, he quickly skirted the issue to become irate about his adolescent daughter's "sinful" transgression of the traditional code of ethics, namely her secret romance with a fantasized boyfriend!

Therapist Ethnicity: Cultural and
Object-Relations Perspectives

There is some documentation on the advantage of matching the ethnicity of the therapist with that of Asian American patients (Atkinson, Maruyama, and Matsui, 1978). It is also my experience that Asian American parents and children come to the Asian American therapist with an *a priori* trust. This seems to be based on their perception that a commonly shared cultural heritage and uprooting experience will automatically enhance the therapist's empathy and competence. This trust appears to speed up the initial positive transference necessary to foster a working alliance between the therapist and the child and/or the cooperation of parents.

Lien, a seventeen-year-old Vietnamese female refugee, was referred to me by the school principal because of an overdose of aspirin following an argument with her American teacher. Lien came to the evaluation with a belligerent and fearful attitude, "because I'm not crazy," but she quickly changed her demeanor when she was introduced to a Vietnamese refugee-therapist. Our commonly shared ethnic background and refugee experience not only helped Lien to quickly lower her guard but also enhanced her trust in my understanding and competence. Indeed, not only did Lien agree to see me "for two or three sessions only" (as she initially put it) but later asked to continue the therapy for the next several months. She worked on the rather superficial issue of cultural conflict between her and her American teacher and volunteered also to "dig" deeper into the painful issues of early losses of her father through death and of her mother through abandonment.

However, there are also some disadvantages to the therapist-patient matching, and some clinicians have observed opposite phenomena. Some Vietnamese American and Chinese American children and/or parents would rather select a Western therapist because they do not trust the Vietnamese American and Chinese American therapist's adherence to the principle of confidentiality. Indeed, confidentiality is not uncommonly stressed as a poorly understood principle in some Asian cultures.

In Lien's case, her aunt and uncle as legal guardians were reportedly "extremely leery" of Lien's "spilling of her guts" to a Vietnamese outsider who could easily spread "vicious gossip" about their family's private matters to the Vietnamese community in the city. They kept putting more and more pressure on Lien to stop seeing the therapist until a forced, premature termination of Lien's therapy occurred.

The main obstacle for an Asian American therapist is the temptation to get sidetracked by the seemingly prominent role of external cultural conflict in the etiology of Asian American youths' distress and their family dysfunction (as in the cases of Kim and Lien). This narrow focus on cultural symptoms may lure the therapist away from exploring the underlying deeper issue of object losses that can have a far-reaching impact on the vicissitudes of these childrens' and adolescents' development, and, in turn, on symptom formation. By the same token, the Asian American parents' noisy complaints about cultural conflict between themselves or between the child and themselves may be the initial clues that the parents' own deeper issues may really be at stake. The dynamics that sometimes underlie Asian American therapists' shortsightedness around such issues may reside in their unconscious identification with their Asian American patients' repressed ambivalence toward their common cultures of origin. Indeed, culture is often experienced emotionally by immigrants—therapists and patients alike— as a symbolic representation of their internalized object representation (Stein, 1984). Motherland and fatherland are universal metaphors that are charged with the same emotional intensity one feels toward one's parents: all may be unconsciously perceived by immigrants and refugees as having failed to provide security, safety, and nurturance to their children. Therefore, it is no surprise that the threat of reemergence of the deeply repressed ambivalence toward "the objects of one's devotion" (Stein, 1984, p. 278) may prompt the Asian American therapist and child-patient alike to unite in an unconscious collusion. Together they "culturalize" the child's symptoms and "deuniversalize" the painful meanings of cultural loss and object loss.

With regard to white child therapists, in addition to a good knowledge base about Asian culture, the two main ingredients vital to success in treating Asian American children and adolescents are very similar to those of Asian American therapists: first, an exquisite sensitivity to the transcultural attributes of the child-patient, such as his or her narcissistic vulnerability, sense of powerlessness and helplessness, and metaphoric style of communication; and second, the adept application of psychodynamic theories, especially the relational model, to the understanding of the Asian American child's psychopathology and to the choice and implementation of therapeutic interventions. The success of the white child fellow in the treatment of Dien described above was a good illustration.

Conclusion

The interaction between developmental and cultural processes is a complex phenomenon that shapes the individual's psychological health and/or psychopathology. Psychological potentials and deficits are relative concepts reflective of and congruent with cultural values and prohibitions. Thus, the fundamental differences between Eastern and Western cultures pose major implications for the treatment of first-generation Vietnamese American and Chinese American children and adolescents. These "living-between-two-cultures" youths are more vulnerable to intensified intergenerational conflicts and identity struggles. Therefore, effective psychotherapeutic strategies with these youths should aim at narrowing the cultural gap in order to integrate the psychological potentials unique to each of these cultures.

In my view, Western-developed object-relations theory seems to be the most appropriate theory to bridge the vast differences between Eastern and Western cultures, because it is built on universal human conditions: the prolonged biopsychological dependency of the human infant and the relational dimension of the human existence.

To validate this conceptual framework, I have explored and illustrated with case vignettes the theoretical and clinical value of applying object-relations theory to the developmental processes, intergenerational conflicts, and identity struggles of first-generation Vietnamese American and Chinese American children and adolescents and their parents. The above discussions have major implications for my stance on the relative importance of therapist ethnicity.

Finally, I wish to conclude this chapter with a positive message to both Vietnamese American and Chinese American patients and their therapists. The psychological realities of cultural conflicts and identity struggles that burden many Vietnamese and Chinese immigrants and refugees do not necessarily have to translate into psychopathologies. Indeed, they offer unprecedented opportunities for psychological growth: the integration of the Eastern "familial-self" with the Western "individual-self" (I-self) into an enriching "expanding self" (Roland, 1988).

References

Atkinson, D. R., Maruyama, M., and Matsui, S. "Effects of Counselor Race and Counseling Approach on Asian-Americans' Perception of Counselor Credibility and Utility." *Journal of Counseling Psychology*, 1978, *25*(1), 76–83.

Blos, P. "The Second Individuation Process of Adolescence." *Psychoanalytic Study of the Child*, 1967, *22*, 162–186.

Bourne, P. "The Chinese Student—Acculturation and Mental Illness." *Psychiatry*, 1975, *38*, 269–277.

Ching, J.W.J., and others. "Changing Role Perceptions: A Follow-Up of Normal Adolescent Development." Unpublished manuscript.

Ganesan, S., Fine, S., and Lin, T. Y. "Psychiatric Symptoms in Refugee Families from South-East Asia: Therapeutic Challenges." *American Journal of Psychotherapy*, 1989, *43*, 218–228.

Jacobson, E. "Adolescent Moods and the Remodeling of Psychic Structures in Adolescence." *Psychoanalytic Study of the Child*, 1961, *16*, 164–183.

Kakar, S. "Psychoanalysis and Non-Western Cultures." *International Review of Psycho-Analysis*, 1985, *2*, 441–448.

Mahler, M. S., Pine, F., and Bergman, A. *The Psychological Birth of the Human Infant*. New York: Basic Books, 1975.

Marsella, A. J., Kinzie, D., and Gordon, P. "Depression Patterns Among American College Students of Caucasian, Chinese, and Japanese Ancestry." Paper presented at the Conference on Culture and Mental Health in Asia and the Pacific, Honolulu, Hawaii, Mar. 1971.

Ng, M. L. "Psychoanalysis for the Chinese: Applicable or Not Applicable?" *International Review of Psycho-Analysis*, 1985, *12*, 449–460.

Nguyen, N. A. "Living Between Two Cultures: Vietnamese Children in America." Paper presented at the 11th international congress of the International Association for Child and Adolescent Psychiatry and Allied Professions, Paris, July 1986.

Nguyen, N. A., and Williams, H. L. "Transition from East to West: Vietnamese Adolescents and Their Parents." *Journal of the American Academy of Child and Adolescent Psychiatry*, 1989, *28*(4), 505-515.

Pande, S. K. "The Mystique of 'Western' Psychotherapy: An Eastern Interpretation." *Journal of Nervous and Mental Disease*, 1968, *146*, 425-435.

Roland, A. "Psychoanalysis Without Interpretation: Psychoanalytic Therapy in Japan." *Contemporary Psychoanalysis*, 1983, *19*(3), 499-505.

Roland, A. *In Search of Self in India and Japan: Toward a Cross-Cultural Psychology.* Princeton, N.J.: Princeton University Press, 1988.

Slote, W. H. "Psychodynamic Structures in Vietnamese Personality." In W. P. Lebra (ed.), *Transcultural Research in Mental Health.* Honolulu: University Press of Hawaii, 1972.

Slote, W. H. "The Intrapsychic Locus of Power and Personal Determination in a Confucian Society: The Case of Vietnam." In W. H. Slote (ed.), *The Psycho-Cultural Dynamics of the Confucian Family: Past and Present.* International Cultural Society of Korea (ICSK) Forum Series no. 8. Seoul, Korea: ICSK, 1986.

Sommers, V. "Identity Conflict and Acculturation Problems in Oriental Americans." *American Journal of Orthopsychiatry*, 1960, *30*, 637-644.

Spitz, R. A. *The First Year of Life: A Psycho-Analytic Study of Normal and Deviant Development of Object-Relations.* New York: International University Press, 1965.

Stein, H. F. "Misplaced Persons: The Crisis of Emotional Separation in Geographical Mobility and Uprootedness." *Journal of Psychoanalytic Anthropology*, 1984, *7*(3), 269-292.

Sue, D., and Frank, A. "A Topological Approach to the Psychological Study of Chinese and Japanese American College Males." *Journal of Social Issues*, 1973, *29*(2), 129-148.

Sue, S., and Sue, D. W. "The Reflection of Culture Conflict in the

Psychological Problems of Chinese and Japanese Students." Paper presented at the convention of the American Psychological Association, Honolulu, Hawaii, 1971.

Tobin, J. J., and Friedman, J. "Intercultural and Developmental Stresses Confronting South-East Asian Refugee Adolescents." *Journal of Operational Psychiatry*, 1984, *15*, 39–45.

Wong, C. K. "The Unseen Tears of Children: A Chinese Boy Who Vomited for 14 Months." *Canadian Journal of Psychiatry*, 1988, *33*(8), 751–753.

PART FOUR

Working with American Indian Children and Adolescents

11

Multidimensional Therapy: A Case Study of a Navajo Adolescent with Multiple Problems

MARTIN D. TOPPER

Introduction

The treatment of American Indian adolescents can be complex and difficult. Like all young people, they must confront the developmental tasks of adolescence. However, the achievement of separation from the family of biological origin and the development of an independent adult identity can be severely complicated for many by factors such as economic underdevelopment on reservations, limited access to publicly funded support services, incongruity between traditional American Indian cultures and the culture of the dominant society, and the social and medical consequences of all of the above.

This chapter describes a broad-based clinical approach to the treatment of mental and emotional illnesses among American Indian adolescents that focuses on the environmental context and medical status of the patient as much as on the patient's mental and emotional condition. The approach is referred to as "multidimensional" because it views the patient from the perspective of several

The opinions expressed in this chapter are those of the author and do not necessarily reflect those of the Indian Health Service or the U.S. Environmental Protection Agency.

dimensions of human existence (medical, psychological, socioeconomic, and cultural-historical) in its attempt to develop an interdisciplinary method of evaluation and treatment.

My approach to therapy requires that the therapist initially coordinate a structural interdisciplinary evaluation of both the patient and the context in which the patient lives. This structured evaluation is followed by the development of an equally formal treatment plan that specifically targets interventions toward those areas of the patient's medical and psychological condition and those aspects of the patient's environmental context that are delaying reaching the developmental landmarks that the patient must achieve to become a functioning adult member of his or her culture.

If the evaluation reveals dysfunction within the family system, a process-oriented intervention like family therapy (Minuchin and Fishman, 1981) or extended family therapy (Topper and Curtis, 1987) can be employed as one of several interventions in the treatment plan. Furthermore, because one of the dimensions of evaluation is cultural-historical, it is clear that both cultural content and context must be considered when defining the goals of treatment and evaluating its outcome.

Therefore, the approach described in this chapter is multidimensional not only with respect to the dimensions of the patient's life but also in that it relies on techniques from all four types of therapy. This eclecticism leads to a method for evaluation and treatment that is universally applicable yet culturally sensitive. It assumes that psychological development is a universal phenomenon and that many mental and emotional disorders are categories of illness that have cross-cultural validity. On the other hand, this approach draws a great deal of its strength from the fact that it applies assumptions about evaluation and treatment in a manner that takes account of both the context of the patient's life and the content of his or her culture.

The reasons for approaching evaluation and treatment so broadly arise partly out of my personal experience and the unique clinical opportunities that exist on the Navajo Indian reservation. I spent nearly two years living in the household of a traditional Navajo medicine man prior to undertaking postdoctoral training in clinical mental health care. During this period, I was exposed to a very different philosophy of healing from that found in Western cultures. The Navajo philosophy does not view healing as a discreet set of practices through which the stricken are diagnosed and thus separated from society so that their specific disorders can be treated by specialists. Instead, it views healing as a process through which the patient gains strength and achieves "cure" through reintegration with his or her spiritual, social, and cultural context.

While I shared the daily lives of the medicine man and his household and attended a variety of traditional healing ceremonies, often referred to in English as "sings," it became clear to me that the function of the medicine man's treatment was to restore a balance between the patient and his or her environment (Topper, 1987; Sandner, 1979). Perhaps Geertz put it best when he said, "The sustaining effect of the sing . . . is to give the stricken patient a vocabulary in terms of which to grasp the nature of his distress and relate it to the wider world" (Geertz, 1973, p. 105). Even if I had not chosen to become a clinician among the Navajo, this experience with the medicine man would have still convinced me, as similar experiences have convinced Hammerschlag (1988), that healing involves more than identifying and treating disorders. Healing involves the culturally appropriate reestablishment of the patient as a functioning participant within the social context from which he or she came and to which he or she must return. Therefore, the lessons taught by the medicine man included both the need to be sensitive to the traditions and symbols that form the content of the patient's culture and an understanding that healing and long-term recovery require that the patient be placed in balance with his or her social context in a manner that is compatible with those traditions and symbols.

Another reason that this chapter describes a broad approach to education and treatment is that the Indian Health Service (IHS) facilities where I was employed provided a broad range of patient services. In addition, the IHS, as the primary provider of medical, mental health, medical-social, and other clinical services, was vitally interested in and actively promoted integration of services for its patient population. Therefore, this encouraged a multidisciplinary approach toward the patient and the family that provided me with a unique opportunity to integrate what I had learned about healing from the medicine man with the practice of Western clinical mental health care.

The end result of these experiences is the approach described in this chapter. It represents an attempt to view the patient as a continually developing individual who is embedded in an ever-widening set of social systems. My approach owes its emphasis on development to Nemiroff and Colarusso, who both played important roles in my clinical education. Their approach toward the patient can best be seen in their statement that "the major developmental themes of childhood (or adulthood) are never completely mastered or resolved. . . . Do we ever stop refining our sense of self and identity?" (Nemiroff and Colarusso, 1990, pp. 100-101).

Along with an emphasis on development, I have borrowed heavily from the concept of "systems" as described by Minuchin and Fishman (1981). However, I do not use the family systems approach only as a therapeutic technique but also as a metaphor to translate the medicine man's view of how the patient is related to the world at large into a method for clinical care. If a family is composed of many different holons, then the patient's life is composed of many dimensions, one of which (the socioeconomic) contains the family. If the patient is to be healed as a whole person (in the manner that the medicine man seeks to heal a patient), the therapist must assess where the patient is in relation to all of the dimensions of his or her life and develop a treatment plan that seeks to restore balance and harmony in as many of these dimensions as possible. It is only in this way that the patient can be cared for in a manner that promotes both development and improved functioning in the context of the economic, social, and cultural systems in which he or she must live. Just as the family therapist seeks to improve the functioning of the family by restoring and adjusting the balance between the holons, the medicine man seeks to cure the patient by restoring the balance between the patient and the spiritual forces that control the Navajo universe. In the same way, the goal of a therapist using the multidimensional approach is to understand what is happening broadly in the patient's life and then use a variety of interventions to help the patient and his or her family utilize available resources to achieve a more stable adjustment to their world.

Related Trends

The multidimensional approach owes its origins not only to my experiences, even though unique, but also to others who have perceived that broad-based approaches are frequently needed. Therefore, the multidimensional approach can also be seen to draw its origins from several trends in contemporary patient care. The first is a general tendency toward interdisciplinary treatment, most often referred to as "holistic health care." This trend represents a response to the problems of patient management created by the rapid specialization in medical treatment over the past several decades, which leads to losing track of the patient as an individual. Second, the multidimensional approach arises from trends already established in the field of mental health, and especially in the field of alcohol treatment. Both Westermeyer (1976) and Chafetz (1983) clearly demonstrate the need for bringing the skills of a variety of specialized practitioners together in the development of a treatment regimen for patients who abuse alcohol. Alcohol abuse, mental and emotional illnesses, and many medical disorders as well are not simple, discreet biomedical disturbances; they are disruptions of a human life that have far-reaching medical, psychological, socioeconomic, and even cultural consequences.

The multidimensional approach also draws significant impetus from the work of Kleinman (1980), who argues that "the biomedical framework must be united with the ethnomedical framework in some overarching integration. That integration, which is not available at present, would reshape the medical model to include social and cultural questions and methods and would radically alter the program of health sciences and the professions that carry it out" (p. 375).

Kleinman refers to a broad theoretical integration of the two frameworks. However, the beginning of such an integration was already under way on the clinical level with the emergence of the team approach in alcohol abuse treatment and a number of other forms of mental health care. Why, therefore, is it not possible to add a cultural dimension to achieve an elementary integration of the biomedical and ethnomedical frameworks on the level of clinical practice? If the medicine man treats patients on a cultural level, why cannot the clinician? I proceeded in this direction (Topper, 1985) when I built on multidisciplinary efforts at cross-cultural alcohol abuse treatment employed by Navajo Area Indian Health Service staff. The case reported is the result of going a step further and taking the multidimensional approach previously reported on (1985) for the treatment of adult Navajo alcohol abusers and applying it to the treatment of delayed development in a Navajo adolescent whose disruptive behavior only minimally involved the abuse of alcohol. In doing so, I attempted to take previous work and give it broader relevance to the field of cross-cultural mental health care.

Environmental Issues with an Impact on Treatment

When treatment is provided to Navajo adolescents, two environmental issues have a special impact on the evaluation and development of the treatment plan: the general shortage of ancillary resources due to the economic underdevelopment of the Navajo reservation and problems generated by the differences between traditional Navajo culture and the culture of the dominant society. Obviously, all environmental variables are important. However, these two directly affect the therapist's ability to work with the patient and the rest of the therapeutic community on the reservation. Therefore, dealing with these issues up front is critical to the success of any treatment plan.

The shortage of ancillary resources can affect both evaluation and treatment. Although funding for specialized services for adolescents has increased on the Navajo reservation in the past few years, the underdevelopment of the local economy has meant that there are practically no private providers. Adolescents with special needs are eligible for federal and tribal services, but the median age of the rapidly growing Navajo population is only seventeen years (Broudy and May, 1982), and there is a high incidence of family disruption due to economic underdevelopment. Therefore, federal and tribal service providers often have large caseloads and significant waiting periods for nonemergency services and placements in residential facilities. This situation requires a well-thought-out plan for case management, making the multidimensional approach especially useful.

The multidimensional approach is also well suited to clinical environments where there are significant cultural differences between the cultures of the clinic staff and the patient population. This is because it includes a cultural dimension in both its evaluation and treatment components. In multidimensional evaluation the evaluator specifically attempts to develop an understanding of the level of traditionality of patients and how their traditional beliefs and practices might influence their understanding of the affliction from which they are suffering. In the area of treatment, the cultural dimension helps the clinician identify culturally acceptable treatment goals, determine if any proposed treatment modalities might be unacceptable to patients, and identify sources of family and community assistance that might promote the patients' recovery. These sources of assistance, of course, include their performance of healing ceremonies.

For example, Navajo patients utilize traditional Navajo ceremonies, ceremonies of the American Indian church, and fundamentalist Christian prayer ceremonies to seek relief from a broad variety of medical and psychological disorders. Important outcomes of these spiritual interventions include the identification of members of the household, the extended family, and the community at large with the patient; a concomitant increase in support for the patient; and, at the very least, a marked reduction in the patient's levels of anxiety (see Topper, 1987, for a detailed description of traditional Navajo healing).

Description of the Multidimensional Approach

As stated above, the multidimensional approach views the patient from the perspective of four basic dimensions of human existence: medical, psychological, socioeconomic, and cultural-historical. These dimensions correspond to the Western view of the human being as an amalgam of biological, psychological, social, economic, and cultural traits that either may be examined individually or may be viewed as they function together as part of a human system.

In this manner, the multidimensional approach combines principles from both Western health care and traditional Navajo treatment. It utilizes the specialized approach to mental health care in a way that integrates many specialties into a larger whole to provide a therapeutic approach more culturally compatible with the patient's experience. The multidimensional approach is not an attempt to duplicate the medicine man's effort; it is merely a way of organizing Western specialties to bridge the differences in the definition of therapy of the Western therapist and the Navajo patient.

The multidimensional approach, as employed by the author, has two major components. The first is evaluation. Patients are evaluated according to all four dimensions in order to develop an integrated and holistic picture of their medical and psychological condition and of their participation in the social, economic, and cultural systems in the community where they reside. The purpose is, therefore, to identify the problems confronting patients, to assess their functioning in the local community, and to determine how effectively they utilize the resources that are available to help resolve their daily problems.

The evaluation begins with the medical dimension. A review is made of the medical history and of any current acute or chronic medical problems the patient is experiencing. Special attention is accorded problems that can affect mental and emotional status either directly by causing a biochemical imbalance or neurological dysfunction or by the creation of a disability that inhibits social or occupational functioning or development. In addition, it is important to note any conditions that might affect mental health treatment, such as sensitivities to medications.

Once the medical evaluation is completed, the evaluation process focuses on the psychological dimension, which consists of a recording of the presenting complaint, psychological history, and a mental status exam. If any questions concerning educational disability, organicity, or diagnosis arise, testing by a child psychologist is indicated, along with a request that the testing psychologist provide specific recommendations as to appropriate kinds of interventions.

Data gathered along the medical and psychological dimensions provide a core of information about the patient's status as an individual. These dimensions describe how the adolescent is developing and if he or she has any medical or psychological disability, both of which are critical for understanding the kinds of socioeconomic and cultural stresses on the patient's life and evaluating how he or she is reacting to them.

Data gathered along the socioeconomic and cultural-historical dimensions investigate the kinds of environmental stresses that have an impact on the patient and provide an understanding of the patient's capacities to cope with stress. These assessments provide the evaluator with an idea of how well the patient is functioning in the context of other people and how capable his or her environment is of providing the basic nutrients—shelter, support, and opportunities—necessary for an adolescent of his or her culture to achieve the normal developmental landmarks defined by that culture. In cultures where there is rapid cultural change or considerable dislocation, analysis along these two dimensions provides clear insight into how such changes and dislocations increase stress, contribute to delays in development, and promote medical, social, and/or psychological pathology.

Evaluation along the cultural-historical dimension can be especially important. It provides a framework for integrating the data gathered along the other three dimensions by providing a means of understanding their meaning in terms of the daily experiences of the patient and the members of his or her residence group as members of their culture. This kind of information can be vital because symptoms and syndromes can have very different meanings in different cultures. In addition, there may be traditional native treatments that can either be a distinct adjunct or contraindication to modalities that a Western therapist might employ.

A knowledge of the definition of illness, treatment, and acceptable outcome in the patient's culture can also help the therapist negotiate treatment goals and develop a treatment plan that is compatible with the realities of the patient's life-style and expectations of what constitutes appropriate care. For example, traditional Navajos live in isolated extended family encampments that are frequently as much as thirty to fifty miles from the nearest health care facility. This, coupled with high rates of unemployment and a corresponding shortage of transportation, often makes it difficult for patients to come into the clinic for frequent appointments. The isolated patterns of residence coupled with the requirements of a subsistence economy based on sheepherding also make it difficult for many of these Navajos to undergo frequent traditional healing ceremonies. The Western mental health treatments that are most compatible with the resources and life-styles of traditional Navajo patients are thus those that are geared toward periodic intervention rather than those, like psychoanalysis, that require multiple sessions each week.

Once the multidimensional evaluation and initial treatment plan are completed, multidimensional treatment begins. Three basic types of intervention are employed simultaneously: medical intervention, psychotherapy, and environmental intervention. When used together, they make it possible for the therapist to have a broad impact on the patient's life and treat a variety of stresses that have contributed to the development of the patient's mental or emotional disorder.

The Case of Jonathan

Perhaps the best way to describe multidimensional treatment is through the presentation of a case that demonstrates how it can be used to bring a number of diverse but related resources together to facilitate a positive outcome for even the most challenging patients. This previously unreported case is that of Jonathan, a Navajo adolescent who was sixteen years old at the time he was first seen in the mental health clinic.

Jonathan was a complex patient whose history demonstrated problems in all of the dimensions. Furthermore, these problems interacted with each other in a synergistic manner. Any one of Jonathan's problems could have potentially caused a developmental delay, but taken together, they created a situation that would likely have been impossible to overcome without professional intervention.

To begin with, Jonathan had neurological deficits that greatly limited his psychological and social functioning. At the age of two he suffered from pneumonia and a high fever, which caused him to be hospitalized. During this illness, he developed generalized tonic-clonic seizures that persisted after the pneumonia had been treated. The neurologist's opinion was that Jonathan had developed a permanent generalized seizure disorder and that he also suffered from a right cerebral dysgenesis and a left hemiparesis.

Jonathan's medical condition had major psychological impacts. At age six, upon entry to school, it was learned that he was both educationally and emotionally impaired. Psychological testing indicated that he functioned at the borderline level, with an IQ of approximately 70. He also had significant deficits in visual-motor coordination. In addition, he displayed a striking inability to use his hands in a coordinated fashion in the performance of manual tasks like tying knots. These deficits persisted throughout childhood and adolescence and continued at least until the age of twenty, when he was last seen in the clinic by the author.

In addition to his learning and coordination deficits, Jonathan suffered from a number of emotional disorders that were a result of high levels of anxiety. He was agoraphobic and complained of psychogenic pain when under stress. He also displayed marked problems in adjustment when he went to live in the dormitory of a local Indian boarding school. He became particularly anxious and defensive when he was in the company of strangers, and he was capable of becoming violent when he was ridiculed because of his disabilities or felt trapped by circumstances. In addition, he suffered from a mixed personality disorder with avoidant and antisocial features.

It is difficult to determine if Jonathan's emotional problems resulted directly from organic causes or if they were a result of many years of trying to cope with neurological disabilities and the negative reactions of others to these disabilities. In either case, the net result was that Jonathan presented a complex and difficult challenge.

It was inevitable that he would develop problems in social adjustment. These difficulties were reflected in Jonathan's level of mental and emotional development. At age sixteen he should have been entering late adolescence and should have been developing a separate adult identity and gradually forming occupational preferences. His attention should have been shifting away from his family toward the establishment of a more independent life-style, including an eventual marriage. This is as true of traditional Navajo development as it is for the development of Western adolescents (see Topper and Schoepfle, 1990).

However, Jonathan did not fit the expected pattern. His limited intellectual capacities had caused his social skills to be consid-

erably underdeveloped. In addition, his lack of coordination and
left-sided hemiparesis made him an object of disdain among his
peers. His response was to become withdrawn and dependent upon
his parents and upon parental surrogates who could either gratify
his needs or see to it that others would provide him with what he
desired.

Jonathan was quite insistent when seeking gratification of
his needs. When attempts at manipulation failed, he reacted with
violence or other antisocial behavior. Fortunately, he had sufficient
insight that he could relate the undesirable consequences of such
acts to his own behavior. A brief stay in jail, for example, was
sufficient to prevent repetition of an episode of intoxication and
disorderly conduct. On the other hand, he was not able to form deep
and lasting relationships outside of his family or form a romantic
relationship with a member of the opposite sex. In the traditional
Navajo reservation community where his family lived, this placed
distinct limitations on his future possibilities, because it would be
very difficult for him to marry and move in with his wife's family
in the traditional Navajo manner.

Furthermore, Jonathan faced a number of economic problems. His parents made their income from raising a small flock of
sheep at a traditional Navajo sheep camp, and his father also had
a wage-labor job with a railroad that passed through the reservation. Although this gave the family more cash income than some
nearby households, Jonathan was one of thirteen siblings and his
family did not have sufficient funds to provide him with specialized
care. If he was to get what he needed, a program that combined
available federal, tribal, state, and local resources would have to be
created for him.

In addition to this lack of family resources, community resources both off and on the reservation were in short supply. Jonathan's home community had an unemployment rate that season-
ally varied between 35 and 50 percent; the local economy of the off-
reservation town where he went to school had an unemployment
rate that remained at around 11 percent. These high rates of unemployment affected Jonathan in two ways. First, both communities
lacked the kind of specialized care he needed. Second, when Jonathan became an adult, it would be very unlikely that he would be

able to find any employment, let alone a working environment that could accommodate his special needs and provide self-fulfillment and self-support.

Culturally, Jonathan's medical condition created an especially difficult issue. Seizure disorders are considered by traditional Navajos to be caused by incest (Reichard, 1950), and people with seizures are often shunned. There was once a traditional healing ceremony called "Moth Way" that would remove this stigma, but it is no longer practiced. Therefore, it was doubly imperative that a medical way of controlling Jonathan's seizures be found, although it would not be possible to remove the stigma. Finally, complicating all his other problems, Jonathan faced a major cultural barrier in his adolescent development. Jonathan came from a relatively unacculturated and isolated extended family with a lifestyle that quite closely followed traditional Navajo customs. On the one hand, this placed Jonathan in a position where he did not experience significant problems with the "between-two-worlds" conflict identified by Kluckhohn and Leighton (1963) and described in its clinical implications for Navajo adolescents by this author and Curtis (Topper and Curtis, 1987). Instead, he had a very limited knowledge of life in the wage-work agency towns on the reservation or the border towns. Because of his illness and disability, he had been sheltered within the social safety net of his traditional extended family. When he was not living at home, he lived in an on-reservation boarding school where he received special attention from the dormitory aides because of his condition. It is little wonder that he developed an adjustment disorder when he transferred to the high school dormitory in an off-reservation border town. He was not emotionally prepared to cope with the multicultural border-town environment or with the multicultural staff at the off-reservation dormitory, who did not provide him with the additional attention he had come to expect. In short, he was culturally unsynchronized with many of his peers and with the new environment. Furthermore, he lacked the mental and emotional resources for rapid acculturation.

Jonathan presented at the clinic in a rather dramatic fashion. His family brought him in under restraint after he had become violent at home prior to being taken back to school. He was very angry about having to return. Specifically, his complaint was that the other boys teased him, especially in the locker room after physical education class. He was on the point of being asked to leave school because of his oppositional and avoidant behavior.

Jonathan expressed his anger through refusal to take his seizure medications. This caused him to have occasional seizures, which required the dormitory and clinic staff at school to provide him with the attention that he desired. He often came to the clinic complaining of a pain in his nose. Medical examination, however, found that the "nose pain" had no medical origin, although he apparently had had pre-ictal olfactory aura on one or two occasions.

Given all of his problems, it was clear that it would be very difficult for any one person to help Jonathan. He needed so many kinds of assistance that a network of resources would have to be assembled if he was to have any chance to successfully complete the developmental tasks of adolescence. This need for coordination was evident in both the immediate situation and over the long term.

Something had to be done immediately to help Jonathan adjust to life in the dormitory so his development could continue. Obviously, he was not going to be able to stay at home. The question became how to use the resources at hand to develop an immediately effective safety net to support his adjustment in the boarding school and at the same time promote his development toward independence.

The immediate intervention involved creating a plan of action and getting all of those who took care of Jonathan to play a role in assuring that medical, psychotherapeutic, and environmental interventions were initiated and consistently applied. First, Jonathan needed to return to the dormitory and he and the family needed to come to the mental health clinic for an evaluation of the family situation. At that session, it became clear that Jonathan had many caretakers. The next step was to learn who these people were and how they related to him. From that point, it was possible to enlist their aid in the development of an overall plan to modify Jonathan's environment sufficiently to allow him to continue at school and remain on a path that would lead toward achieving whatever level of independence his disability would allow.

There were several types of caretakers. First, there was the medical staff of the Indian Health Service Unit that provided medical care for Jonathan's home community and for the dormitory: doctors, nurses, and other clinic-based staff plus community health and mental health staff. The community health nurse was extremely important since she knew the dormitory staff and could frequently visit the dormitory to see that the staff were complying with any plan that might be developed.

The next group of caretakers was the dormitory staff, both professionals and nonprofessionals. The nonprofessionals were responsible for the preparation of meals, the conduct of recreational activities, and the maintenance of the facility itself. A professional principal headed the staff, and there was also a counselor who assisted students with everyday problems.

A third group of caretakers was located at the high school where Jonathan was enrolled in the special education program. His primary on-site caretaker was the special education teacher, who worked very closely with him to define educational goals that he could achieve as he worked toward graduation from the program. The school also employed an educational psychologist who periodically tested Jonathan, evaluated his condition and progress, and helped set long-term educational goals. The third caretaker at the school was Jonathan's counselor. This person proved to be invaluable in the treatment because he, like the community health nurse, was willing to serve as a point of contact between the therapist and the school and facilitate the development of a cooperative attitude among the staff.

The fourth and final group of caretakers was composed of the members of Jonathan's extended family. Since Jonathan resided about fifty miles from home for most of the year, the use of extended family therapy as part of his day-to-day treatment was not possible. However, the support of the extended family for the treatment process and for the goals of treatment was vital, and their aid was enlisted. Of the many members of his extended family, two were most important for the success of Jonathan's treatment.

Jonathan's mother acted as a spokesperson for the immediate family. It was she who voiced the agreement for the initial treatment plan at the family interview at the outset of treatment, and it was she who voiced agreement to the final disposition of the case some

four years later. She also served as a mediator of tensions that sometimes arose among Jonathan and other family members.

The cousin who lived near the dormitory provided a more
intermittent role later in the treatment. A relationship evolved between Jonathan and his cousin in which Jonathan would spend
considerable time on weekends at his cousin's home watching
sports on television. This provided him with an alternative to the
tense atmosphere of the dormitory where the other boys never did
fully accept Jonathan and to the more adult recreational activities
of the local community (which included drinking).

Once the caretakers were identified and their roles were defined, the immediate intervention could be designed. It was agreed
by Jonathan, the family, and the therapist that Jonathan was to
remain in the dormitory. The high school agreed to allow him to
be excused from physical education. The community health nurse
would work with the dormitory on issues of medication compliance
and counsel the staff about being supportive to Jonathan. The high
school counselor would provide on-site counseling for Jonathan
and support to the school staff on a day-to-day basis. The family
agreed to take Jonathan home for visits and vacations. The therapist
would see Jonathan twice a month and would provide overall case
coordination and support for the caretakers. In this way, medical,
psychological, and environmental interventions were combined to
create a situation that would allow Jonathan to remain in school
until the therapist could get to know him and his capabilities better
so that a more refined, longer-term approach could be developed for
his care.

The long-term plan did not suddenly appear when a critical
mass of data had been collected. As in any other form of mental
health care, it gradually evolved through adjustments to the initial
treatment plan in each of three areas of intervention—medical, psychological, and environmental.

The goal of the medical intervention was to get Jonathan to
comply with his medication and bring his seizures under control.
Although a great deal of effort was put into this, his aversion to the
side effects of his seizure medication was such that his compliance
was episodic. Consultation with a consulting psychiatrist led to use
of a seizure medication that was less sedating. This change had an

unforeseen psychological benefit—it led to an improvement in his ability to control his violent outbursts.

The plan called for psychotherapy as the second major intervention. Due to Jonathan's limited intellectual capacity, therapy employed a counseling approach that focused on practical issues such as Jonathan's relationships at the dormitory and at school. His thought processes were slow, and any attempt to use interpretation to promote insight only increased his anxiety. The school counselor suggested that Jonathan might benefit from the use of a manual arts type of therapy, and, although he never was able to use his right and left hands simultaneously due to his hemiparesis, he did get a great deal of satisfaction from being able to design and construct simple abstract metallic sculptures.

Altogether, Jonathan was seen by me for approximately forty sessions over the course of treatment. He also received frequent counseling from staff at the high school and informal counseling at the dormitory. The net result was that he did learn to relate to others in a more mature fashion, was less anxious, and was more capable of satisfying his own needs in an appropriate fashion. He was much less demanding and aggressive by the time treatment was terminated.

In addition to these efforts at psychotherapy and counseling, Jonathan underwent a broad set of psychological tests to confirm his diagnosis, evaluate his progress, and assess his potential for vocational training. These found that Jonathan's capacities remained diminished, although he had made some increases academically through enrollment in a special education program at the high school. The test results also showed vocational training was clearly possible, and application was made to the tribal vocational rehabilitation program.

The third major intervention in the plan was environmental. Jonathan was to be excused from physical education, and the elimination of this stress brought quick results. Jonathan's aggressive behavior and tendency to be oppositional in school and at the dormitory decreased markedly. Two other interventions were tried. The first was an after-school job at the dormitory. He initially had problems handling the stress of this activity, but the dormitory counselor worked with the staff and Jonathan's self-esteem increased when it became clear that he could perform a job in a controlled environment. The second involved vocational training. At the time mental health treatment was terminated, Jonathan was on the waiting list for placement with the Navajo Vocational Rehabilitation Program. Given his agoraphobia, it was not certain that he would succeed in the program; however, his success at the after-school job indicated it was worth trying.

Up to this point, treatment had employed environmental interventions that allowed him to improve his functioning in the dormitory and in school. The goal was to help him graduate and provide him with skills that would help him function in the increasingly bicultural environment of the Navajo reservation, where it is increasingly important for a young person to be able to interface with the wage-labor economy of the dominant society and successfully hold a job. Placement in tribal vocational rehabilitation, if successful, would be a final step in allowing Jonathan to achieve this independence.

It is clear that with twelve siblings and a mental disability, Jonathan would be unlikely to inherit the family flock and the permit. Since Jonathan was not interested in marriage and could not run a sheep camp by himself, living a traditional Navajo lifestyle of herding and farming as an independent adult was not a viable option. He could live on at the camp as a dependent of his mother or of an inheriting sibling, but, in the long run, continued dependency, even at Jonathan's new, higher level of functioning, would prevent him from achieving the kind of personal growth and development that would allow him to feel a sense of achievement about his life.

After graduation, Jonathan went home to await placement in vocational training. About ten months later, he and his mother came to the clinic requesting that he be evaluated for Social Security disability benefits, which he received a few months later. The final plan was for him to continue on his seizure medication and remain working at the family sheep camp until placement in vocational rehabilitation became possible. He was still awaiting placement when this chapter was written.

Summary

Jonathan's case was both difficult and complex. It cannot be said that he was cured or that he achieved the developmental goal of attaining fully independent adult status. Even if he successfully completes vocational rehabilitation, he will most likely require at least limited supervision on an ongoing basis. On the other hand, it is quite possible that treatment helped avert a tragic outcome, providing enough stability to allow Jonathan to achieve some developmental goals. He graduated from the special education program at the high school, learned to control his temper to the point that he was no longer violent toward his family or his peers, and was able to develop consistent work habits in structured work settings. Although he did not achieve complete independence, given his limitations, he achieved a great deal.

The multidimensional approach, developed as an outgrowth of my personal experience, is not a new or radical departure from the past practice of the multidisciplinary team approach in mental health care; it is an elaboration of that approach built upon the therapeutic emphasis on context found in traditional Navajo healing. It formalizes the team approach and introduces three elements to it.

The first element is a cultural-historical analysis separate from an analysis of the patient's social and economic condition. This allows the therapist to view the beliefs and values that motivate the social and economic actions of the patient and design interventions to fit within the framework of the patient's and his culture's ongoing systems of belief and behavior.

The second new element is the targeting of the synergism that can often exist among the patient's problems. In Jonathan's case, it was very clear that his problems all fed off of one another. His uncontrolled seizure disorder was especially influential in complicating his other problems. With this under control, Jonathan's other problems became more accessible to treatment.

The third and final element is the focus on the caretakers. This goes beyond previous concepts of systems and views the developing child as a person embedded in a system of dependencies that

offer support but also represent relationships from which independence must be achieved if development is to progress. The caretakers
are allies for the patient and therapist to use on a temporary basis
to help attack the problems that produce the synergism. As treatment progresses, however, they, like the therapist, become objects
from whom the patient must separate so that adult status and functioning may be achieved.

Is the multidimensional approach suited only to the treatment of Navajos? No. Although it draws its holistic focus and emphasis on context from traditional Navajo healing, most of its
treatment modalities come from Western health care practices. Its
cross-cultural focus allows it to be modified to include culture-
specific evaluation and treatment modalities from most cultures or
subcultures.

Is the multidimensional approach suitable for all patients?
No. Some patients have much less complicated life situations than
others, and for them the use of the multidimensional approach with
its emphasis on context may be inefficient. The approach is most
effective in complex situations where many institutions and many
caretakers are directly involved in the patient's daily life. American
Indian reservations and inner cities where poor people experience
both family disruption and dependency on multiple state, federal,
and local/tribal agencies for support are especially suited. This
multidimensional approach can also be used for patients with complex problems who are not from inner cities or reservations and in
cases where there are no major cultural conflicts.

References

Broudy, D. B., and May, P. A. "Demographic and Epidemiological
   Transition Among the Navajo." Window Rock, Ariz.: Navajo
   Area Indian Health Service, 1982.
Chafetz, M. E. *The Alcoholic Patient: Diagnosis and Management.*
   Oradell, N.J.: Medical Economics Books, 1983.
Geertz, C. *The Interpretation of Cultures.* New York: Basic Books,
   1973.
Hammerschlag, C. A. *The Dancing Healers: A Doctor's Journey of*

Healing with Native Americans. New York: HarperCollins, 1988.

Kleinman, A. *Patients and Healers in the Context of Culture: An Exploration of the Borderland between Anthropology, Medicine, and Psychiatry.* Berkeley: University of California Press, 1980.

Kluckhohn, C., and Leighton, D. *The Navajo.* New York: Doubleday, 1963.

Minuchin, S., and Fishman, H. C. *Family Therapy Techniques.* Cambridge, Mass.: Harvard University Press, 1981.

Nemiroff, R. A., and Colarusso, C. A. *New Dimensions in Adult Development.* New York: Basic Books, 1990.

Reichard, G. A. *Navajo Religion: A Study of Symbolism.* New York: Pantheon Books, 1950.

Sandner, D. *Navajo Symbols of Healing.* Orlando, Fla.: Harcourt Brace Jovanovitch, 1979.

Topper, M. D. "Navajo 'Alcoholism': Drinking, Alcohol Abuse, and Treatment in a Changing Cultural Environment." In L. A. Bennett and G. A. Ames (eds.), *The American Experience with Alcohol: Contrasting Cultural Perspectives.* New York: Plenum, 1985.

Topper, M. D. "The Traditional Navajo Medicine Man: Therapist, Counselor, and Community Leader." *Journal of Psychoanalytic Anthropology,* 1987, *10*(3), 217-249.

Topper, M. D., and Curtis, J. "Extended Family Therapy: A Clinical Approach to the Treatment of Synergistic Dual Anomic Depression Among Navajo Agency Town Adolescents." *Journal of Community Psychology,* 1987, *15*(3), 334-348.

Topper, M. D., and Schoepfle, G. M. "Becoming a Medicine Man: A Means to a Successful Midlife Transition Among Traditional Navajo Men." In R. A. Nemiroff and C. A. Colarusso (eds.), *New Dimensions in Adult Development.* New York: Basic Books, 1990.

Westermeyer, J. *Primer on Chemical Dependency.* Baltimore, Md.: Williams & Wilkins, 1976.

12

A Cognitive-Behavioral Approach to Drug Abuse Prevention and Intervention with American Indian Youth

JOSEPH E. TRIMBLE

Counseling and psychotherapeutic techniques with American Indians of all ages are fraught with numerous complications. The techniques themselves are built on a model heavily influenced by the wisdom and experiences of North American academicians and practitioners; and the majority of them acquired their knowledge and training in institutions whose structure and function mirror classic European traditions. Consider the following circumstances: (1) almost all, if not all, early American clinicians and counselors were of European ethnic origin; (2) most counseling techniques were spawned in academic environments that largely catered to students

Funding for the preparation of portions of this chapter was provided by Grant DA-03277 from the National Institute on Drug Abuse. The author extends his deepest gratitude and appreciation to Steven Paul Schinke, School of Social Work, Columbia University, for assisting in compiling the material discussed in the latter part of the chapter. Additional support for the chapter was provided by Grant P50 DA 07074 from the National Institute on Drug Abuse funded through the Triethnic Center for Prevention Research at Colorado State University. Correspondence concerning the chapter should be addressed to Joseph E. Trimble, Center for Cross-Cultural Research, Department of Psychology, Western Washington University, Bellingham, Wash. 98225-9089.

who represented many varied generations of European heritage; and (3) most, if not all, of those counselors and clinicians responsible for developing counseling psychotherapeutic theories and techniques were white. Hence, the emergence, promotion, and progressive growth of counseling and psychotherapy theory has been culture bound and "culturally encapsulated" (Wrenn, 1962); the term implies that a cocoon of pretentious reality protects one against the struggle with the multitude of differences that abound in North America.

This chapter begins by emphasizing some of the inherent problems concerning conventional psychotherapeutic and counseling approaches and the traditional American Indian worldview. Knowledge of the problems and incompatibilities is important because a number of clinical intervention models are incorporated into drug and alcohol intervention strategies, including those in some American Indian communities (see Fleming and Manson, 1990).

The chapter presents a detailed description of a cognitive-behavioral approach to drug abuse prevention and intervention. Background information concerning drug and alcohol use among American Indians precedes and introduces the discussion of the intervention strategy. The strategy emphasizes an intervention approach targeted toward the individual and the community: individuals in group settings are recipients yet the community context in which the intervention occurs must be included. Strategies designed for drug and alcohol intervention in American Indian communities cannot focus solely on individuals—most, especially in rural and reservation settings, are sociocentric and are centered around familial and kinship relationships. The strength and presence of relationships are normative and highly valued, and the intervention strategy presented in the chapter builds on this strength. (In this chapter the term *American Indian* does not refer to Alaska natives or Canadian Indians.)

Problems with Conventional Intervention Approaches

For many American Indians and Alaska natives the essence of counseling and clinical theory creates problems. Self-disclosure—talking

out feelings, fears, anxieties, and intrapersonal problems and keeping a scheduled appointment to "talk" with someone who is not
from their culture—represents a small portion of a much more elaborate and extensive list of potential problems (LaFromboise, Trimble, and Mohatt, 1990). To a large extent, though, the most
problematic is the possibility that for many American Indians counseling and clinical intervention techniques may be intrusive, invi-
dious, and presumptuous; that is, the techniques are presented as
though the individual and the community of origin had no effective
means for dealing with emotional and behavioral disorders. On the
contrary, it is safe to conclude that virtually all American Indian
sociolinguistic groups had time-tested approaches for handling
known forms of individual, familial, and community deviations
from a group's prevailing *ethos* and *eidos*. Such approaches for
"classifying and categorizing forms of behavior fit closely within
their world view and the view they [had] of themselves as people"
(Trimble and Medicine, 1976, p. 13). Therefore, mental health and
all that it represents in the conventional psychological and psychiatric literature probably mean very different things to many American Indians (Trimble, Manson, Dinges, and Medicine, 1984). Moreover, many American Indians firmly believe "that 'mental health'
is much more spiritual and holistic than conventional psychological theory would suggest" (LaFromboise, Trimble, and Mohatt,
1990, p. 629).

The incompatibility between conventional counseling and
psychotherapy and the native worldview has received considerable
attention in recent years (Attneave, 1969; Trimble, 1981; Manson
and Trimble, 1982; Trimble and Hayes, 1984; LaFromboise, 1988;
Trimble and Fleming, 1989). Much of the criticism draws attention
to the heavy emphasis that conventional clinical techniques place
on the self-process and self-insight. The emphasis tends to run
against the social ecological flow of one's connectedness to the
American Indian community, the family, and the indigenous native
network (Attneave, 1969; Trimble and Hayes, 1984). Moreover, for
some American Indians the therapeutic value-free environment is
inconsistent with their needs and expectations because they may
need someone to assist them in asserting their traditional values and

belief system and define their problem within the context of that network (LaFromboise, Trimble, and Mohatt, 1990).

Indian Sickness and White Man's Disease

Many American Indians view illness or sickness as emanating from outside the community ("white man's disease") or influenced by some aspect of their traditional view of causality (spirit intrusion, taboo violation, soul loss, ghost sickness, and so on). Traditional healers, shamans, medicine people, and "Indian doctors" typically are assigned the responsibility for treating and curing the "Indian sicknesses." When an individual's problem is believed to emanate from a cause outside the community, then assistance is sought from appropriate health agencies such as the Indian Health Service or urban American Indian health centers (Manson and Trimble, 1982). For example, alcoholism and drug abuse are viewed as white man's diseases and therefore, as the logic goes, it is the white man who is responsible for treating them.

Basing the diagnosis of disease on one or the other sociocultural lifeway presents an interesting problem for the non-American Indian clinician. If a native-oriented, traditional American Indian, for example, is treated successfully by a shaman for alcoholism or drug addiction, the healer is credited with the power to diagnose and treat a white man's disease (Powers, 1986). But if the patient does not respond, then the blame is deflected away from the healer and projected onto public health authorities. Patients never die from "Indian sickness [because] the [healer] is always successful" (Powers, 1986, p. 178). If the patient is treated by a non-American Indian clinician he or she can almost expect to experience failure because from a traditionalist's point of view these clinicians can never heal Indian sicknesses. The clinician is also at a distinct disadvantage in treating clients since the worldviews of patient and therapist are believed to be different and at odds with one another.

The apparent incompatibility between conventional counseling and clinical theory and practice and typical American Indian worldviews is not altogether unsolvable. The debate rolls on. Some small steps have been taken to develop an eclectic blend of divergent viewpoints in an effort to achieve some balance; such efforts are slow in developing and the results await further discussion and debate (LaFromboise, 1989; Beiser, 1985; Hammerschlag, 1988; Speck and Attneave, 1973). The one area, however, that presents the most difficulty is the prevention and treatment of the dreadful incidences of alcoholism and drug addiction occurring among American Indians, especially those in the adolescent developmental life span.

The generalized array of clinical and counseling problems discussed above coupled with the belief that alcoholism and drug addiction are "white man's diseases" compounds the use of effective prevention and intervention techniques and strategies among American Indians. The remaining sections of this chapter focus on the subject of the prevention and treatment of drug abuse among American Indian adolescents. Following a review of the scant literature on the topic, information will be provided describing one approach to intervention that has shown some promise with American Indian youth.

Causes of Drug Abuse

For most American Indians and Alaska natives, alcohol and drug abuse are considered to be their primary mental health and community problem. Sadly, the causal relationship between personal and social problems and the use and abuse of psychoactive substances is not clearly understood. Several theories and anecdotal explanations have been offered, but few have been subjected to the rigors of scientific research (Trimble, Padilla, and Bell, 1987; Mail and McDonald, 1980). Some of the explanations emphasize that drug abuse is a reaction to feelings of powerlessness (McClelland, Davis, Wanner, and Kalin, 1966), peer influence and pressure (Oetting and Beauvais, 1987), need for tension reduction and coping with unpleasant and unwanted feelings (Segal, 1989), need to experiment and try out things that alter consciousness (Segal, Huba, and Singer, 1980), and need to assert and validate one's Indianness (Lurie, 1971).

Incidence and Prevalence of Drug Abuse

Even though sparse results are offered to explain American Indian drug use and abuse, there is no lack of opinion and data describing its incidence and prevalence. Mail and McDonald (1980) identified and compiled over 950 annotated citations dealing solely with alcoholism; they note that "the indicators used for assessing problem drinking among Native Americans are by necessity mostly indirect and very unsatisfactory" (p. 2). Lobb and Watts (1989) compiled a more current summary of the literature on American Indian alcohol use; they show that the literature tends to be more multidisciplinary than ever and that a number of once firmly held notions about American Indian drinking behavior are being challenged.

Watts and Lewis (1988) point out that "the subject of alcohol and native (sic) American youth has been a long, tortured second trail of tears" (p. 81). More than any other American ethnic group, American Indian youth and adults appear to bear the brunt of alcohol and drug abuse problems. The most extensive study on drug use and abuse among American Indian youth was conducted by Oetting and his colleagues at Colorado State University (Oetting, Edwards, and Beauvais, 1989). Over a ten-year period the researchers found that alcohol clearly was the most abused drug. Marijuana, tobacco, inhalants, stimulants, and cocaine ranked among the next most used drugs.

Oetting and his colleagues indicate that lifetime use has increased since 1975, the year they began their comprehensive study. Some of their more interesting findings show that (1) 75 percent of American Indian youth beyond the sixth grade have tried marijuana; (2) 30 percent of their respondents have tried inhalants; (3) one youth in twenty has been exposed to heroin; and (4) these youth may be exposed to stimulants, cocaine, sedatives, and tranquilizers at younger ages than non-American Indian youth.

Bernard Segal at the Center for Alcohol and Addiction Studies at the University of Alaska in Anchorage tracked the drug use of Alaska youth from 1977 to 1988 (Segal, 1989). Segal's results closely resemble those obtained by the Colorado State University study group. His results show that Alaska native students have the highest prevalence rate of any Alaskan ethnic group for having tried one or more drugs. Segal maintains that "the bad news is that Alaska's lifetime prevalence for adolescent drug taking behavior contrasts with national findings that reported a 'downward trend in the use of any illicit drugs'" (1989, p. 118).

The abuse of psychoactive drugs by American Indian youth
is not limited to reservation, rural, and village settings as reported
by the Colorado State and University of Alaska studies. All the
indicators reveal that it has reached epidemic proportions in some
American Indian boarding school settings. May (1982) points out
that many such boarding schools are the repositories of high-risk
or problem youth and suggests that the environment is ripe for
facilitating heavy drug use. Some survey results support his conten-
tion. Dinges and Duong-Tran (1989) showed that the lifetime rates
for alcohol use in one boarding school reached 93 percent; 53 percent of their sample were considered to be at-risk for serious alcohol
abuse. In yet another boarding school, King, Beals, Manson, and
Trimble (forthcoming) reported that for 85 percent of the total
school population alcohol was the drug of choice, followed by marijuana (75 percent). Twenty-five percent of the youth reported using
alcohol *every weekend* and over 50 percent indicated that they have
six or more drinks when they drink; of these, 73 percent answered
that they drink until they are "high" or drunk. Using structural
modeling techniques, King and his associates found that the more
youth at the particular school experienced life stress the more likely
they were to experience depression and/or to use alcohol and drugs.
The limited number of surveys concerning drug use in Indian
boarding schools warrants serious attention, since about 20 percent
of the total American Indian student-age youth are likely to be in
attendance (U.S. Department of the Interior, 1988).

Alcohol use and abuse among Indian youth has received considerable attention in recent years due largely to the reported heavy
use rates over many decades (see Oetting, Edwards, and Beauvais,
1989), but unfortunately, little attention has been directed toward
understanding the use and abuse of other psychoactive substances.
As of 1988, there were only fourteen journal publications exclusively devoted to the American Indian drug use topic; nine were
commentaries and literature reviews that attempted to draw attention to the problem (Trimble, 1988). Most of the drug and alcohol
studies focus on rural American Indian youth. Therefore, little is
known about those residing in America's urban settings where close
to half of the total American Indian population is, and one can only

speculate about the incidence and prevalence of drug use among the youth of this group.

Prevention and Intervention

Published accounts of alcohol and drug abuse prevention and intervention approaches are restricted to a few researchers and practitioners. The paucity of published articles concerning the topic belies the attention and concern expressed by tribal and village leaders and residents. Therefore, there may be an enormous gap between the number of published accounts of prevention and intervention efforts and those that have occurred and are occurring in dozens of American Indian communities. Most community efforts are rarely carefully documented or subjected to the rigors of scientific research principally because the sponsors and community residents are most concerned about local outcomes. An example may help. In the mid 1980s a married couple residing on the Alkali Lake reserve in British Columbia, Canada, openly declared their resolve to achieve total sobriety from alcohol among themselves, relatives, and close friends. In time, along with a good deal of pain, persistence, and patience and the support of many, the couple was able to move the community of nearly 400 to a level where slightly over 90 percent declared abstinence from alcohol; before the couple's initiative around 95 percent of the adult residents were heavy drinkers or alcoholics ("Indian Substance Abuse . . . ," 1987). The success of the Alkali Lake residents might not have achieved any noteworthy attention if the story had not been documented in a film entitled *The Honour of All*. The Alkali Lake experience occurred without the aid of a grant, the use of measurement tools to evaluate the effectiveness of the intervention, and the scrutiny of outsiders interested in the phenomenon for research purposes. By all standards, the Alkali Lake residents intervened and prevented alcoholism from totally destroying their valued community. Above all else, the experience confronted the despair of community alcoholism with hope and commitment that things can change.

In the late 1980s the United States Office of Substance Abuse Prevention (OSAP) began supporting numerous projects that emphasized preventive-intervention efforts in communities through-

out the country. The OSAP administrators were specifically interested in supporting the development of innovative intervention
models that emphasized high-risk youth. By 1988 OSAP had
awarded eighteen grants that targeted communities with sizable
American Indian and Alaska native populations; some twenty-four
tribes and villages were represented in the prevention activities.
Fleming and Manson (1990) conducted an extensive evaluation of
the characteristics and effectiveness of the eighteen programs. The
results of their assessment produced some interesting insights concerning the importance and significance of substance abuse prevention and intervention efforts.

Ninety-four percent of the community-based programs emphasized primary prevention activities, developed for the purpose of
preventing a health-related problem from occurring among those
who may be at-risk. Some of the primary activities involved the use
of educational materials, promotion of American Indian identity
and building self-esteem through cultural events, and the creation
of self-help groups. Individual and group therapy and counseling
were found in 88 percent of the projects. Secondary and tertiary
levels of prevention emphasize the use of counseling and psychotherapy; hence the activities are intended to prevent a problem from
intensifying and to intervene in hope of alleviating the problem.

Because the eighteen programs were based at the community
level, the opinions of local staff were important in shaping the
project's design to fit local needs and cultural perceptions. Sixty-
one percent of the projects reported that the success of the activities
centered on improving relationships with their respective clients'
families; 56 percent felt that it was important to support and maintain open communications across all levels of the project's
operation.

Fleming and Manson (1990) asked their respondents to identify those factors that placed American Indian youth at-risk for using drugs and alcohol. Eighty-eight percent singled out poor self-
esteem and parental abuse of alcohol as the greatest contributors to
high risk. The respondents also identified additional contributing
factors, including peer and friends' use of drugs; abuse, neglect, and
family conflict; sexual abuse and emotional and psychological difficulties; previous suicide threats or attempts; and alienation from

the dominant culture's social values. The researchers also asked their respondents to identify factors that presumably prevented one from using and abusing drugs. Protective factors listed included a well-defined spiritual belief system; a positive sense of self-worth; the ability to make good decisions about personal responsibilities; and the ability to act independently of others' influences. The respondents also believed that one's friends and peers who act in healthy and responsible ways can serve as models for those youth who are at-risk.

Basically, Fleming and Manson demonstrated that some American Indian community members had a good sense for those social and psychological factors that contribute to drug use; they also recognized those factors that are essential to preventing the problems from occurring or getting worse. More to the point, many American Indian communities appear to have keen insight into drug and alcohol abuse problems and the commitment and knowledge necessary to intervene. Communities may require technical and expert assistance in certain phases of prevention and intervention programs; however, such assistance is not an absolute necessity.

Additional available evidence demonstrates that many other American Indian communities are actively involved in preventing substance abuse. Owan, Palmer, and Quintana (1987) surveyed nearly 420 schools from Head Start to the secondary school level with large American Indian and Alaska native enrollments and 225 different tribal groups who were receiving grant support for alcohol and drug abuse projects from the Indian Health Service. Both the school and community respondents indicated that alcohol and drug abuse education was a major priority followed by a concern for building self-esteem and developing effective coping and decision-making skills. Owan, Palmer, and Quintana (1987) draw some important conclusions that emphasize the need for "early intervention to combat alcohol and substance abuse among Indian youths" (p. 71) and emphasize the point that American Indian youth need strong families in order to promote positive self-esteem, identity, and values. "Weak families," they argue, "produce uprooted individuals susceptible to 'peer clusters' prone to alcohol and substance abuse" (p. 71).

A Cognitive-Behavioral Approach to
Prevention and Intervention

During the past decade we have been exploring a blend of conventional psychological theory and local indigenous cultural lifeways and thoughtways in an effort to prevent Indian adolescent drug and alcohol use (Schinke and others, 1985; Schinke and others, 1988). Because of the unique bicultural and sometimes multicultural demands placed on American Indian youth, prevention-intervention approaches must strike a blend between psychological theory and the unique cultural circumstances. As a consequence of the blend, American Indian youth should be able to learn biculturally effective competence skills that "blend the adaptive values and roles of both cultures in which [youth] were raised and the culture by which they are surrounded" (LaFromboise, 1982, p. 12).

Learning biculturally competent skills allows American Indian youth to make known their desires and preferences in both American Indian and non-American Indian social milieus. Elaborating on the subject, LaFromboise and Rowe (1983) emphasize that "a socially competent, bicultural assertive lifestyle involves being benevolently interested in the needs of the group, socially responsible to perpetuate a belief system that highly values personal rights and the rights of others, self-confident . . . and decisive" (p. 592). The subgoals of bicultural competence theory as outlined by LaFromboise and Rowe center on knowledge and skills in communication, coping, and discrimination, which serve as the core elements of our prevention approach.

Merging the learning of new thought patterns with the expression of appropriate behaviors to generate biculturally competent skills actually builds on cognitive and behavioral principles drawn from social learning theory in psychology (Botvin and Wills, 1985; Schinke and Gilchrist, 1984). Briefly, these principles emphasize the relationship between our actions and thoughts and the social environment that witnesses and reacts to our actions. Ordinarily, most people act in ways that produce some form of what we believe to be positive reinforcement. In the course of our transactions with others, we achieve degrees of success that subsequently lead to beliefs about our efficaciousness (self-efficacy), our ability to function effectively in social settings (self-mastery), and our sense of worth as an acceptable person (self-esteem). We can also acquire knowledge and skills by observing the behaviors of others—presumably the more significant the others are in our lives, the greater the influence on learning appropriate and effective actions. Social learning theory, therefore, is often referred to as observational learning.

The tenets of social learning theory can be organized around an instructional framework to accelerate the learning of new information and new life skills. Social learning theory also can be fused with certain fundamental counseling skills to equip adolescents with the ability "to handle current problems, anticipate and prevent future ones, and advance their mental health, social functioning, economic welfare, and physical well-being" (Schinke and Gilchrist, 1984, p. 13). Therefore, a prevention strategy can be organized that emphasizes "the way the individual combines information into a judgement of perceived behavioral pressure, . . . inoculation against drug use, . . . and efforts to modify other aspects of the intimate culture" (Huba, Wingard, and Bentler, 1980, p. 24). Youth, whether they are at a high risk or not, can learn to inoculate themselves against peer pressure to engage in dysfunctional behavior such as drug and alcohol use, using some of the very components used by peers to promote drug use (information, communication, and support networks).

Components of Life Skills Training

In our drug abuse prevention training and research, the methods and approaches are organized in such a way that they can be used by American Indian youth and conducted by American Indian paraprofessionals, teachers, counselors, and parents. The methods center on providing information intended to change knowledge and attitudes, assisting with problem solving, providing opportunities to formulate and use coping statements, improving interpersonal communication skills, and promoting the organizing of supportive "peer clusters" and social networks.

Social modeling, another inherent fundamental principle of social learning theory, forms the nexus of the prevention effort. The use of social modeling is grounded in the finding that "Indians have an overabundance of opportunities for learning and for performing 'drinking' behaviors. . . . In this case excessive drinking would not be deviant behavior, it would conform to the expected modes of excessive drinking and the undesirability of nondrinking" (Escalante, 1980, p. 201). Peers do affect drug use behavior among youth. Plant (1975), for example, found in his survey that "all respondents attributed their first drug experiences to the direct influence and encouragement of friends" (p. 76). Similarly, Oetting and Beauvais (1986) concur with Plant. Because of results of almost a decade of drug use survey research among American Indian youth, the Colorado State University researchers argue that actual drug use is directly and intimately linked to involvement with peer clusters.

Oetting, Edwards, and Beauvais (1989) point out that peers help teach a youth how to use drugs, often provide the drugs, and provide personal and emotional support for using drugs" (p. 23).

History and Background

In the early 1980s a cognitive-behavioral skills enhancement program designed to prevent drug use among American Indian adolescents was implemented under controlled conditions in the Pacific Northwest (Schinke and others, 1985; Gilchrist, Schinke, Trimble, and Cvetkovich, 1987). To assist in organizing and implementing the project and in designing the cultural components of the training curriculum, an American Indian advisory committee was formed; the formation and use of such a committee is an absolute must for any prevention-intervention effort. In keeping with local Coast Salish tradition in the Northwest, the project was named *La-quee-biel* (to prevent) by a prominent American Indian doctor (shaman) from one of the participating reservations. The intent was to determine the feasibility of blending social learning theory with local cultural lifeways and thoughtways and to assess the impact of the blended perspective.

The twelve-member board met regularly to review, critique, change, and approve the implementation plans, curriculum, and intervention materials. The board also assisted in identifying communities where the intervention eventually took place and monitored the pilot testing of the intervention materials. During the course of the intervention phase of *La-quee-biel*, the board was provided with progress reports and summary analysis of the research findings.

During the period from the fall of 1984 to the spring of 1985, a total of 102 American Indian youth participated in the prevention effort at three intervention sites (one urban and two rural). Much information was collected from the youth in an effort to assess the effectiveness of the intervention approach. Overall, the analysis of the measures modestly supports the potential for a bicultural competence skills intervention approach among American Indian youth. Gilchrist, Schinke, Trimble, and Cvetkovich (1987) report that at a six-month follow-up the adolescents who received the skills enhancement program had lower rates of alcohol, marijuana, and inhalant use when compared with their peers who did not receive the skills training. Although the number of youths who participated in the intervention approach was relatively small, the overall effort generated a good deal of enthusiasm from a number of constituent groups.

Organization and Implementation

The use of our bicultural skills enhancement approach occurs in four phases: (1) establishing community collaborative relationships and formation of an advisory or steering committee; (2) designing the intervention and curriculum to accommodate and incorporate local American Indian values, customs, and lifeways; (3) training local indigenous community paraprofessionals; and (4) conducting the intervention scheme with local American Indian youth. The following discussion presents the essential components of the third and fourth phases.

Training Paraprofessionals

Local Indian community residents, especially parents, tribal leaders, and those with paraprofessional training in mental health and substance abuse fields, are invited to serve as small group leaders. For about two months the small group leaders and training staff meet for sixteen two-hour sessions to review and study the content and approaches needed to conduct the cognitive-behavioral prevention scheme. The training curriculum emphasizes an orientation to the problem, rationale for using the cognitive-behavioral approach, knowledge of drug and alcohol use among American Indian youths, problem solving, decision making, self-instruction, personal coping, interpersonal communication, homework, and small group dynamics. The essential focus of each of the training components is highlighted below.

Orientation and Rationale. The trainers emphasize the history, incidence, and prevalence of drug abuse in the United States. Attention then is directed to the nature of drug abuse among American Indians, giving sufficient attention to social learning theory and the cognitive-behavioral perspective. An attempt is made to demonstrate the linkages between American Indian drug use and the core principles of the cognitive-behavioral prevention approach.

Drug Knowledge. Our early training efforts revealed that many American Indians had misconceptions, inaccurate knowledge, and stereotypic views about drugs and alcohol. Hence, some time is devoted to providing the group leaders with factual information about the recreational and medicinal uses of drugs frequently used and abused by American Indian youth. Such factual information is a key element in the cognitive-behavioral approach.

Drugs and American Indian Youth. The instruction of drug and alcohol information must be structured to reflect an adolescent's orientation to learning. During this training element group leaders learn the importance of relating drug and alcohol use to the daily experiences of American Indian youth. Moreover, group leaders learn to create a nonjudgmental atmosphere in which youth feel comfortable discussing their personal experiences and asking questions about drug use without fear of being criticized or reprimanded.

Problem Solving. Group leaders are provided instruction in recognizing drug use problems, developing solutions to deal with the problems, and applying problem-solving steps. In essence, the paraprofessionals learn to use the problem-solving strategies on themselves and then teach them to one another. In this component, the trainers provide feedback, offer praise, and give suggestions where needed.

Decision Making. Problem solving of any kind requires one to identify and make appropriate decisions. In this component, trainers and group leaders review a series of short case studies and subsequently generate and rank solutions. Each solution to the individual's problem in the case history is reviewed thoroughly. Group leaders also attempt to master the decision-making process even to the extent of incorporating it into their own lives. The following example is a sample vignette typically used in the exercise:

> Fifteen-year-old Lonnie and his friends get stoned during the school lunch hour. Lonnie likes his friends and wants to stay buddies with them, yet he knows his schoolwork fails after he smokes dope. Lonnie defines the problem as feeling he has to go along with the gang. Further specifying the problem, he sees that either he or his friends must change the lunch-hour pattern. Since Lonnie has limited power over his friends and major influence over himself, he reasons that he will be the one to change.
>
> Lonnie generates a range of solutions. He could hang out with his friends and just take a few hits off each joint. That way he might not get too stoned. He could say he has a sore throat. He could stay inside school over the lunch hour. He could pretend to smoke dope but not inhale.

Self-Instruction. There is an intimate almost inseparable relationship among knowledge, problem solving, and decision making and the behavior one chooses to emit. Trainers teach group leaders how to use "inner speech" to guide overt behavior. Group leaders are asked to practice self-instruction in their daily life experiences. A good deal of training time is devoted to sharing self-instructions in small group settings. Self-instruction is a major component of the cognitive-behavioral approach and therefore it must be thoroughly learned.

Personal Coping. This training component often generates lively discussion and active participation, in part because many people believe that moderate forms of drug and alcohol use can help one to deal with stress. Group leaders are taught how coping self-statements (a form of self-instruction) and activities help people enact responsible, unpopular decisions. Group leaders are asked to generate thoughts and corresponding actions and then adhere to them, such statements as: "Even though I really want to get loaded, I'll feel awful later." "I've handled problems like this before." "The

pressure is getting bad; I'm going outside and taking a long walk."
Coping with problematic and potentially stressful life events involves advance planning and even rehearsal, so group leaders are
asked to act out their coping strategies through role-play and psy-
chodrama. The activities centered in this component help group
leaders to assess their own coping skills and assist them in practicing the instruction of effective skills to others.

Interpersonal Communication. In this component, self-
instruction and personal coping strategies are linked to the development of interpersonal communication skills. Group leaders learn
and act out nonverbal and verbal behaviors that mirror drug-
avoidance knowledge and intentions. Group leaders role-play youth
who are attempting to stay away from drugs. Trainers serve as an-
tagonists, coaches, and sources of feedback. In many sessions, American Indian group leaders actually relive their adolescent experiences with drug and alcohol use, and many come face to face with
the peer pressures they themselves have encountered in social situations. A good deal of individual practice is required in this component; trainers and small group members must be convinced that the
individual's refusal skills are genuine and determined.

Homework. Group leaders and eventually the youth themselves must practice learning self-instruction, problem-solving, and
decision-making skills. Homework emphasizes the learning process
and reinforces use of the skills. Trainers negotiate assignments with
the group leaders to practice drug prevention activities in the natural environment. Group leaders are asked to expand their drug
knowledge by searching out up-to-date materials, referral sources,
and community programs. During training sessions group leaders
spend some time reviewing their progress on their out-of-session
assignments. Finally, they devote some time to rehearsing the training of youth to negotiate their eventual homework activities.

Small Group Dynamics. Group leaders must learn the basic
elements of small group leadership, merging the cultural norms
concerning small group processes with those known to be effective
in the general social sciences literature. During the training, group
leaders watch, practice, and teach all of the cognitive-behavioral
prevention components. At strategic junctures, the trainers relate
small group experiences to generalized situations so that the group

leaders can lead youth through the prevention activities. Trainers emphasize group confidentiality, subgroup sabotaging, homework, faking, and what to do with youth who arrive high on drugs and alcohol.

When the training of the group leaders is completed, they have learned essentially all of the components of the cognitive-behavioral prevention program. They have received the basic rudiments of group dynamics, interpersonal communication, and problem-solving skills. Throughout the training group leaders are encouraged to modify the small group techniques with those culture specific norms and values particular to their community. In forging a blend between two sources of knowledge, the group leaders mold a style that captures the basic knowledge of human dynamics and those cultural norms that operate best in the community.

Prevention Program

The components of the cognitive-behavioral prevention-intervention program are basically those learned by the group leaders during their training. Youth of similar ages are trained in ten-member groups, which meet twice weekly for fifteen two-hour sessions over two months. Group leaders, with the assistance of resource people, use didactic methods, guest speakers, audiovisual materials, discussion, experiential procedures, and homework to work through the basic components. The goal of the training is to assist American Indian youth to infuse cognitive-behavioral prevention into everyday avoidance of drugs.

Early in the training, youths are introduced to the acronym S.O.D.A.S. It stands for *Stop* (what's happening in the situation?), *Options* (what are my options?), *Decision* (what decision can I make now?), *Act* (how can I act on my decision?), and *Self-praise* (I must praise myself for making a positive, healthy decision). Buttons, posters, leaflets, and small soda-pop cards blazoned with the S.O.D.A.S. acronym are circulated among the youths. In the course of the training, especially during the self-instruction component, youths are encouraged to use the acronym to guide them in their thoughts and actions. Experience tells us that youth remember the S.O.D.A.S. acronym long after they complete their training; many actually refer to the training as the "S.O.D.A.S. project" or that "S.O.D.A.S. person" (referring to the person who coordinated the training).

Activities are listed in Table 1. An abbreviated description of the sessions is presented below using the program's components as guidelines. It should be pointed out that most of our prevention-intervention conducted over the past six years occurred in community-based settings such as neighborhood facilities, tribal centers, and tribally controlled schools; in a few instances local public school administrators offered the services of their facilities. Use of tribal facilities, however, appears to provide an atmosphere most conducive to trust; such locations also enhance the perceived cultural relevance of the training.

Orientation. Group leaders lay out the ground rules and emphasize punctual attendance, confidentiality, active participation, honesty, positive feedback, and a nonjudgmental atmosphere. An overview of the substance of the fifteen sessions is presented.

Knowledge of Drugs. Discussion emphasizes the nature of various kinds of psychoactive drugs. Films, slides, videotapes, and overheads are used to supplement the didactic process. Instructional self-tests, take-home brochures, and summary facts sheets are circulated. For homework youths are asked to gather supplemental drug information from home and community resources. To emphasize and promote positive attitudes, guest speakers are also invited to discuss their personal successes in life that occurred through nondrug use means.

Problem Solving. Based on their own training experiences, group leaders present material to help youth understand problem solving to gain an awareness of its usefulness in personal, daily situations. Youths are encouraged to identify and discuss problem-solving approaches in small group sessions.

Decision Making. Based on the solutions generated from the problem-solving component, youths are asked to judge the solutions, develop a plan to implement them, and estimate and discuss others' reaction to them. Youths learn that problems can be broken down into small manageable segments. Through the process youths learn that drug and alcohol problems are commonplace but that they can be managed.

Table 1. Schedule of the Cognitive-Behavioral Skills
Prevention Program.

Sessions	Topics
1	Introduce program rationale.
2	Discuss fictions concerning American Indian drinking and drug use. Discuss the impact of stereotypes on behavior. Complete a self-esteem promotion activity.
3	Review health education information on drugs and alcohol through games, films, handouts, and posters.
4	Discuss factors that encourage drug use. Introduce peer guest speaker to share personal reasons for rejecting drug use.
5	Discuss the role of values in decision making. Complete activities to encourage identification of personal values. Introduce the S.O.D.A.S. problem-solving method.
6	Focus on the "S" (Stop) and the "O" (Options) of the S.O.D.A.S. model. Teach students to identify tough situations and cope with stress. Practice brainstorming techniques.
7	Focus on the "D" (Decide). Practice consideration of personal goals, personal values, and drug-alcohol facts during decision making. Use S.O.D.A.S. to solve drug and alcohol problems.
8	Focus on the "A" (Act—communication skills) and the "S" (Self-praise). Use communication skills.
9.	Use comic books and overhead projector to practice using the S.O.D.A.S. model to generate refusal statements for tobacco, alcohol, marijuana, and inhalant abuse.
10	Use participation videos for students to practice S.O.D.A.S.-generated refusal statements (S.O.D.A.S. and response prompts).
11	Students create their own answers (S.O.D.A.S. prompts but no response prompts) for participation video situations in Session 10 and engage in group practice.
12	Generalize use of S.O.D.A.S. to nondrug and nonalcohol problems. Use puppets and story boards to practice skills.
13	Provide additional practice by working with other students to create a S.O.D.A.S. "commercial" on videotape.
14	Finish videotaping. Review drug-alcohol facts. Introduce adult guest speaker from tribal alcohol treatment program. Obtain student evaluation of the program.
15	Summarize S.O.D.A.S. Outline plans for follow-up. Discuss termination concerns. Enjoy a farewell party.

Self-Instruction. Essentially youths are taught the value of inner speech using one's daily routines as an example. Group leaders model the self-instruction process; inner speech is used to describe an activity one is engaging in and identify the feelings associated with it. Group leaders rehearse the activity with the youths, eventually leading them to discuss thoughts for implementing drug use avoidance decisions. Practice, feedback, and support are essential to achieving success with this activity. An example may help illustrate the interaction that occurs between the group leader and a youth:

Leader: "Sharon, why don't you run through the self-instructions for carrying out your decision? Practice what you'll say to yourself when your friends start doing drugs and want you to join in. Describe the situation as you imagine it will happen."

Sharon: "OK. Pretend like me and the girls are over at Ronnie's. We're just sittin' 'round, listenin' to records. Ronnie comes out of her bedroom carrying her stash box. Everybody is gonna get high, and I don't want to."

Leader: "All right. Does everyone have the scene? Sharon, say out loud self-instructions you will be able to use. Don't be embarrassed. We're your friends. Nobody will poke fun at you."

Sharon: (taking a deep breath) "Oh, oh. Ronnie's got her stash. The girls are gonna smoke. Ronnie will probably pass around white crosses like she usually does. I don't want to do none of that stuff. I know I can turn it down. When Ronnie brings the stash by me, I'll say 'Uh, uh, not for me, Ronnie. I'm not doing much dope these days.' If Ronnie or anyone else makes trouble I'll say 'Hey, back off!' and will get up and go to the john. When the hassle is over I'll say 'Sharon, you're cool. You didn't do any dope and everything turned out just fine!'"

Leader: "Super! Those are great self-instructions, Sharon. Let's go through the scene again. This time whisper your self-instructions."

Sharon: "OK." (Sharon subvocalizes the same thoughts.)

Leader: "Swell! Now say the self-instructions inside your head."

Sharon: (Sharon sits silently for a moment.)

Leader: "Real good. Anyone have feedback for Sharon?"

Rhonda: "Yeah, I do. Those are neat things to say, Sharon, but when you think them, don't close your eyes. The girls might think you've gone weird. If you gotta give yourself time to think, why not look down at the floor a minute?"

Leader: "Good suggestion. Anyone else?"

Personal Coping. Youths are given opportunities to identify and practice coping responses that will assist them in maintaining their drug avoidance decisions. Inner thoughts concerning refusal skills must be turned into proactive and positive overt behaviors. It is important that youths practice the personal coping procedures until they achieve some sense of mastery.

Interpersonal Communication. Group leaders introduce this component by discussing postures, expressions, gestures, and verbalizations that occur in drug-using situations with other people. Styles of nonverbal and verbal communication skills used among American Indians are discussed. Group leaders indicate that subtle cues can unintentionally lead people to encourage one another's drug use. Even when motivated, youths especially may have trouble refusing invitations to use drugs. Leaders also discuss and model communication patterns that unambiguously show drug-avoidance decisions. Youths practice their styles in dyads and then engage in group feedback sessions. Exhibit 1 is an example of one of the structured situations used in the session. Group leaders move from subgroup to subgroup giving youths feedback, coaching, and praise. The youths' comfort and skill in structured situations signals their readiness to handle individual problems with substance abuse. Group leaders and youths continue to identify ways to take charge of temptation and pressure. Continued practice and rehearsal can inoculate youths against the obstacles to drug avoidance.

Homework. Homework ties together all previous components and moves drug prevention into homes, schools, jobs, peer

Exhibit 1. An Example of Interpersonal Group Communication.

Act out this problem in your subgroup. Use postures, looks, and words like the leaders used. Give feedback after each practice. Remember to be positive and helpful. Switch roles so everyone can practice.

You and your friends are hanging out at the Seven-Eleven. Dave wants you to go with him to Bernie's and score some dope. You don't want to.

Dave: "Hey, let's you and me cut to Bernie's. He's got some fine weed."

You: _____

Dave: "What are you sayin'?"

You: _____

Dave: "What's the matter with you?"

You: _____

Dave: "Quit stalling. Let's go."

You: _____

Dave: "Some friend you are!"

You: _____

Dave: "Are we together or not?"

You: _____

---

groups, and communities. It may even lead to parental involvement. Homework assignments are negotiated at every session and monitored at the beginning of the following session, although youths must know that the responsibility for completing them rests with them. Group leaders in turn provide social reinforcement for successfully completed assignments, respond directly to noncompletion, and ignore fabricated reports.

Examples of the types of homework we have used include (1) obtain additional information about drugs and alcohol; (2) tell someone at home or school about a guest speaker's presentation; (3) practice problem-solving and decision-making skills in real-life situations; and (4) report on situations where someone's refusal skills have been successful. The assignments provide opportunities for the youth to practice and polish their skills. They also provide forms of prognostic information that can raise interesting discussion questions: (1) Do youths think drug-avoidance decisions can be carried out? (2) If so, how will they deal with responses from other people? (3) Are youths entertaining a range of options and contingency plans? (4) What if decisions are greeted unexpectedly? (5) Can they handle a physical response? (6) How about decisions that meet with disinterest and silence?

The final session of the intervention is set aside for reviewing all of the basic components of the training and celebrating the completion of the program. Youths are given certificates at a small awards ceremony, followed by a blessing from a spiritual elder from the local community. Then a small feed is arranged where parents, community leaders, and concerned residents are invited to share in the success of the youths' experience.

Did *La-quee-biel* work? Did our cognitive-behavioral prevention plan have an impact on the drug-avoidance skills of the youth? The answers to both questions are in the affirmative. The group leaders and youth did learn something; analysis of our data collection tells us so (Gilchrist, Schinke, Trimble, and Cvetkovich, 1987; Schinke and others, 1988). But the prevention-intervention methods must be approached with a degree of healthy skepticism. Part of our assessment plan involved a three- and six-month followup, and in some instances we painfully learned that some of our youth did engage in drug use at least at an experimental stage. One twelve-year-old user told us: "I really liked the S.O.D.A.S. course. I learned a lot and I thought I could handle my friends. At home it's different. My mom drinks and smokes and so does my uncle. I see them drunk all the time and it hurts because it's my mom. And I say 'They do it so it must not be so bad.' I'm confused sometimes." Youths can learn and benefit from the program; however, for the training to be effective it must have home and community support. Teaching youths prevention skills within the context of a community rife with drug and alcohol use is likely to create emotional tension for them, cause them to question what is normative, and erode respect and allegiance to kin.

Conclusion and Implications

The chapter begins with a discussion of the problems of using conventional and traditional forms of psychotherapeutic and counseling interventions with American Indians and Alaska natives. Numerous points are made. One must recognize that culture-specific forms of psychological and behavioral intervention and prevention had existed in American Indian communities for centuries. Vestiges of traditional healing and treatment ceremonies persist to this day, although many have been revised to accommodate contemporary life-styles. Use of conventional clinical intervention approaches in culturally distinct communities must forge a blend with the local *ethos* and *eidos* in order for some modicum of success to occur.

Emphasis is subsequently placed on the alarming prevalence and incidence of drug and alcohol use in American Indian communities. Some epidemiological data are provided to demonstrate the essence of the problem. Summary information is provided showing that numerous American Indian communities are working through a variety of prevention and intervention schemes in an effort to deal with drug and alcohol use. At a general level it is clear that the communities rely heavily on the conventional wisdom and methods of the substance abuse research field; however, the community resource people recognize that intervention schemes must be adjusted to fit local tribal-specific customs and norms.

The chapter proceeds to a discussion of cognitive-behavioral prevention, bicultural competence skills, and social skills enhancement. All three perspectives have been brought together to form a drug use prevention-intervention strategy tailored for use with American Indian youth. Descriptions of the theory and history of the strategy and details describing the training of local indigenous community people as group leaders are presented, along with the key components of the cognitive-behavioral prevention plan. This is followed with a description of the plan; examples and a table are included to illustrate unique aspects.

As a stand-alone prevention-intervention strategy, the cognitive-behavioral perspective probably would not be very useful. The content of the components, exercises, interpersonal communication styles, and didactic approaches must be adjusted to fit the cultural lifeways of a community. Local people also must be included in the planning and curriculum adjustment and modification phase. And they should also be trained to serve as group leaders. The cognitive-behavioral skills enhancement prevention strategy, therefore, can be used in many culturally different communities; it does lend itself to translation into Spanish for use with Latino populations.

Our prevention strategy is adaptive, flexible, and amenable to revision to accommodate different cultural perspectives. At one level the strategy focuses on youth at the individual level; yet when viewed from another perspective the strategy requires the cooperation of many. And this is the strategy's major strength. We have learned that the community where the training occurs must be collectively supportive, must take a stand against local drug and alcohol abuse, and must be active in promoting prevention and intervention approaches that meet local needs.

References

Attneave, C. L. "Therapy in Tribal Settings and Urban Network Intervention." *Family Process,* 1969, *8,* 192–210.

Beiser, M. "The Grieving Witch: A Framework for Applying Principles of Cultural Psychiatry to Clinical Practice." *Canadian Journal of Psychiatry,* 1985, *30,* 130–141.

Botvin, G. J., and Wills, T. A. "Personal and Social Skills Training: Cognitive-Behavioral Approaches to Substance Abuse Prevention." In C. S. Bell and R. Battjes (eds.), *Prevention Research: Deterring Drug Abuse Among Children and Adolescents.* NIDA Research Monograph no. 63, pp. 8–49. Washington, D.C.: U.S. Government Printing Office, 1985.

Dinges, N. G., and Duong-Tran, Q. *Indian Adolescent Mental Health Screening Project: Replication and Cross-Cultural Validation. Final Report to the Mental Health Program.* Portland, Oreg.: Portland Area Mental Health Service, Indian Health Service, 1989.

Escalante, F. "Group Pressure and Excessive Drinking Among Native Americans." In J. O. Waddell and M. W. Everett (eds.), *Drinking Behavior Among Southwestern Indians: An Anthropological Perspective.* Tucson: University of Arizona Press, 1980.

Fleming, C., and Manson, S. *Substance Abuse Prevention in American Indian and Alaska Native Communities: A Literature Review and OSAP Program Survey.* Rockville, Md.: Office of Substance Abuse Prevention, 1990.

Gilchrist, L., Schinke, S., Trimble, J., and Cvetkovich, G. "Skills Enhancement to Prevent Substance Abuse Among American Indian Adolescents." *International Journal of the Addictions*, 1987, *22*(9), 869-879.

Hammerschlag, C. A. *The Dancing Healers: A Doctor's Journey of Healing with Native Americans*. New York: HarperCollins, 1988.

Huba, G. J., Wingard, J. A., and Bentler, P. M. "Applications of a Theory of Drug Use to Prevention Programs." *Journal of Drug Education*, 1980, *3*, 15-28.

"Indian Substance Abuse Provisions Included in Omnibus Antidrug Act." *NIHB Health Reporter*, 1987, *4*(5), 1-4.

King, J., Beals, J., Manson, S., and Trimble, J. "A Structural Equation Model of Factors Related to Substance Abuse Among American Indian Adolescents." *Drugs and Society*, forthcoming.

LaFromboise, T. D. *Assertion Training with American Indians: Cultural/Behavioral Issues for Trainers*. Las Cruces, N.M.: State University, Educational Resources Information Center Clearinghouse on Rural Education and Small Schools, 1982.

LaFromboise, T. D. "American Indian Mental Health Policy." *American Psychologist*, 1988, *43*, 388-397.

LaFromboise, T. D. *Circle of Women: Professional Skills Training with American Indian Women*. Newton, Mass.: Women's Educational Equity Act Publishing Center, 1989.

LaFromboise, T. D., and Rowe, W. "Skills Training for Bicultural Competence: Rationale and Application." *Journal of Counseling Psychology*, 1983, *30*, 589-595.

LaFromboise, T., Trimble, J., and Mohatt, G. "Counseling Intervention and American Indian Tradition: An Integrative Approach." *Counseling Psychologist*, 1990, *18*(4), 628-654.

Lobb, M. L., and Watts, T. D. *Native American Youth and Alcohol: An Annotated Bibliography*. Westport, Conn.: Greenwood Press, 1989.

Lurie, N. O. "The World's Oldest On-Going Protest Demonstration: North American Indian Drinking Patterns." *Pacific Historical Review*, 1971, *40*, 311-332.

McClelland, D., Davis, W., Wanner, E., and Kalin, R. "A Cross-

Cultural Study of Folk Tale Content and Drinking." *Sociometry,* 1966, *29,* 308-333.

Mail, P. D., and McDonald, D. R. *Tulapai to Tokay: A Bibliography of Alcohol Use and Abuse Among Native Americans of North America.* New Haven, Conn.: HRAF Press, 1980.

Manson, S. M., and Trimble, J. E. "American Indian and Alaska Native Communities: Past Efforts, Future Inquiries." In L. Snowden (ed.), *Reaching the Underserved: Mental Health Needs of Neglected Populations.* Newbury Park, Calif.: Sage, 1982.

May, P. A. "Substance Abuse and American Indians: Prevalence and Susceptibility." *International Journal of the Addictions,* 1982, *17,* 1185-1209.

Oetting, E., and Beauvais, F. "Peer Cluster Theory: Drugs and the Adolescent." *Journal of Counseling and Development,* 1986, *65*(1), 17-22.

Oetting, E., and Beauvais, F. "Peer Cluster Theory, Socialization Characteristics, and Adolescent Drug Use: A Path Analysis." *Journal of Counseling Psychology,* 1987, *34*(2), 205-213.

Oetting, E. R., Edwards, R. W., and Beauvais, F. "Drugs and Native-American Youth." *Drugs and Society,* 1989, *3*(1/2), 1-34.

Owan, T., Palmer, I., and Quintana, M. *School/Community-Based Alcoholism/Substance Abuse Prevention Survey.* Rockville, Md.: Indian Health Service, Office of Health Programs, Alcoholism/ Substance Abuse Program Branch, 1987.

Plant, M. *Drug Takers in an English Town.* London: Tavistock, 1975.

Powers, W. K. *Sacred Language: The Nature of Supernatural Discourse in Lakota.* Norman: University of Oklahoma Press, 1986.

Schinke, S., and Gilchrist, L. *Life Skills Counseling with Adolescents.* Baltimore, Md.: University Park Press, 1984.

Schinke, S., and others. "Preventing Substance Abuse with American Indian Youth." *Social Casework: The Journal of Contemporary Social Work,* 1985, *4*(66), 213-217.

Schinke, S., and others. "Preventing Substance Abuse Among American Indian Adolescents: A Bicultural Competence Skills Approach." *Journal of Counseling Psychology,* 1988, *35*(1), 87-90.

Segal, B. "Drug-taking Behavior Among School-Aged Youth: The

Alaska Experience and Comparisons with Lower-48 States."
Drugs and Society, 1989, *4*(1/2), 1–174.

Segal, B., Huba, G. J., and Singer, J. L. *Drugs, Daydreaming and Personality: A Study of College Youth.* Hillsdale, N.J.: Erlbaum, 1980.

Speck, R., and Attneave, C. *Family Networks: Retribalization and Healing.* New York: Random House, 1973.

Trimble, J. E. "Value Differentials and Their Importance in Counseling American Indians." In P. Pedersen, J. Draguns, W. Lonner, and J. Trimble (eds.), *Counseling Across Cultures.* (2nd ed.) Honolulu: University Press of Hawaii, 1981.

Trimble, J. E. "Emerging Strategies in Conducting Cross-Cultural Substance Abuse Research." Paper presented at an invited conference on conducting cross-cultural substance abuse research sponsored by the National Institute on Drug Abuse, Rockville, Md., 1988.

Trimble, J. E., and Fleming, C. "Providing Counseling Services for Native American Indians: Client, Counselor, and Community Characteristics." In P. Pedersen, J. Draguns, W. Lonner, and J. Trimble (eds.), *Counseling Across Cultures.* (3rd ed.) Honolulu: University Press of Hawaii, 1989.

Trimble, J. E., and Hayes, S. "Mental Health Intervention in the Psychosocial Contexts of American Indian Communities." In W. O'Conner and B. Lubin (eds.), *Ecological Approaches to Clinical and Community Psychology.* New York: Wiley, 1984.

Trimble, J. E., Manson, S. M., Dinges, N. G., and Medicine, B. "American Indian Conceptions of Mental Health: Reflections and Directions." In P. Pedersen, N. Sartorius, and A. Marsella (eds.), *Mental Health Services: The Cross Cultural Context.* Newbury Park, Calif.: Sage, 1984.

Trimble, J. E., and Medicine, B. "Influence of Theoretical Models on Research on Mental Health Among Native Americans." In J. Westermeyer (ed.), *Anthropology and Mental Health.* Amsterdam/Lesse, Netherlands: Moltune, 1976.

Trimble, J. E., Padilla, A., and Bell, C. (eds.). *Drug Abuse Among Ethnic Minorities.* DHHS Publication no. ADM 87-1474. Rockville, Md.: National Institute on Drug Abuse, 1987.

U.S. Department of the Interior. *Report on BIA Education: Excel-*

lence in Indian Education Through Effective Schools Process.
Washington, D.C.: U.S. Government Printing Office, 1988.
Watts, T. D., and Lewis, R. G. "Alcoholism and Native American
Youth: An Overview." *Journal of Drug Issues,* 1988, *18*(1), 69–
86.
Wrenn, G. C. "The Culturally Encapsulated Counselor." *Harvard
Educational Review,* 1962, *32*(4), 444–449.

13

Treating American Indian Victims of Abuse and Neglect

DIANE J. WILLIS
ANTONIA DOBREC
DOLORES SUBIA BIGFOOT SIPES

Child abuse and neglect, including sexual abuse, can have a negative impact on a child's cognitive, behavioral, and psychosocial development (Willis, Holden, and Rosenberg, 1991). With 2.4 million children reported as abused in 1989, the first report of the U.S. Advisory Board on Child Abuse and Neglect (1990) called the problem a national emergency. This chapter presents a brief review of what is known about child abuse and neglect in Indian country, reviews the special role of American Indians in the federal government, discusses special considerations in working with sexually abused children and families both on and off reservations (including the use of healing ceremonies), and presents three treatment models for working with the sexually abused child. The chapter concludes with suggestions on when to reunify the family after sexual abuse has been reported and either the child is removed from the home or the offending parent leaves.

Although serious economic, social, and medical problems exist among American Indians, we must bear in mind that the limited information available indicates that American Indian communities experience child abuse and neglect at approximately the same rate as do non-American Indian communities. Nevertheless, there is wide variation in the estimated prevalence of child maltreatment within American Indian communities. This variation may be reflective of the methods of defining child abuse and neglect, a lack of uniform reporting requirements, the social or political factors experienced by individual tribal communities, and the historic and distinctive relationship between American Indian tribes and the federal government.

American Indian families, however, must contend with aspects of their environment that may or may not relate to increased indices of child maltreatment, particularly in certain tribal groups. The high rate of alcoholism among certain tribes coupled with poverty, economic insecurity, poor educational achievement, multiple home placements of children, and dysfunctional parenting add to the problem. Early in life in some American Indian homes, children are exposed to heavy drinking, loss of parental figures, frustration, and poor socioeconomic conditions that mitigate against their attaining a sense of well-being. This, of course, is not true of all tribes nor of all American Indians. We do know that American Indian students drop out of school at a very high rate. Fifty percent of American Indian youth drop out of reservation schools and 85 percent drop out of urban schools (Task Force Five on Indian Education, 1976). Without education, economic insecurity prevails among American Indian young adults, assuring them of a lower wage income.

The cycle of poverty is high among American Indians. It has been established that maltreatment is seven times more likely to occur in families with incomes less than $15,000 than in families with incomes above that level (National Center on Child Abuse and Neglect, 1988), so we can be sure that "poverty makes child maltreatment much more likely" (U.S. Advisory Board on Child Abuse and Neglect, 1990, p. 17). Among many tribes the severity of sociocultural stress associated with the inability to provide for one's family can be great.

Crowding due to the lack of housing may have much to do with mental health problems among American Indians. Studies have shown clearly that overcrowding in households negatively influences the organization of family roles and, in particular, is positively related to sibling friction, child neglect and abuse, and overall family breakdown. The extent to which these relationships exist among American Indians with varying cultural backgrounds is not known.

Incidence of Child Abuse

Child sexual abuse does occur in Indian country, and it is a serious problem. In one adolescent health survey administered by the Indian Health Service (IHS), approximately 20 percent of the respondents reported incidents of sexual abuse (Indian Health Service, 1991). However, again, adequate statistics on the overall incidence of child abuse and neglect in Indian country are lacking.

The number of American Indian children placed in foster care as a result of abuse is not clear since we do not know how many of these children are placed voluntarily. We know that in states with large American Indian populations, as many as 25 to 35 percent of American Indian children are removed from their families and placed in foster care (Unger, 1977). In other states, however, such as Florida, the incidence of child abuse is quite low.

Lujan, DeBruyn, May, and Bird (1989) reviewed a small number of studies dealing with child abuse and neglect among American Indians. They found that among some tribes neglect is more frequently reported than other types of abuse, that the incidence of maltreatment varies widely from one tribe to another, that child abuse and alcoholism are closely related in some tribes, and that some tribes inflict serious injury (and even death) on children as a result of physical abuse but do not sexually abuse them (p. 450). In Lujan, DeBruyn, May, and Bird's (1989) secondary data analysis of child abuse and neglect records, they found that "alcohol abuse was present in 85% of the neglect cases and 63% of the abuse cases" (p. 449). The results of their analyses also demonstrated that 65 percent of the population sample both abused *and* neglected their children. Piasecki and others (1989) surveyed federal human service providers in selected locations in Arizona and New Mexico who were either providing mental health care to children and adolescents, recommending mental health care, or had known abuse and neglect cases in their caseloads. Of the 1,155 identified children, aged from birth to twenty-one years, 67 percent were described as abused or neglected. These authors concluded that there was a relationship of abuse or neglect to severe chaos in the family and that the children had more psychiatric problems and greater drug use than nonabused children.

Special Considerations: American Indians and the Government

Because many American Indians are reared in families in which harsh discipline may be used, they may not distinguish child abuse. Therefore, many American Indian adults, including tribal personnel, may not recognize child abuse problems. In addition, tribal elders may prematurely return children home before adequate psychological interventions are carried out. Most private, federal, state, and local human service agency personnel are unaware of the history and background of American Indian communities and do not possess the understanding and skills to work effectively with American Indian victims and their families. Responding to American Indian children who have been abused requires culturally appropriate, relevant, and responsive training for personnel working in such programs.

Before discussing treatment issues related to child sexual abuse in Indian country, governmental, child welfare, and health systems issues must be understood by the mental health worker, especially as they relate to laws governing American Indian children and families.

The historic and distinctive relationship between the federal government and American Indian tribes presents different challenges for American Indians than for the general population and other minority groups in the United States. The condition of the American Indian population, however, is as much a reflection of their poor economic, social, and educational status as it is of their uncertain and often strained relationship with federal and state governments. Tribal governments or coalitions of tribes provide various human services and child care programs with funding from the federal Bureau of Indian Affairs (BIA) under Public Law 93-638, the Indian Self-Determination and Education Assistance Act, and Public Law 95-608, the Indian Child Welfare Act. Additional services are provided by the BIA, Indian Health Services (IHS), and local and state public welfare agencies. The various systems tend to provide services in a "picket fence" fashion (Wright, 1978), with little consideration given to coordination and collaboration in serving American Indian children and families. Consequently, because of a lack of clear understanding of roles and responsibilities of various entities that have authority to act upon allegations of domestic violence and child sexual abuse, assistance is often not given. Although this manner of service delivery is evident in education, health, and welfare services to American Indians, it is particularly problematic in the delivery of services in cases of child physical and sexual abuse and other domestic violence.

As a result of the previously mentioned public laws, a variety of parallel service systems have been developed within Indian country that address health, education, and welfare concerns. The public law that has the greatest effect upon the development and delivery of protective services for American Indian children has been the Indian Child Welfare (ICW) Act of 1978. Its passage is the most significant action that the Congress of the United States has taken to preserve American Indian families and communities. The passage of the act was spurred by the concern among American Indians and child welfare professionals about the experience of American Indians with the country's child welfare system (Plantz, Hubbell, Barrett, and Dobrec, 1989). Plantz and colleagues pointed out four primary concerns: the disproportionately large number of American Indian children who are being removed from their families; the frequency with which American Indian children are placed in non-American Indian substitute care and adoptive settings; the failure of public agencies and courts to consider legitimate cultural differences when working with American Indian families; and the serious lack of services to the American Indian population.

In thirteen years, there has been progress in implementing the act. A number of public agencies and state courts are complying with its requirements. Some states (Oklahoma and Minnesota) have enacted legislation and many have entered into state and tribal agreements and service contracts that supplement or augment the act. The major weakness in implementing the act has been the limited efforts at the federal level (Department of Interior, Bureau of Indian Affairs) to institute performance standards and monitor or enforce compliance by state courts and public agencies. The limited federal effort has produced uneven implementation of the act across geographic areas and governmental levels with regard to specific provisions. At some governmental levels, in fact, noncompliance is quite pronounced (Plantz, Hubbell, Barrett, and Dobrec, 1989).

Although tribes can be identified by distinct cultural and indigenous language groups, there are diverse patterns in degrees of assimilation, social systems, legal systems and, tribal government administrations. The availability of services for child victims of crime depends upon the degree of tribal sophistication in law enforcement and human service delivery and relationships developed with local, state, and federal authorities. American Indians, as citizens of the state in which they reside, have the right to access services provided by the state, tribal, and federal governments if they meet eligibility requirements. States often are reluctant to intervene in situations regarding American Indian children and families because of a belief that their needs are already being satisfied by a tribal or federal agency, or in situations where jurisdiction is a question. Unless there is an existing working relationship between state, tribal, and federal agencies, communication and coordination of services is often limited.

The following case example illustrates the conflict between jurisdictions as it affects treatment of child sexual abuse.

A fourteen-year-old girl was reported to the school counselor because of alleged sexual abuse by her natural father, with whom she lived. The school counselor contacted the Indian Child Welfare worker, who had no previous experience or training in sexual abuse investigations. The county human services department declined to become involved due to lack of jurisdiction. The FBI was contacted, who stated that they could not respond immediately but recommended to the counselor to proceed with the investigation. The tribal/BIA police were contacted to assist but refused due to lack of training in that area. The ICW worker made an appointment for a medical examination, interviewed the girl at school on three separate occasions, and submitted an investigative report to the FBI. When the FBI received the report and read it, they declined to prosecute due to the inadequate evidence in the report.

The tribal court prosecutor was contacted but declined to prosecute due to the lack of authority in a major crime. The ICW worker again contacted the FBI and asked for assistance. The FBI responded by going out and interviewing the girl, contacting the alleged perpetrator, and proceeding with their own investigation.

Approximately five weeks later, the FBI declined to prosecute, stating that the initial investigation by the ICW had been done so poorly that the evidence could not be used in the federal court system. The case never went to court.

It is in the area of criminal jurisdiction that most of the controversies among the federal government, the various states, and American Indian tribes have arisen. For example, to determine which of the three has jurisdiction in a criminal matter, one must first establish what crime was committed, whether the alleged perpetrator was an American Indian, in which state the crime occurred, and what tribal laws and treaties apply, if any. In the area of civil jurisdiction, American Indian governments have the power to regulate their own affairs as well as all activities occurring within their territory. Although the Indian Child Welfare Act protects children from mass movement out of the tribe and adoption in non-American Indian homes, it also has multiple problems. For example, ICW workers may not have proper credentials or knowledge in the area of child abuse, as demonstrated in the above case example. Likewise, American Indian courts may not understand the seriousness and impact of abuse and may return children prematurely to their natural home.

These jurisdictional complications can pose serious problems for children. For example, a father in a metropolitan area (non-American Indian land) molested and physically abused his daughter, and the evidence was conclusive both by child report and by physical examination. The father fled to his family's American Indian land and requested ICW involvement so that the child was transferred to a foster home within the tribal area. Neither the ICW worker nor the American Indian judge carefully reviewed the records or understood the seriousness of the allegations, and the child subsequently was returned home. No additional services or court plan was included, so that neither the father nor the daughter received treatment.

A second problem tribes combat is the lack of American Indian foster homes, or the approval of American Indian foster homes that are equally as dysfunctional as the natural home. Third, in some tribes, the belief that children should not be separated from their parents is so strong that children do not receive the protection they need. Tribal interference occurs in the ICW office where workers are pressured to return children to their homes. Also, the ICW worker may be frustrated by the lack of services she or he can obtain for the family; this renders the investigation and recommendations for treatment moot. Even if services are available, the American Indian courts do not exert sufficient leverage to insist that the family regularly attend treatment. Given this background on the unique aspects of child abuse in American Indian country, we will now focus on the effects of child sexual abuse and the treatment methods mental health professionals might utilize to help victims.

Effects of Child Abuse

Children who are victims of child sexual abuse report experiencing sex-related fears, trait anxiety, intrusive thoughts, feelings of stigmatization, global adjustment problems, and shame or guilt (Friedrich, Urquiza, and Beilke, 1986; Wolfe, Gentile, and Wolfe, 1989). Adults incestuously abused as children report a high incidence of sexual dysfunction (Giaretto, 1976), depression (Gold, 1986), poor self-esteem and increased drug and/or alcohol abuse (Gelinas, 1983), prostitution or running away (James and Meyerding, 1977), and adolescent pregnancy (Herman, 1988). The consequences on children can result in internalizing and/or externalizing behaviors (Haugaard and Reppucci, 1988).

A history of physical neglect, emotional maltreatment, and physical abuse has an important impact on a child's socio-emotional development over and above the impact of poverty or welfare dependency alone. Maltreatment has an impact on the child's secure readiness to learn (Aber, Allen, Carlson, and Cicchetti, 1989). Indeed, the insidious nature of neglect and emotional maltreatment may have more far-reaching consequences on the child's development than physical maltreatment, since it imparts the message to the child that he or she is neither valued nor loved.

Effective Treatment of Sexual Abuse
in American Indian Children

Generally, social services, assistance, and treatment for child abuse victims must be sought out in rural, remote localities, where American Indian victims and family members are virtually alone, as very few mental health treatment programs or private services are accessible. More than likely, members of reservation communities are socially, economically, and environmentally isolated and the few available services are overburdened and severely limited in what

they can provide. In order to seek justice, treatment, and other appropriate services, American Indian children and their families
must traverse a number of confusing and conflicting jurisdictions
without assistance, support, and guidance, a process that alone may
serve to revictimize families involved in child maltreatment.

As with other populations, American Indian victims are seldom subject to random maltreatment. Most of the time, an offender
is known to the victim, making intervention, treatment, and prose-
cution more difficult. The child victim is placed in more than a
double bind. Family or extended family supports may be absent or
nonfunctional. Both the victim and the perpetrator often have familiarity with the same human service, law enforcement, and judi-
cial providers. This systematic handicap further compounds the
American Indian victim's psychological or emotional state: feelings
of fear, anger, guilt, shame, and grief, complicated by the shattering
of self-esteem. Victims often feel abandoned by their family, their
community, and the "system."

Effective treatment is not easy to come by, as there are certain
barriers to treatment both on and off reservations, including lack of
transportation and lack of telephones. Families often live great dis-
tances from IHS clinics or other mental health clinics and have
difficulty getting to the appointments. Indian families prefer to use
IHS clinics and tend to distrust non-Indian service providers. However, the main barrier to treatment, aside from a lack of transportation, is accessibility of mental health services by trained, qualified
professionals. American Indian children and youth who have access
to mental health services can receive therapy from social workers,
mental health technicians, and occasionally psychologists. However, many professionals have little or no specific training in treatment of children and youth who have been physically or sexually
abused.

Culturally Sensitive Therapy

The culturally sensitive therapist will recognize that the American
Indian has had little contact with mental health personnel.
Members of a tribe may distrust non-American Indian personnel
because of discrimination and oppression they have experienced in

the past, and they will generally be distrustful of the therapist, at least in the beginning. Therapy may be nontraditional in that it may not be one-on-one therapy in the therapist's office but may be scheduled in the home of the client. This may include not only the immediate family but also the extended family, especially the grandparents. It is important to remember that the American Indian family is not just a single nuclear family but is rich and varied and may extend across several households and include grandparents, aunts, uncles, or nonkin who have become members of the family. The therapist working with children who have been sexually abused will often see the child while the child is in foster care. The child may also be distrustful, but, generally, therapy and therapy issues with American Indian children will not be different from those with non-American Indian children. When one begins working with the family for reunification, however, cultural differences may arise, because many American Indian families resist cultural assimilation. Because of the multitude of tribes (400 plus), therapists in a given locale may need to familiarize themselves with the customs and healing ceremonies of the tribes in their area. Ho (1987) provides an excellent general overview of family therapy with ethnic minorities, including background information about the culture of the American Indian, Asian/Pacific, black, and Hispanic American.

The remainder of this chapter will focus on therapy issues arising as a result of abuse, especially sexual abuse, and what the therapist needs to help the children address during the period of therapy. However, before discussing specific treatment models that apply to American Indian children and youth, we will review cultural factors that influence the course of treatment. Since most incidents of sexual abuse involve a father or stepfather abusing a female child, illustrations often will refer to the perpetrator as male and the victim as female. However, it is important to note that female perpetrators also can sexually abuse male children.

First and foremost, sexual abuse by a father or stepfather is grounds for removal of the child from the home unless the father or stepfather moves out and the mother believes the child's story and is willing to protect the child. A number of factors may occur that place stress upon the family and may even cause the child to recant her story. Within American Indian cultures, family bonds are extremely strong and important, and understanding this phenomenon is essential to providing effective treatment. For instance, on self-contained reservations where people know each other or are related to each other, the child's report of molestation may cause friction among family members. Since cultural or spiritual activities involve interaction among family members, the friction can be felt by all immediate and extended family members. For example, an adolescent girl living with her mother on one reservation reported that her uncle, living with the child's grandmother across the square, molested her. The mother reported the incident to the tribal police, who interviewed the adolescent and subsequently arrested the uncle. The adolescent's grandmother refused to believe the molestation occurred and would not speak to her daughter and granddaughter. The friction generated by the grandmother's lack of support and belief later caused the adolescent to recant her story. To her, it was more important to maintain peace in the family and to reestablish the relationship with her grandmother than to maintain her story.

Second, it is important to realize that sex or sexuality is not an acceptable topic to discuss openly among American Indians, especially on reservations. In child abuse prevention/education meetings, it takes time and patience to build trust before others will open up to discuss sexual abuse, which is considered a cultural taboo.

Third, some tribal leaders do not believe children should be separated from their families and may interfere with the investigation process after allegations of sexual abuse. For example, a physician performing medical examinations on Head Start children found a case of sexual abuse based not only on the physical findings but also on child report. The physician reported the incident to Indian Child Welfare, who investigated and with the tribal police removed the child from the home. The parents, evidently having influence with tribal leaders, complained and the ICW worker subsequently was fired. Unsuccessful attempts then were made to eliminate medical exams of Head Start children. These are rare but very real issues that mental health workers must work around. Education and public awareness of the effects of child abuse, including child sexual abuse, are effective ways to combat the problem of tribal interference.

Including the entire family in treatment efforts may be effective in some tribes. The Navajo family unit is quite strong and somewhat different from the dominant culture. Including the Navajo family in the treatment may well mean including grandparents, aunts, uncles, and cousins. Within the Navajo tribe, all family members are expected to support each other. If a child or adolescent has a problem and is in need of help and support, the extended family takes part in offering this assistance. This often makes it difficult for "outsiders," such as mental health providers, to gain cooperation from the immediate family because it is not culturally acceptable to accept nonfamily assistance for problems. In the Navajo tradition, the extended family assumes the role of "counselor." The medicine man also serves as a counselor, religious leader, and doctor—for the family or child to decide to see a mental health professional over a medicine man may create guilt on their part. The mental health provider must work hard to gain the family's trust and thus may find it helpful to work cooperatively with the medicine man.

Some centers (such as the Seattle Center) have begun to use culturally sensitive mental health practitioners coupled with an American Indian spiritualist. As a result of this trial, two things have occurred. First, American Indians began using the service. Second, the mental health problems with which they presented were more serious in terms of the stress they caused, so that *physical* health of the American Indians was also affected. As an outgrowth of these services, home visits were made by mental health counselors, who found that the stress on the family had certainly affected the children; for example, some children five to six years old were found to be comatose from spray paint sniffing. Another large population that began utilizing the Seattle Center services were American Indian children who had been victimized by the state foster care and adoption agencies. These children were being raised in non-American Indian homes and were coming to the Seattle Center Indian Mental Health program with severe identity and behavioral problems.

Finally, within the more traditional families the use of healing ceremonies can be very beneficial for the child or adolescent who has been harmed by sexual abuse. Mental health professionals are not the healers in these ceremonies; indeed, their role might be to encourage such a ceremony. It is important that mental health professionals, when suggesting tribal healing practices as a method of treatment, take care to recognize the protocol of the tribe. Tribal healers and helpers typically do not need to have detailed accounts of what has happened to an individual in order to assist them. Even in very public rituals leading to a renewal of the spirit, individuals do not need to disclose events.

Mental Health Treatment Models

While understanding the importance of cultural beliefs, that is, whether the family makes use of healing ceremonies or of a medicine man, the mental health professional also needs to be trained in psychological methods of treatment. Although numerous treatment methods may be utilized for victim/survivors of child sexual abuse, only three of the more successful will be discussed in this chapter because these models seem to have more applicability for the presenting symptoms of victims. The first model, developed by Finkelhor and Browne (1985), provides a conceptual framework for therapy addressing the initial and long-term traumagenic dynamics of child sexual abuse. The second model concerns treatment of a post-traumatic stress disorder (PTSD) that can develop as a result of child sexual abuse. The third model is parallel group treatment of children and their mothers developed by Damon and Waterman (1986).

Traumagenic Dynamic Model

Finkelhor and Browne (1985) postulated that people who have been sexually abused may experience one of four trauma-causing factors, which they called traumagenic dynamics: (1) traumatic sexualization; (2) stigmatization; (3) betrayal; and (4) powerlessness. When treating children who have been molested, the therapist must assess specific dynamics that may be present in the child. Finkelhor and Browne (1985) suggest that the therapist ask how traumatically sexualizing the experience might have been, determined by the nature of the attack (for example, fondling, intercourse), how long the abuse occurred, and the degree of participation of the child. Traumatic sexualization may be viewed in children who seem preoccupied with sex and who act out sexually. For instance, a four-year-old male child was following girls into the restroom at school and trying to touch their genitals. He pulled his pants down and showed his penis or his rear to the little girls. He seemed more preoccupied with this sexual activity than he was in performing normal developmental tasks in the preschool. Older children and youth may become preoccupied with having babies or may become promiscuous.

The degree of stigmatization related to sexual abuse also depends upon the length of time the abuse persisted, age of the child, reaction of family members to disclosure, and who knew about the abuse. Stigmatization refers to the child's sense of isolation and feeling of guilt and shame over the abuse. Children who have been sexually abused may feel very different from others and experience lowered self-esteem.

The traumagenic dynamic of betrayal depends upon the closeness of the perpetrator to the child (father-daughter, uncle-niece, friend of the family-child), how the perpetrator engaged the child, and whether or not the child told others (for example, the mother) but received no assistance or was not believed. The sense of betrayal adds to a child's feelings of grief and depression, anger, hostility, or mistrust of men.

Assessing the dynamic of powerlessness includes considering the duration of the abuse, whether or not force or threats were used, and so on. The feeling of powerlessness ensues when the child's body is invaded against his or her will, causing anxiety or fear and a host of other emotional symptoms. A case example involves a nine-year-old American Indian female whose stepfather entered her bedroom when her mother was playing bingo, forced her to undress, threatened to kill her mother if she told, and proceeded on a regular basis to fondle her and lie on her. The shame and guilt the child felt, coupled with the fear and anxiety over the threats, set her apart at school and made her feel different, angry, and alone.

Once assessment of the traumagenic dynamics is completed, treatment might focus on areas of greatest trauma. If the trauma is exhibited by a child sexually acting out in school, the treatment can focus on diverting the child's interest onto more appropriate developmental tasks. If the child (or adolescent) feels guilty or ashamed and feels stigmatized, the treatment of choice may be in a peer group setting. In this manner, the child recognizes that he or she is not alone or different, can get support from others who have been molested, and can begin to learn that the abuse was not his or her fault even if he or she enjoyed it.

Any of the traumagenic factors can be addressed in individual and/or group therapy. Whether children are seen in groups on reservations or in urban, off-reservation settings, group treatment is most beneficial if the children have a few sessions of individual treatment first. Depending upon the severity of the abuse, age of the child when the abuse first started, duration of the abuse, relationship of the perpetrator, and response of the (usually) maternal figure, the child may require individual treatment supplemented with group treatment at a later time. Not only are the traumagenic issues dealt with during treatment but other issues may need to be played out or discussed. Sgroi (1982) synthesized ten treatment issues often seen in abused children and adolescents: (1) the child's sense of feeling damaged, that is, the "damaged goods" syndrome; (2) guilt, including the child's sense of responsibility for the sexual abuse, for disclosure, and for disruptions that might occur in the family as a result of disclosing the abuse; (3) fear; (4) depression; (5) low self-esteem and poor social skills; (6) repressed anger and hostility that often is not seen early in treatment; (7) inability to trust; (8) blurred role boundaries and role confusion; (9) pseudomaturity and failure to complete developmental tasks; and (10) decreased self-mastery and control (a feeling of being powerless). Faller (1988) discussed treatment issues that may need to be addressed in some children and youth, including (1) loss of trust, (2) altered body image, (3) guilt feelings and feeling responsible, (4) anger, (5) depression and self-destructive behaviors, (6) understanding the meaning of the sexual abuse, and (7) strategies for self-protection.

Many of these treatment issues (Sgroi's and Faller's, for example) can be subsumed under Finkelhor and Browne's (1985) traumagenic dynamics. A part of treatment must include prevention education, that is, teaching the child to be more assertive, how to say no, whom to tell, and what to do if the threat of sexual abuse reoccurs. The following case is an illustration:

Recently, one of the authors was asked by a tribal judge to do a court-ordered evaluation on a seven-year-old female American Indian child, to evaluate the child's emotional and learning problems subequent to a history of sexual molestation. The child had been in foster care two years and no charges had been filed against any alleged perpetrator. The evaluation included a basic intellectual and psychoeducational assessment coupled with a diagnostic play interview, sexual abuse interview, and objective and projective testing.

An in-depth history of the child was obtained from the foster mother. The history revealed that this child entered the foster home quite filthy, malnourished, with head lice, unable to perform simple developmental tasks for her age, unsocialized, sexually acting out, fearful of American Indian men, and with persistent nightmares. Initially, she was functioning in the borderline to mild range of retardation. Two years later, she was functioning in the average range of intelligence but was still unable to read or to recognize all twenty-six letters of the alphabet. Indeed, academically she was performing at a beginning kindergarten level on most tasks with splinter skills at a beginning first-grade level. Objective testing suggested both internalizing (anxiety and depression) and externalizing (impulsive-hyperactive) behaviors as well as learning problems.

The sexual abuse interview confirmed sexual molestation of a sadistic nature and by multiple American Indian men. The child reported being tied to a bed, whipped, having a gun placed in her mouth and the trigger pulled, and being molested and used to orally stimulate the perpetrator. The abuse occurred over a long period of time. The child's sleep problems persisted and she reported that she did not like to go to bed. Her greatest fear was having to leave her foster mother, and she emphatically reported that she did not want to return home.

The child presented with all of the dynamics reported by Finkelhor and Browne (1985): traumatic sexualization, stigmatization, betrayal, and powerlessness.

The problem with providing treatment to a child like this one is more the norm in treating American Indian children. First, this child is being treated in a rural community by a mental health technician unfamiliar with specific treatment modalities that are effective in treating sexually abused children and also unfamiliar with the specific dynamics presented by children who have been molested. Second, in this case the child lives in the community where she sees the perpetrators. Third, the perpetrators have never been arrested or charged with any crime. Had this case been investigated in a metropolitan area (and perhaps on non-American Indian land), the perpetrators would have been arrested and, in all likelihood, charged with a crime and sentenced to prison. Two years after the molestation of this child, no arrests have been made and there is the possibility that this child will be returned to her natural home.

In this case, and in many cases, the psychologist may become a consultant to the therapist, rather than provide the therapy directly. Articles such as the ones referenced in this chapter may be sent to the mental health technician to read, and telephone consultation may occur between the therapist and consultant and the psychologist consultant and foster parent. Periodic appointments may also be made with the foster parent and therapist to aid them in their treatment and care of the child. Finally, the psychologist consultant can offer his or her services to tribal courts and the FBI, especially if he or she evaluated the child and can serve as an expert witness.

Early in treatment, it is important to reduce the child's sense of guilt and feeling of wrongdoing by imparting to the child that he or she did nothing wrong and in fact did the right thing to tell someone about the abuse. The child must be helped to understand that children generally are supposed to obey adults but that some adults do things that are wrong and when they do, it is the adult's fault, not the child's. Often the child has conflicting feelings about the perpetrator; that is, he or she loves (or likes) the person and may have enjoyed the closeness. The therapist accepts this fact and works to reduce whatever sexualized trauma has occurred. An important therapy goal is to help the child return to a normal developmental track, free of abuse and free of preoccupation with sexual issues.

Post-Traumatic Stress Disorder Model

A second treatment modality focuses on relieving the child of stress and anxiety symptoms. Specifically, PTSD symptoms experienced by children and youth who have been sexually abused include intrusive thoughts, flashbacks, recurrent distressing dreams, persistent efforts to avoid anything associated with the trauma or numbing of general responsiveness, and symptoms of increased arousal such as sleep disorders, irritability or anger, hypervigilance, and concentration problems. The preceding case example illustrates classic PTSD symptoms. The intensity of the PTSD symptoms seems to be dependent upon the severity of the abuse and the availability of emotional support.

Wolfe, Gentile, and Wolfe (1989) studied seventy-one sexually abused children and their mothers on a variety of measures; results of the study supported a PTSD symptom model. Deblinger, McLeer, and Henry (1990) used a cognitive-behavioral treatment program for sexually abused children suffering from PTSD and noted significant improvement in the children and youth on posttreatment measures. The treatment approach described by the authors required the participation of the child and the nonoffending primary caretaker. The sessions were time limited to twelve treatment sessions (although children may need to be seen longer), and the cognitive-behavioral methods included "gradual exposure, modeling, education, coping and prevention skills training" (p. 748). Within the twelve sessions, Deblinger, McLeer, and Henry (1990) moved the children through three modules. Module I consisted of two sessions of modeling/coping skills where relaxation skills and mediated self-talk helped the children cope with their anxiety. Module II, consisting of six sessions, gradually exposed the child to abuse-related memories and stimuli that could be expressed through doll play, drawing, letter writing, and a variety of other techniques. Module III consisted of two sessions of education/prevention training where issues addressed included "clear communication, body ownership, the touching continuum, the right to say no, getting away, telling until someone listens, and secrets" (p. 749). Two final sessions presented and reviewed material.

The nonoffending parent intervention consisted of three modules. Module I involved two sessions devoted to education/coping. The goal was to reduce the emotional conflicts the parent might be experiencing, such as guilt or anger, and to emphasize to the parent the role she plays in the recovery and long-term adjustment of the child. Module II included two sessions focused on communication, modeling, and gradual exposure to help the parent provide an atmosphere conducive to open and nonshameful discussions of the abuse. Areas covered during the sessions included "listening, age appropriate communication, expression of feelings, encouraging questions, problem sharing, overcoming abuse-related avoidance, and maintaining open communication" (Deblinger, McLeer, and Henry, 1990, p. 749). Module III involved six sessions focused on behavior management skills and assigned reading from chapters of Patterson's (1975) *Families*.

Post-traumatic stress symptoms must be treated directly with the child, but realistically many mental health care providers on reservations or within IHS clinics will require specialized training to be able to move children effectively through this disorder. In addition, many American Indian parents tend to be passive and noninterfering in their child rearing; therefore, teaching behavior management techniques to the more traditional American Indian mother will take time. Basic education of the mother and grandparents about their role in protecting the child, their influence in aiding the child's adjustment, and their understanding of the child's symptoms will be extremely beneficial.

Parallel Group Treatment

In addition to individual play therapy or individual therapy in the case of older children or adolescents, group treatment is extremely helpful. An excellent description of parallel group treatment of children and their mothers is described by Damon and Waterman (1986). These therapists take children and their mothers in parallel group treatment through thirteen issue-related modules, dealing with the following issues (p. 248).

1. The Right to Say "No"
2. What Happens When You Say "No"?
3. Private Parts
4. Who Can You Tell?
5. Anger and Punishment
6. What Happens When You Tell?

7. What Happened to You?
8. Fault and Responsibility
9. Separation
10. What Happens to the Perpetrators?
11. Integration of Positive and Negative Feelings toward the Perpetrator
12. What If the Denial is Maintained?
13. Sex Education

These modules deal with most issues of concern to children (and parents), and proceeding through the modules helps alleviate the child's sense of isolation, guilt, anxiety, stigmatization, betrayal, and powerlessness.

When to Reunite the Family

Since there is no known "cure" for incest, just as there is no known "cure" for alcoholism, Herman (1988) suggested that a family be reunited only when the father accepts responsibility for his behavior, recognizes the adverse effect that molestation can have on children, apologizes to his daughter in front of the family, and promises not to molest his child again. Herman (1988) reported that the decision regarding return of the father to the family must rest solely with the mother, and that, as therapists, it is not our decision, nor should it be our intent, to preserve the marriage. Indeed, the criteria of therapeutic success, once the mother-daughter relationship is restored, "is the child victim's subjective feeling of safety and well being, the disappearance of her distress symptoms, and the resumption of her interrupted normal development" (Herman, 1988, p. 187). If the father returns to the home, and the therapist feels the mother will protect her daughter at all costs and the daughter is old enough to tell, then the child may be safe. However, in the case of young children and/or depending upon the degree of threat to the child, outside supervision may need to continue indefinitely. Enlisting the support and help of the extended family may be critical, so, during treatment of the child, the extended family members may be receiving educational information about the effects of abuse upon the child. During time spent with extended family, it is often helpful to show the films *Wildfire*[1] (1991) and *The Bridge*[2] (1990), which explore the impact of child abuse and child sexual abuse on adult women and men in the American Indian community. These films are also helpful in educating tribal law enforcement personnel and ICW workers.

Summary

This chapter illustrates the many challenges to providing mental health services to American Indians, many of which do not necessarily exist for other minority groups. Associated with those challenges, American Indians have had the least access to mental health care of any ethnic minority group in the United States. The families are at great risk for child abuse and neglect due to a high rate of poverty, unemployment, and low educational status, which results in stress and family dysfunction. Providing mental health services to American Indian children and youth may be different from providing services to other ethnic groups due to the special relationship of American Indians to the federal government. The incidence of child maltreatment in Indian country is discussed, along with the effects of maltreatment upon the cognitive, social, and emotional functioning of the child. Effective treatment of child abuse with the American Indian community must include recognition of the importance of cultural beliefs and practices. Along with the emphasis on cultural differences, the chapter presents three effective models for treating sexually abused children, as well as suggestions on when to reunite the family. Education of tribes for public awareness of the effects of child abuse upon the developing child will help to combat the problems of child maltreatment. When families become more economically secure and attain higher educational status, this, too, will decrease the incidence of child abuse and neglect.

[1]American Indian Community Awareness: A Campaign to Combat Child Abuse and Neglect. Three Feathers Associates. P.O. Box 5508, Norman, Okla. 73070.
[2]Program for Aid to Victims of Sexual Abuse. 424 W. Superior Street, Suite 202, Duluth, Minn. 55802.

References

Aber, J. L., Allen, J. P., Carlson, V., and Cicchetti, D. "The Effects of Maltreatment on Development During Early Childhood: Recent Studies and Their Theoretical, Clinical, and Policy Implications." In D. Cicchetti and V. Carlson (eds.), *Child Maltreatment: Theory and Research on the Causes and Consequences of Child Abuse and Neglect.* New York: Cambridge University Press, 1989.

Damon, L., and Waterman, J. "Parallel Group Treatment of Children and Their Mothers." In K. MacFarlane and J. Waterman (eds.), *Sexual Abuse of Young Children.* New York: Guilford, 1986.

Deblinger, E., McLeer, S. V., and Henry, D. "Cognitive Behavioral Treatment for Sexually Abused Children Suffering Post-Traumatic Stress: Preliminary Findings." *Journal of the American Academy of Child and Adolescent Psychiatry,* 1990, *29,* 747–752.

Faller, K. C. *Child Sexual Abuse: An Interdisciplinary Manual for Diagnosis, Case Management, and Treatment.* New York: Columbia University Press, 1988.

Finkelhor, D., and Browne, A. "The Traumatic Impact of Child Sexual Abuse: A Conceptualization." *American Journal of Orthopsychiatry,* 1985, *55,* 530–541.

Friedrich, W. N., Urquiza, A. J., and Beilke, R. "Behavioral Problems in Sexually Abused Young Children." *Journal of Pediatric Psychology,* 1986, *11,* 47–57.

Gelinas, D. J. "The Persisting Negative Effects of Incest." *Psychiatry,* 1983, *46,* 312–332.

Giaretto, H. "Humanistic Treatment of Father-Daughter Incest." In R. Helfer and H. Kempe (eds.), *Child Abuse and Neglect: The Family and the Community.* Cambridge, Mass.: Ballinger, 1976.

Gold, E. R. "Long Term Effects of Sexual Victimization in Childhood: An Attributional Approach." *Journal of Consulting and Clinical Psychology,* 1986, *54,* 471–475.

Haugaard, J. J., and Reppucci, N. D. *The Sexual Abuse of Children: A Comprehensive Guide to Current Knowledge and Intervention Strategies.* San Francisco: Jossey-Bass, 1988.

Herman, J. "Father-Daughter Incest." In F. Ochberg (ed.), *Post-*

Traumatic Therapy and Victims of Violence. New York: Brunner/Mazel, 1988.

Ho, M. K. *Family Therapy with Ethnic Minorities.* Newbury Park, Calif.: Sage, 1987.

Indian Health Service. *IHS Primary Care Provider,* 1991, *16*(2), 17–26.

James, J., and Meyerding, J. "Early Sexual Experience and Prostitution." *American Journal of Psychiatry,* 1977, *134,* 1381–1385.

Lujan, C., DeBruyn, L. M., May, P., and Bird, M. E. "Profile of Abused and Neglected American Indian Children in the Southwest." *Child Abuse and Neglect,* 1989, *13,* 449–461.

National Center on Child Abuse and Neglect. *Study Findings: Study of the National Incidence and Prevalence of Child Abuse and Neglect.* Washington, D.C.: National Center on Child Abuse and Neglect, 1988.

Patterson, G. R. *Families.* Webster, N.C.: Psytec, 1975.

Piasecki, J. M., and others. "Abuse and Neglect of American Indian Children: Findings from a Survey of Federal Providers." *American Indian and Alaska Native Mental Health Research,* 1989, *3,* 43–62.

Plantz, M. C., Hubbell, R., Barrett, B. J., and Dobrec, A. *Indian Child Welfare: A Status Report.* DHHS Publication no. (OHDS) 89-30014. Washington, D.C.: U.S. Government Printing Office, 1989.

Sgroi, S. M. (ed.). *Handbook of Clinical Intervention in Child Sexual Abuse.* Lexington, Mass.: Lexington Books, 1982.

Task Force Five on Indian Education. *Final Report to the American Indian Policy Review Commission.* Washington, D.C.: U.S. Government Printing Office, 1976.

Unger, S. (ed.). *The Destruction of American Indian Families.* New York: American Association of Indian Affairs, 1977.

U.S. Advisory Board on Child Abuse and Neglect. *Child Abuse and Neglect: Critical First Steps in Response to a National Emergency.* Washington, D.C.: Department of Health and Human Services, 1990.

Willis, D. J., Holden, E. W., and Rosenberg, M. (eds.). *Prevention of Child Maltreatment: Development and Ecological Perspective.* New York: Wiley, 1991.

Wolfe, V. V., Gentile, C., and Wolfe, D. A. "The Impact of Sexual Abuse on Children: A PTSD Formulation." *Behavior Therapy,* 1989, *20,* 215–228.

Wright, D. S. *Understanding Intergovernmental Relations.* North Scituate, Mass.: Dunbury, 1978.

14

Conclusion: Improving the Prospects for Ethnic Minority Children in Therapy

JOAN D. KOSS-CHIOINO
LUIS A. VARGAS

Somehow it seems to fill my head with ideas—only I don't exactly know what they are!
—Alice, on reading the Jabberwocky,
Through the Looking Glass,
Lewis Carroll, 1977, p. 23.

Ethnic minority children and adolescents can experience therapy much as Alice experienced the meaning of the Jabberwocky, that is, as stimulating but disturbing and out of the range of their feeling and understanding. The intent of this book has been to describe the development of psychotherapeutic interventions with such children and adolescents through the use of a culturally colored "looking glass" so that therapy will not be a Jabberwocky experience. In turn, as psychotherapists gain a greater awareness of the influence of culture on psychological problems and their solutions, we expect that they, unlike the Red Queen, will develop ways to understand the child's culture of origin.

This chapter is the result of equal contributions by both authors.

In Chapter One, our introduction, we presented a model with which to describe the cultural responsiveness of psychotherapies. The model comprises two sets of dimensions: culture and structure. The two cultural dimensions consist of content and context; the structural dimensions consist of form and process. All psychotherapies have these dimensions; however, the cultural dimensions that are embedded in most psychotherapeutic approaches pertain to Western values, concepts, and traditions. Therapists usually are not fully aware of cultural content or context in their work, or how the cultural dimensions interrelate with those of process and form. In developing culturally responsive psychotherapies, therapists can make alterations within any of these dimensions that can have a pervasive and significant impact in developing cultural responsiveness. This can produce a therapy in which the dimensions are interrelated. For example, therapists who emphasize cultural context as a primary dimension, such as Costantino, Malgady, and Rogler (1986) in Cuento Therapy, secondarily interrelate cultural context with form and process. Although the cultural dimensions may be their major foci, the structural dimensions become secondary foci in developing a therapy that is culturally responsive.

The aim of this concluding chapter is to examine and compare how the twelve authors in this book went about the task of conceptualizing and developing their approaches. Our overall objective is to suggest ways in which therapists can modify existing approaches or create new ones that will better serve their ethnic minority child and adolescent clients.

Diverse Approaches to Cultural Responsivity

In meeting our general criteria, each author creatively developed unique approaches to his or her task. Despite individual variability in how they presented their clinical work, their solutions can be compared by using the model we developed in the first chapter. In these comparisons, we first make note of the dimensions each author emphasizes as his or her primary foci. An author may also focus secondarily on other dimensions. The second step in our description is to indicate which dimensions, either primary or secondary, are interrelated by the author in carrying out his or her psychotherapeutic approach, to augment the quality of cultural responsiveness and make its effect more pervasive. Since the structural dimensions are most often ethnocentrically constructed (Cushman, 1990), intentionally relating the cultural dimensions to them changes their role in the therapy. Examples of how the cultural dimensions can be intentionally infused into one or both structural dimensions are described below in our brief review of how each author modified or innovated his or her psychotherapeutic approach.

Table 2 categorizes the foci of culturally responsive modifications in terms of which are primary or secondary in each author's presentation. Obviously, the task of developing psychotherapy as culturally responsive is not limited to one particular strategy, as illustrated by these therapist-authors.

Table 2. Authors' Clinical Approaches Using the Descriptive Multidimensional Model.

Clinical Approach by Chapter and Author	Culture		Structure	
	Content	Context	Form	Process
2 Jones	Secondary	Primary	Primary	Secondary
3 Jackson Westmoreland	Secondary	Primary		
4 Greene	Secondary	Primary	Primary	Secondary
5 Martinez Valdez	Primary	Secondary	Primary	Primary
6 Cervantes Ramírez	Primary	Secondary	Secondary	Primary
7 Morales	Secondary	Primary		Primary
8 Chao	Primary	Secondary	Secondary	Primary
9 Ho	Secondary	Primary	Primary	Primary
10 Nguyen	Primary	Primary	Secondary	
11 Topper	Primary	Secondary	Primary	
12 Trimble	Primary	Primary	Primary	
13 Willis Dobrec Sipes	Secondary		Primary	

In the clinical approach taken by Arthur C. Jones in Chapter Two, which focuses on treating middle-class African American adolescents, cultural context and form receive primary emphases. For Jones, issues around identity and self-esteem, resulting from pervasive societal racism, assume a central place in psychotherapy. In addition, he structures the formal aspects of his approach to directly address other issues, such as intergenerational conflicts, separation-individuation, and identity confusion. Jones begins the work by seeing the parents and adolescent separately, followed by joint family sessions. He employs a teaching style to educate all family members about what he perceives as important, unconscious dynamics in the parent-child relationship. Additionally, he brings in cultural content and process as secondary foci. As a consequence of his primary focus on racial identity issues, Jones specifically introduces variations in presenting problems as influenced by conflictual attitudes toward black or white identity. Moreover, he focuses on family process as related to identity issues of the adolescent client by facilitating understanding between the parents and the adolescent about the nature of their conflict.

Helen L. Jackson and George Westmoreland, in Chapter Three, examine salient issues in therapy for African American children and adolescents in foster care. Their primary focus is on cultural context with regard to racial identity, as related to psychological development. They emphasize the interaction of developmental tasks and presenting problems with the competencies and racial experiences of the black child. Cultural content becomes a secondary focus, specifically in relation to the values and attitudes of the child's family of origin and how these relate to the positive or negative adjustment of the child in his or her foster home. These authors do not directly attend to relationship patterns between therapist and client, and they do not elaborate about how the form or process of the psychotherapeutic work should be altered to accommodate cultural issues. Yet they address a much-ignored, problematic area in mental health, giving important insights and direction for the therapist who provides services to ethnic minority children and adolescents in foster care.

In Chapter Four, Beverly A. Greene primarily focuses on the role of racial socialization in relation to cultural context and form.

This is best illustrated by her emphasis on psychohistorical issues such as racism, severance from the culture of origin, loss of freedom, and the economic disadvantage of African Americans. Her prescription of the use of racial socialization as a therapeutic tool is primary; however, she does not give us a description of the therapeutic process that can alleviate behavioral and emotional problems related to negative racial socialization. On the other hand, it is important to note that Greene's approach highlights how to enhance adaptive strength in children through an emphasis on positive racial socialization.

In Chapter Five, Kenneth J. Martinez and Diana M. Valdez describe a therapist-facilitated transactional contextual model of play therapy, which emphasizes the process of empowering the Hispanic child. Their use of the word *contextual* is more inclusive than ours, in that their description of contextual factors (economic, political, racial, social, and spiritual) includes in large part what we refer to as cultural content (for example, their use of Mexican American toys and motifs). Cultural content is primary, but it is interrelated with context. Both, in turn, are interrelated with the form dimension, which is illustrated by their focus on Hispanic materials, playroom decorations, music, games, and language. In addition, they advocate the technique of therapist-facilitated play as a specific, formal adaptation of the Hispanic patterns of interpersonal relationships. Process is also a primary focus. This is evident in the attention they give to resistances expressed by the child, as well as in their description of the process through which these resistances are negotiated. Martinez and Valdez emphasize the importance of the child's integrating, in a positive way, cultural and familial aspects of identity and self-image. Their approach may elicit strong reactions from some, especially traditional psychodynamic and client-centered play therapists, because of its emphasis on therapist facilitation. In our opinion, however, it is precisely this aspect of their model that especially heightens its value as a culturally responsive approach.

Joseph M. Cervantes and Oscar Ramírez discuss in Chapter Six the relevance of another set of psychohistorical experiences among Latino children and adolescents, that is, the merging of Mexican Indian and Latino spirituality and its relationship to the behavioral and emotional problems children and adolescents present. Their primary point of departure is based on cultural content—the emergence of a "mestizo" (Indian and Latino) worldview and spirituality—which they suggest is significantly related to familial and interpersonal relationships. Although their approach implies a strong emphasis on cultural context, this is secondary to that on cultural content. Cervantes and Ramírez focus primarily on culturally responsive clinical process, as is evident in their description of treatment. For example, they specifically point to the use of culturally patterned imagery to interpret the voices Pelón hears. In fact, the way they deal with his "voices" illustrates their in-depth consideration of process issues. In the same vein, their description of the influence of the philosophy of curanderismo on family relationships also falls within the process dimension. They make secondary use of culturally responsive form when they suggest that some of the healing practices of curanderos might be utilized in the treatment of Latino children. They imply a parallel between a safe therapeutic environment and the mestizo value of familial balance and harmony. Thus, their chapter offers an approach different from that of several of the other authors in that it views emotional and behavioral problems as rooted in a culturally unique and multigenerational psychohistory.

In Chapter Seven, Armando T. Morales describes his Latino gang intervention approach as "biopsychosocial." His primary focus is on culture as context, as is best illustrated in his explanation of why gangs develop, and cultural content is secondary. For example, he attends to the subculture of the gang as an ethnic variation on a social theme, as illustrated by his description of how Hispanic gang members are organized. His clinical cases provide ample opportunity to examine how he incorporates cultural issues into the processual aspect of therapy. For example, he describes how he facilitates a therapeutic alliance with gang members by being particularly sensitive to the symbols of the subculture. When working with Flaco, he inquires about the youth's teardrop tattoo, recognizing that such body marks symbolize pain resulting from memorialized, traumatic life events. In this chapter we can learn from the work of a therapist who has been very successful at engaging and treating Latino gang members, clients who have often been dismissed as "not appropriate for therapy."

In Chapter Eight, Christine M. Chao offers a clear exposition of her clinical approach with Southeast Asian families. She emphasizes the primacy of cultural content, including customs, traditions, and values, such as filial piety, aspects of traditional healing, the role of the healer, and ways of celebrating birthdays. She also considers cultural context with regard to the effects of immigration and generational differences. More than other authors, she specifically takes cultural heterogeneity among Asian Americans into account. In her special approach to working with Asian American children, Chao emphasizes the integration of cultural content and process variables, especially in her description of how therapists and clients relate with one another. She does this with a poetic sensitivity that conveys an exquisite appreciation of Asian American cultures. For her, process supercedes form. However, she does attend to formal aspects of psychotherapy in a culturally responsive way by giving special attention to family members' views of traditional healers and causes of emotional problems.

Man Keung Ho's model in Chapter Nine attends directly to cultural context, in relation to the impact of the dominant cultural environment on the Asian American child. He does not devote as much attention to cultural content (for example, the values and traditions of Asian Americans). However, he emphasizes form in his focus on selecting the appropriate modality for particular types of clients and in describing the bases for these decisions. His model also places primary emphasis on process, as illustrated by the glosses on the case he describes, which refer to the meanings of therapists' and clients' behaviors. Ho's presentation of his model is both informative and instructive in offering a culturally responsive parallel to Lazarus's (1989) multimodal approach to psychotherapy.

In Chapter Ten, Nga Anh Nguyen approaches the task of culturally responsive psychotherapy by first exploring the interface between developmental processes and cultural context in treating first-generation Asian American children and adolescents. Her attention to variables such as the scheduling of developmental landmarks and cultural loss illustrate her extensive use of cultural content. However, her treatment of cultural heterogeneity and emphasis on the impact of situation on behavior reveal her use of cultural context to be a primary focus. Although Nguyen describes herself as a "universalist," she gives ample descriptions of the way in which even the form of psychodynamic therapy can be culturally adapted for Asian American clients while the manner in which it is applied, that is, its process, is left unchanged. Nguyen's approach is thus based on a premise that a universalistic approach to carrying out psychodynamic psychotherapy with Asian American youth can be culturally responsive.

Martin D. Topper, in Chapter Eleven, presents a multidimensional model for therapy with American Indian youth based upon his description of Navajo medicine as holistic. In this sense, the dimension of cultural content is primary, since he bases his approach upon the Navajo ethos. His perspective is particularly interesting because it is culturally responsive while contained within a mental health delivery system that commonly ignores culture as a significant factor. This model is an excellent description of how a therapist who is culturally aware can modify existing services and approaches. Topper's primary emphasis on form is found in his high degree of specification of the use of multidimensional interventions geared to the adolescent's problems. Secondarily, his approach focuses on cultural context as illustrated by the clear recognition of the need to creatively orchestrate a large health care system as it relates to family and community variables. He also attends to culture as content as he gains rapport with his young client by understanding how Navajo culture views and treats seizure disorders.

In Chapter Twelve, Joseph E. Trimble presents a cognitive-behavioral skills enhancement program to prevent drug abuse among American Indian adolescents. He clearly frames the prevention and treatment of drug abuse problems in culturally contextual terms; yet he also views them as having significant cultural content. For example, he describes the impact of cultural and personal values on the self-esteem of his clients. His model, which goes by the acronym of S.O.D.A.S., is primarily form-dominant in its adaptation to the culture in which he works. Because it is highly instructional in its application, it does not lend itself to cultural accommodations at the process level. On balance, his model is both easy to learn and to apply, which makes it valuable for use by a wide range of health professionals.

In Chapter Thirteen, Diane J. Willis, Antonio Dobrec, and Dolores Subia BigFoot Sipes describe cultural accommodations to the treatment of abused American Indian children. Their approach secondarily emphasizes cultural content, in its recognition that interpersonal and spiritual activities among family members may be affected by the sexual molestation of a child, but it also can be used therapeutically to assist in treating the client. Few cultural context variables appear in their description of treatment; however, culture *is* addressed in their definition of the problem. Their primary focus is on the dimension of form, as illustrated by their suggestions regarding how to culturally adapt three models for treating sexually abused American Indian children. They imply, rather than specify, that these interventions should be accommodated to the cultural background of clients.

Conclusion

Our review of the different approaches to developing culturally responsive approaches to psychotherapy with ethnic minority children and adolescents reveals interesting commonalities within each of the four large ethnic populations represented in this book. A common theme among the authors who treat African Americans is racism and racial identity, as both the cause and the solution to their problems. Among those who describe psychotherapeutic approaches to Hispanic Americans, a common thread is the need to synthesize the diverse psychohistorical experiences of Hispanic peoples as a vehicle for culturally responsive interventions. In contrast, the authors who work with Asian Americans focus largely on the effects of experiences of immigration and acculturation, particularly on cultural conflict between their clients and members of the mainstream society, who differ radically in worldview. Finally, the authors who treat American Indians share a "sociocentric" perspective; that is, a high value is placed on kinship and community and the embeddedness of individuals in these groups as a salient, underlying characteristic of their clients' behavior. They thus approach psychotherapy through an emphasis on building on preexisting adaptive strengths inherent in American Indian traditions.

We appreciate the fact that cultural responsiveness in psychotherapeutic interventions with ethnic minority children and adolescents can be reached by many avenues and different strategies. What we consider most important is not which avenue is taken but rather the clear description of the ways in which a particular approach becomes culturally responsive. It is this degree of specificity that will allow future investigators to assess whether particular cultural adaptations to psychotherapeutic interventions actually result in more positive outcomes.

References

Carroll, L. *Through the Looking Glass*. New York: St. Martin's Press, 1977.

Costantino, G., Malgady, R. G., and Rogler, L. H. "Cuento Therapy: A Culturally Sensitive Modality for Puerto Rican Children." *Journal of Consulting and Clinical Psychology*, 1986, *54*, 639–645.

Cushman, P. "Why the Self Is Empty: Toward a Historically Situated Psychology." *American Psychologist*, 1990, *45*(5), 599–611.

Lazarus, S. S. *The Practice of Multimodal Therapy: Systematic, Comprehensive and Effective Psychotherapy*. Baltimore, Md.: Johns Hopkins University Press, 1989.

Name Index

311

Subject Index

A

Abuse, child sexual: among American Indians, 276-299; background on, 276-278; case examples of, 281, 282, 289-290, 291-292; cognitive-behavioral model and, 293-294; and criminal jurisdiction issues, 281-282; culturally sensitive therapy for, 284-288; effects of, 283, 296; before foster care, 52-53, 57-58; and gang member, 143-144; and government services, 278-283; incidence and prevalence of, 276-277, 278; mental health treatment models for, 288-295; parallel group treatment for, 294-295; and play therapy, 95, 96-97; post-traumatic stress disorder model for, 292-294; and reuniting family, 295-296; summary on, 296; traumagenic dynamic model for, 288-292; treatment issues for, 290-291; treatment problems for, 283-284

Acculturation: and Asian names, 166-167; impact of, 11; levels of, and treatment modalities, 189-190, 194-195, 199, 200; and spirituality, 123

Adolescents: and cultural loss and object-relations theory, 214-216; gang membership by, 129-154; in middle-class African American families, 25-42; multidimensional therapy for, 225-245. *See also* African American youth; American Indian youth; Asian American youth; Ethnic minority youth; Hispanic American youth

Advocacy, by therapist, 164

African American youth: of Caribbean origin, 77; cases with, 26-34, 35-36, 38-39, 46, 51-53, 56, 57-58, 74-77; and cultural values, 69; in culturally responsive psychotherapies, 5, 9, 10, 16, 23-81, 303-304, 308; in foster care, 43-62; in gangs, 137; in middle-class families, 25-42; ra-

319

and treatment by, 226, 231, 232–
234; for gang members, 141–142,
151–152; goals of, 55–59, 228,
295; as inner heart expert, 158–
162; mothering by, 163–164;
need for Southeast Asian, 179–
180; racial socialization as tool
for, 71–77; as Red Queen, 5; and
spirituality, 120–122
Therapy. *See* Culturally responsive
psychotherapies; Treatment
modalities
Traditional healing: and inner
heart issues, 160–161, 171–175;
by medicine men, 226–228, 287.
See also Spirituality
Transactional contextual model,
for play therapy, 89–90
Transcultural Family Institute,
case at, 193–200
Transference: and Asian American
clients, 162, 163–164, 177–179;
and gang members, 142
Traumagenic dynamic model, and
child sexual abuse, 288–292
Treatment modalities: and acculturation levels, 189–190, 194–
195, 199, 200; applications of,
182–203; background on, 182–
183; case example of, 193–200;
characteristics and advantages
of, 183–185; and conceptualization of problem, 191–192; conclusions on, 200–201; ethnicity
factors in, 187–193; for gang
members, 141–150; integrative,
211–212; and language issues,
190–191; multidimensional, 225–
245; and native culture, 187–189;
pathology and motivation related to, 193; play therapy as,
85–102; selecting, 185–187; for
self-esteem and identity, 26–34
Tsotsio (South Africa), 132

U

United Kingdom, gangs in, 132

U.S. Advisory Board on Child
Abuse and Neglect, 276, 277, 298
U.S. Commission on Civil Rights,
136
U.S. Department of the Interior,
252, 274–275, 280
Urban areas, gang behavior in,
129–154

V

VACUUM factors, 141
Venezuela, emigrant from, 98–99
Victim system, African American
adolescents in, 36
Victims of Sexual Abuse, 296n
Vietnam: doctors in, 163; herbalists
in, 171; psychologists in, 160;
reeducation camp in, 166
Vietnamese American youth: and
acculturation, 166–167; first-
generation, 204–222; in gangs,
138; and religion, 169; treatment
modality for, 193–200. *See also*
Asian American youth
Violence: in Asian American family, 193–200; and gang behavior,
129–154; multidimensional therapy for, 235, 236, 237–238, 243
Vitelloni (Italy), 132

W

Washington, D.C., middle-class Af-
rican American families in, 40
Watergate break-in, as gang activ-
ity, 131
Watsonville, California, gangs in,
134
Wechsler Intelligence Scale for
Children-Revised (WISC-R), 88
Wholeness, achieving, 110
Witchcraft (Brujería), 110–111

Z

Zoot suit riots, 130